MW00622606

"Once again Gerald Bray has n ... his great writing style in a book that not only demonstrates that theology was the core matter of the Reformation but also what that theology was, where it came from and how it functioned. This book is a wonderful help to understand the reformers and their message and to see the relevance of Reformation theology."

Herman Selderhuis, president of the Theological University Apeldoorn, director of Refo500

"Here is an excellent book by a master historian, a study which places the Reformation and its theology in the context of the church and culture in which it happened. A fine companion to the Reformation Commentary on Scripture."

Timothy George, founding dean of Beeson Divinity School of Samford University, general editor of the Reformation Commentary on Scripture

"Taking an approach that is both accessible and knowledgeable, Bray dexterously weaves an engaging tapestry, orienting readers to the key Reformation-era theologians and their insights. His themes range from the sources of authority in the Reformation churches to the complexities of church-state relations, helping modern-day readers engage with the leading theological issues in early modern western Christianity."

Karin Maag, director of the H. Henry Meeter Center for Calvin Studies, Calvin College

"It is impossible to understand the Reformation without a clear comprehension of the changing social and geopolitical landscapes of the sixteenth century, the driving importance of a number of complex theological issues, and the sometimes tangled interplay between the two. In *Doing Theology with the Reformers*, Professor Gerald Bray offers a most excellent and integrated overview of Reformation history and doctrine that will serve equally well as a solid introduction to the field and as an engaging read for anyone wanting to further thicken up their knowledge of the period and its developments. With his characteristic accessibility, Professor Bray moves seamlessly from the macrosweep of early modern European history to the nuanced details of particular religious debates, interacting with the major persons, texts, regions, and emphases as he even-handedly narrates the theological story of the Reformation. With plenty of direct connections to present day religion and culture in the West, this volume will profit all its readers at multiple levels."

Tim Patrick, principal, Bible College of South Australia

"The list of useful books produced by Gerald Bray just keeps growing. In this book, written in Dr. Bray's characteristically accessible style, we are given an excellent introduction to the world of the Reformers and their key theological contributions. More than that, he shows how those contributions still affect us, not only through the Reformers' own writing but also through the confessions of the Reformation churches. What is remarkable is the breadth of understanding of the Reformation world that is evident throughout the book and the evenhanded treatment it provides of the theology of each branch of the Reformation. Here is a reliable introduction that is enjoyable to read. Those with a detailed knowledge of the subject will appreciate how well it has all been brought together, though there is no doubt room for disagreement on one or two particulars. Those who are just beginning to discover the riches of the Reformation will be thankful for such a helpful guide. Here is a challenge to do theology with the Reformers, for we cannot ignore their effect on our own grasp of the biblical gospel. Dr. Bray's book is a fine example of how to do just that."

Mark D. Thompson, principal, Moore Theological College

"Gerald Bray is an expert guide to the theology of the Protestant reformers of the sixteenth century, and this volume surveys the terrain in which they labored with his characteristic skill and verve. Let him take you on a tour of the theological landscape of Luther, Calvin, Cranmer, and others and inspire you with the ideas and doctrines that brought light to Europe five hundred years ago."

Lee Gatiss, director of Church Society, author of *Light After Darkness*

GERALD L. BRAY

DOING THEOLOGY
WITH THE REFORMERS

IVP Academic

An imprint of InterVarsity Press
Downers Grove, Illinois

InterVarsity Press
P.O. Box 1400, Downers Grove, IL 60515-1426
ivpress.com
email@ivpress.com

InterVarsity Press® is the book-publishing division of InterVarsity Christian Fellowship/USA®, a movement of students and faculty active on campus at hundreds of universities, colleges, and schools of nursing in the United States of America, and a member movement of the International Fellowship of Evangelical Students. For information about local and regional activities, visit intervarsity.org.

Cover design, image composite, and interior design: Cindy Kiple
Images: Protestant Reformers: Protestant Reformers, c.1654 (oil on panel), English School, (17th century) / Bridgeman Image

ISBN 978-0-8308-5251-2 (print)
ISBN 978-0-8308-6583-3 (digital)

Printed in the United States of America ♾

InterVarsity Press is committed to ecological stewardship and to the conservation of natural resources in all our operations. This book was printed using sustainably sourced paper.

Library of Congress Cataloging-in-Publication Data

Names: Bray, Gerald Lewis, author.
Title: Doing theology with the reformers / Gerald L. Bray.
Description: Downers Grove, IL : InterVarsity Press, [2019] | Includes index.
Identifiers: LCCN 2019013107 (print) | LCCN 2019017131 (ebook) | ISBN
   9780830865833 (eBook) | ISBN 9780830852512 (print : alk. paper) | ISBN
   9780830865833 (digital)
Subjects: LCSH: Reformed Church—Doctrines.
Classification: LCC BX9422.3 (ebook) | LCC BX9422.3 .B73 2019 (print) | DDC
   230/.42—dc23
LC record available at https://lccn.loc.gov/2019013107

P 25 24 23 22 21 20 19 18 17 16 15 14 13 12 11 10 9 8 7 6 5 4 3 2 1

Y 39 38 37 36 35 34 33 32 31 30 29 28 27 26 25 24 23 22 21 20 19

Contents

Preface

THIS BOOK IS DESIGNED TO ACCOMPANY the Reformation Commentary on Scripture series, which endeavors to provide a representative selection of the biblical exposition practiced by the main Protestant reformers of the sixteenth and seventeenth centuries. This companion volume is not a systematic theology, nor does it lean toward one branch of the Reformation as opposed to another. Rather, its purpose is to introduce readers to the world in which the Reformation took place, to the mindset of those who led it and gave it direction, and to the way in which the initial burst of spiritual energy and enthusiasm was gradually codified into the confessional statements that now form the basis of denominational identities in the Protestant world.

Most people agree that the Reformation began when Martin Luther published his Ninety-Five Theses just over five hundred years ago, on October 31, 1517, although the conditions for its success were already in place and the movement itself did not accelerate until a few years later. Once it started, it was impossible to channel the outburst of theological energy in a single direction, and different strands of thought appeared, each claiming the banner of Reformation. For the most part, Luther's immediate followers clustered around him during his lifetime, but even among them tensions quickly emerged and divisions began to surface. As this book demonstrates, present-day Lutherans represent only one of those strands and cannot be regarded as Luther's only, or even principal, heirs. The Swiss Reformers, some of whom were contemporaneous with Luther, lived in a different mental environment and produced at least three distinct kinds of Reformation more or less independently of Luther—the Zwinglians of Zurich, the Calvinists of Geneva, and the Anabaptists. The first two eventually merged into one and have now claimed the term *Reformed* for themselves, whereas the third has survived in different guises. The original Anabaptists had multiple origins and are represented today by Mennonites, Hutterites, Amish, and others more than by Baptists, who are best described as Protestants of a broadly Calvinistic type who have adopted elements of Anabaptism without becoming Anabaptists in the true sense. Then, of course, there are the Anglicans, members of the Churches of England and Ireland who also adopted an essentially Calvinistic position, though with certain characteristics setting them apart from the rest.

All of these different strands of Reformation thought appear in this volume and are treated with equal respect. Martin Luther inevitably has pride of place since the Reformation as we know it would not have happened without him. John Calvin also dominates the scene, as he did in the second generation of Protestantism, particularly outside of Germany. The controversies that developed among the later Reformers largely concerned the interpretation of these giants' legacies. An introductory volume like this one must therefore concentrate on them and their followers while allowing for influences from other quarters that affected the course of debate. Readers should bear in mind that this book is about the theology of the Protestant reformers, not about the Reformation as such. In the sixteenth and seventeenth centuries, theology was the preserve of academics, all of whom were male. Other voices were occasionally heard, but they were exceptional, and only rarely did women or laymen have much impact on what the Reformers taught. Secular rulers, including women, often determined what kind of Reformation their countries would adopt, but their role was usually limited to accepting or rejecting particular doctrinal positions formulated by others. As time went on, even theologians aligned themselves more and more with one established tendency or another, a pattern clearly seen in the confessional movement of the late sixteenth and early seventeenth centuries. It is in that form that the Reformers' theology has reached us today, and understanding that process must be a major aim of a book like this. Detailed studies of particular people and movements are readily available elsewhere, but pursuing these matters responsibly demands a good foundation in the basic lines of theological thinking that shaped the Reformation, which is the present study's primary concern.

Until quite recently, those who wrote about the Reformation almost always did so from a confessional perspective that tended to glorify one tradition at the expense of the others. The ecumenical spirit of our time has made it possible to overcome this tendency to a large extent, and it has also made it possible to be critical of our traditional "heroes of the faith" when criticism is deserved. That does not mean we repudiate them; rather, we can now see them as men and women who had to struggle for their beliefs and were not always entirely successful in the attempt. At the same time, the Protestant Reformation was a fundamental factor in shaping the modern world, which owes much to the truths rediscovered by the Reformers of the sixteenth century. Their achievement must not be forgotten or downplayed.

Today even Roman Catholics, who until recently were almost uniformly hostile to the Reformation, are often inclined to recognize people like Luther and Calvin as doctors of the church universal rather than as founders of sectarian and essentially heretical theological traditions. Virtually everyone now accepts that the late medieval church had become a vast institution that no longer reflected the principles of primitive Christianity but apparently lacked the means or the will to reform itself. The Reformers' inability to agree about how best to renew the church may be regarded as unfortunate, perhaps even as tragic. Rome itself was eventually obliged to adopt its own Reformation, but it was too late to repair the breach, which in some ways was made worse when Rome consciously adopted anti-Protestant principles. The Eastern Orthodox churches were courted by both sides, but they never embraced a movement that they did not understand and regarded as fundamentally alien to their own theological outlook. However we look at this history, we must live with the consequences. The Western church that was a unity in 1500 is now divided into numerous denominations, each of which has its own traditions, outlook, and (if we are honest about it) prejudices that characterize it and tend to perpetuate division whether anyone likes it or not. To borrow a literary analogy, Humpty Dumpty has fallen apart and will not be put back together again, and there can be no return to an imaginary golden age before that fall. In this book we seek to explain what happened and why, not to justify or celebrate one point of view but to increase our understanding and in the process to promote a spirit of charity toward one another that should be the hallmark of every Christian, regardless of what side of the divide we now find ourselves on.

—Gerald Bray

ONE

The Education
of a Reformer

A Changing World

The late fifteenth century was a time of great social and intellectual ferment in western Europe. Many significant changes had occurred over the millennium since the collapse of the Roman Empire in the West, but by 1500 there was a growing feeling that a fundamentally new era in human history was dawning. In 1453 the Eastern Roman (Byzantine) Empire, which had struggled on for centuries, finally succumbed to the Ottoman Turks, who then conquered most of the Balkan Peninsula and were soon poised to threaten both Germany and Italy. As Muslims, the Turks were an existential danger to the Christian countries of Europe, and fear of them was widespread. Meanwhile, at the other end of the continent, the dwindling remnants of Muslim rule in Spain were in their death throes. The marriage of Ferdinand of Aragon to Isabella of Castile united their two crowns and allowed them to pool their resources for the final push toward the south. It took a number of years, but on January 2, 1492, the last emir of Granada surrendered to the forces of Christian Spain.

That event gave an ambitious Genoese sea captain his chance. Christopher Columbus had been trying to convince the Portuguese to finance an expedition to the west, where he believed there was a sea route to India that would bypass the Ottoman Empire, but the Portuguese were preoccupied with their own expeditions down the coast of Africa and were not interested. Prompted by the fall of Granada, Columbus made his appeal to Queen Isabella, who in the euphoria of the moment was prepared to indulge Columbus's fantasies. The rest, as we know, is history. Within a few years, both Spain and Portugal were carving out worldwide colonial empires—the first stage of what we now call globalization. As Christian kingdoms, they were concerned to preach the gospel as they went, and the papacy was involved in their expansion from the start. Missions to the heathen made their appearance on every continent, and there was a real sense that the evangelization of the entire world was at hand, despite the ever-present Turkish menace.

The consequences of this expansion were dramatic. Having been peripheral and quite poor by European standards, Spain suddenly became fabulously wealthy and found itself as the arbiter of Europe's destiny. In the year Columbus sailed, a Spaniard was elected pope (thanks to the influence that Spanish money could buy) and in 1519 the king of Spain was elected Holy Roman emperor—the head of what was then the largest European state, covering Germany, the Netherlands, Switzerland, and Northern Italy, with much else besides. In economic terms, the influx of huge quantities of American gold and silver caused rampant inflation, which transformed the prospects of most Europeans. New products were also introduced, most notably the potato, which rapidly became a staple of the European diet. Its nutritional qualities improved people's health at a time when mortality rates were still very high, which led to a population boom that further unsettled the traditional way of life. But returning Spanish soldiers also introduced strange new diseases like syphilis, which heightened the risk inherent in sexual intercourse and provided moralists with an excellent topic for frightening hearers.

When Columbus landed in the Bahamas, Martin Luther (1483–1546) was a month short of his ninth birthday. We do not know when he first heard of the new discovery, but it is safe to say that its effects were sinking in during his adolescent years. The impact of this can only be imagined. Whatever Luther had learned about the world as a boy suddenly had to be modified or discarded in light of recent events. For the first time, nations and countries not mentioned in the Bible came into view and had to be reckoned with. Were the American Indians (as the Spaniards dubbed them) fully human? If they were, why were they not mentioned in the genealogies found in the Old Testament? What about Africans and Asians, many of whom had developed religions and civilizations completely foreign to the Christian world? These and similar questions plagued the Iberian nations for decades, and although these previously unknown people were eventually recognized as humans created in the image and likeness of God and had also fallen thanks to the sin of Adam, it took some time for them to be evangelized and even longer for them to be integrated fully into the life of the church. It is true that progress was made and some Africans became bishops in the Portuguese colonies within a generation of their conversion, but on the whole this vast expansion of the Christian world passed by most Europeans.

For Martin Luther and his contemporaries, Europe remained the center of the universe, and the Reformation, when it came, would be worked out there rather than anywhere else. But the Protestants' lack of global vision was not true of their Catholic opponents. The missionary priests who fought the Lutherans in Germany belonged to the same religious orders, and on occasion were even the same people, as those who were bringing the message of Christ to the heathen around the world. For them it was all part of a single gospel mission, and many did not hesitate to accuse Luther of being the tool of the devil, whose purpose was to split the church apart in the moment of its greatest triumph.

The need to deal with Luther's rebellion was more urgent than we might assume from our vantage point, because even as he was preaching his message to the Germans, the Ottoman Turks were taking control of Hungary and laying siege to Vienna. There was a very real possibility that the whole of Europe would fall to the forces of Islam, which were making a fresh attempt to secure world domination. Would the ultimate beneficiary of Luther's revolt turn out to be Islam, in the form of the Ottoman Empire? Many people feared that it would, and not without reason.

The new learning. While all this was happening, another development of equal importance was taking place—the invention of printing, which coincided almost exactly with the fall of Constantinople. In the mid-1450s a German printer named Johannes Gutenberg invented movable type, enabling him to produce multiple copies of the same material. As with all new technologies, this was initially an expensive and laborious process, but by 1500 it had caught on, and the ancient tradition of manuscript production had all but died out. The great advantage of printing was that it enabled an infinite number of people to read exactly the same text. Manuscripts, as those who study them know, are almost never identical in every detail, even when they are meant to be copies of one another. Human error inevitably creeps in, which is often reproduced as further copies are made, making the latter version considerably worse than the first. Printed books might contain errors of course, and most do, but at least the misprints are all the same. Printing gave the scholarly world a ready-made platform for discussion and an objective basis for research that it had not previously enjoyed. It was an information revolution that would quickly transform the intellectual climate of Europe, opening new avenues of thought and challenging the accepted verities of medieval life.

By making scholarly works more accessible, printing also fueled an unprecedented demand for knowledge. Scholars ransacked libraries, many of them monastic, for manuscripts that they could publish, and the discovery of different copies of the same works produced the science of textual criticism that still exists today. There was little point in disseminating a text if it was not the best one available, and printing made comparisons between different versions relatively easy. Scholars were able to eliminate inferior editions and propose corrections based on the evidence of other manuscript traditions. Although perfection would never be attained, standards were vastly improved, and in this respect Luther's generation could justly claim to have been better educated than any that had gone before it.

A by-product of the printing revolution was an increased output of books written in the European vernaculars. When manuscripts had been the only form of writing, the few people who possessed them mostly knew Latin. Although it was no longer spoken in daily life, Latin retained its prestige in the church and in the schools of the time, and anyone who wanted to be educated had to learn it. This created a common world of discourse in which priests in Bohemia, for example, could easily read and interact with the writings of John Wyclif (1328–1384) and his followers in England, which they did. So much so, in fact, that some Wycliffite writings have been preserved *only* in Bohemia (part of today's Czech Republic) because the English copies have been lost. Martin Luther learned Latin as a boy and used it throughout his academic career, as did all his contemporaries. They constituted what later came to be called the "republic of letters," an intellectual fraternity that spanned the European continent and paid little attention to national boundaries. Erasmus of Rotterdam (1466–1536) was equally at home in Paris, Cambridge, and Basel, whether anyone in those places understood his native Dutch or not. He would never have dreamed of using his mother tongue to communicate—all his efforts were poured into purifying scholarly Latin so that those who mastered it could speak to one another with an elegance that harked back to the glory days of ancient Rome.

But try as they might, Erasmus and his colleagues could not revive Latin as the spoken language of Europe. Instead, ordinary people increasingly demanded literature in the languages they used and could easily understand. But these vernacular tongues were not properly standardized and lacked technical vocabulary for discussing subjects like theology. Only slowly and sometimes accidentally did the languages of modern Europe emerge as sophisticated vehicles of thought. The process began when the great poet Dante Alighieri used his local Tuscan dialect as the basis for his great epic poem, *The Divine Comedy*, which became the touchstone for creating what we now call Italian. Elsewhere, scholars and writers in different royal courts did much the same for their own languages. Spanish thus arose out of Castilian, French out of Parisian, and English out of the variety of it spoken in London and the Thames Valley.

The development of a standard German language was more difficult because the country lacked a political center that could impose its will on the rest. In the end, Luther's translation of the Bible into his own Saxon dialect laid the foundations for the modern literary language, but it was not universally successful. In the Netherlands a different standard emerged, creating what we now call Dutch, which was able to resist the pull of Luther's Bible. The same thing happened in Switzerland, but only orally, so that today the Swiss Germans speak several dialectical forms of the language but write in the standard one—a confusing situation for foreigners but a living example of the complications that using the vernacular could cause in the sixteenth century.

This situation reminds us that the Protestant reformers found themselves caught between two worlds. As preachers they naturally preferred the vernaculars, which they helped to establish as worthy rivals to Latin. But as scholars they used Latin to reach an international audience. For example, when William Tyndale (1494–1536) went to Wittenberg about 1524 to study under Luther, he had no need to learn German and probably did not do so. Likewise, when Thomas Cranmer (1489–1556) invited men like Martin Bucer (1491–1551) and Peter Martyr Vermigli (1499–1562) to come to England, they did not have to bother learning English, because everybody in Oxford and Cambridge could follow them in Latin. Even when translations of the Bible and prayers were produced for public worship, Latin versions were also on hand for use in the universities and anywhere else where it might have been appropriate. The Reformers were interested in promoting their mother tongues not for their own sake but only in order to communicate the gospel to people in a language they could understand. If that language happened to be Latin, so be it.

This universal bilingualism of the scholarly world must be understood if we are to make sense of the Reformers' writings. What they composed in their own languages was principally intended for domestic consumption by a popular audience. Their Latin works were meant for other scholars and for an international clientele. John Calvin (1509–1564), for example, wrote his *Institutes* in both French and Latin, but it was the latter that circulated more widely and must be regarded as the "official" text, although modern researchers also consult the French versions when clarifying his thought. Similarly, the Thirty-Nine Articles of the Church of England come in two forms—the Latin, which is official, and the English, which is a translation. Where the two differ, the Latin text that prevails, though few modern readers are aware of that.[1]

Today anyone writing in Latin would be thinking in his mother tongue and trying to find a Latin equivalent for whatever he wanted to say, but in the sixteenth century it was usually the opposite.

---

[1]The Protestant reformers were determined to promote the use of vernacular languages, but the hold of Latin was strong. In England it remained the official language of church business until March 25, 1733, and it continued to be the language of theology lectures in the universities until the first decade of the nineteenth century.

The Reformers thought in Latin, at least when discussing theology, and tried to produce vernacular equivalents, some of which were more successful than others. For example, the Latin word *reconciliatio* was rendered in English as "atonement" ("at-one-ment"), which is now standard English, though the word is no longer synonymous with reconciliation. This can cause traps for the unwary. For example, there is a legal maxim stating that "a gentleman is known by his *habitus*." Sometimes *habitus* gets translated as "behavior," which is what a modern person is likely to think, but in fact it means that he is known by his clothing. This is because in the sixteenth century, sumptuary laws prescribed what different classes of people could and could not wear. How they behaved was far less important.

Translation problems of this kind abound and were sometimes disputed even in the sixteenth and seventeenth centuries, particularly when it came to biblical terms. For example, should *ecclesia* be rendered as "church/kirk" or as "congregation"? Both are possible, and the difference between *church* and *kirk* adds an element of dialect usage that is still alive in some quarters. Is *presbyter* a priest or an elder? Can *episcopus* be translated as "bishop," or should some more neutral term be found, like "overseer"? The Latin *iustitia* can be either "justice" or "righteousness" in English, and sometimes the choice is decided along confessional lines—Protestants prefer *righteousness* and Catholics *justice*, probably because it is more Latinate. But the two words are not synonymous, and in reality both must be used according to the context, with the risk that the dimension emphasized by the other English word will be lost in translation. Most notorious of all is *paenitentia*, which can be *penance*, *repentance*, or *penitence* according to context and/or taste. It is not always clear what the original author intended, particularly when the true meaning of *paenitentia* was being debated. The Latin preserves the ambiguity between an outward act versus an inward change of heart, which the English has to resolve by using different words. This means that when we are translating a sixteenth-century document it is sometimes hard to tell which of the various English words captures the author's intended sense most accurately.

How the Protestant Reformation was connected to these developments is controversial. Did the emerging modern world create the conditions that produced the Reformation, or did the Reformation lead to changes that destroyed medieval civilization and ushered in the new era? The question gets even more complicated when we factor in the Renaissance, which was in full flower when Luther began to preach church reform. Was he a product of the new learning (or "humanism," as it was known), or did he oppose it? Did the Reformation ride the wave of intellectual progress symbolized by the invention of printing, or was it in some sense a reaction against it? It is hard to argue that the Reformation brought about the great changes of the late fifteenth and early sixteenth centuries on its own, because by the time it progressed, those changes were already in full swing. Yet it is equally hard to doubt that they had a considerable impact on the spread and acceptance of Luther's message.

One of Luther's contemporaries, Nicolaus Copernicus (1473–1543), made discoveries that helped shatter the prevailing ancient Greek scientific worldview. Luther did not know Copernicus and was unaware of his discoveries, not least because he kept them secret and nobody knew them until after his death. Although Copernicus had nothing to do with the Reformation, and the early Reformers were likely not sympathetic to him, his discoveries made it easier for them to exploit the discomfiture they caused the Roman Catholic Church. At that time it accepted the scientific ideas of the ancient Greeks (particularly those of Aristotle, Ptolemy, and Galen) and based its own official doctrines on them, most notably the belief that in the sacrament of the Lord's Supper, the bread and wine were transubstantiated into the body and blood of Christ. That doctrine made sense only in an Aristotelian universe, where everything was analyzed according to its (variable) form and (invariable) substance. To destroy that way of thinking was to remove the basis for a teaching that lay at the heart of medieval devotion and practice.

The Catholic Church found it impossible to come to terms with this new learning, and even a century later it was still resisting the discoveries of Galileo Galilei (1564–1642), whose unjust sufferings have become the stuff of legend. Protestants did not find it any easier to adjust to the new learning, but they were not held back by a church authority claiming infallibility in doctrinal matters, allowing them to manage a smoother transition from the medieval to the modern way of thinking. The Reformation and the emergence of modern science were parallel developments involving different people. It is misleading to claim that one directly influenced the other, but it is fair to say that both overturned the traditional worldview, which paved the way for a new type of Christianity.[2]

The political scene. The interconnectedness of European politics meant that when Luther defended himself before the Holy Roman emperor, he was speaking to the king of Spain—the effects of that country's American empire were already being felt in Germany, which had recently elected the Spanish monarch as its sovereign. Charles V (I of Spain) dreamed of establishing a universal Christian empire, but his dream would be shattered by the divisions caused by the Reformation. Yet it cannot really be said that the Reformation provided the catalyst that transformed most of Europe into the nation states we know today. A few states, like Denmark and Portugal, had already been united for a long time; others, like England and France, were consolidating themselves and probably would have done so in any case. Germany, however, where the Reformation broke out, remained politically more backward and disunited than anywhere else apart from Italy, which remained uniformly Catholic.

---

[2]See Reijer Hooykaas, *Religion and the Rise of Modern Science* (Edinburgh: Scottish Academic Press, 1972; repr., Vancouver, BC: Regent College Publications, 2000).

The pope would have dearly liked Charles V to crush Protestantism and restore the religious unity of the continent, but it was beyond Charles's power to unite even his own dominions behind him. In Germany, local rulers could defy the center and support rebels like Luther if they wished, and no one could do much about it. States that were already internally centralized could (and did) impose religious uniformity on their populations, but the nature of this uniformity varied from one country to another. Thus we find that Spain and Portugal were able to suppress religious dissent almost completely even as they conquered world empires in the name of the Catholic Church. Conversely, England and the Dutch Republic opted for Protestantism and built their own world empires accordingly, although neither achieved the kind of success that distinguished the Iberian kingdoms. England tried to impose religious uniformity, but in 1689, after a debilitating civil war, it eventually gave up and legislated a limited degree of religious toleration. The much less centralized Dutch Republic permitted a de facto toleration, although it would not be until the nineteenth century that religious freedom would be officially sanctioned in the post-Enlightenment kingdom of the Netherlands.

France was caught in the middle—the center wanted a Catholic state, but its control over many of the outlying regions was weak, resulting in a series of civil wars dominated by the religious question. A stalemate was broken only when the leader of the Protestants, who had inherited the French crown by dynastic accident, converted to Catholicism and granted limited toleration to his Protestant subjects.[3] It took two generations for that tolerance to be whittled away, but the Catholic victory was bought at a high price that eventually made France the first and in many respects most profoundly secular country in Europe. Many Protestants were grudging converts to

---

[3]This was Henri IV (r. 1589–1610), who became a Catholic in 1593 and issued the Edict of Nantes in 1598, granting limited toleration to Protestants. The edict was revoked in 1685.

Catholicism and paid only lip-service to it. As rationalism gained traction in the late seventeenth century, they and others who sympathized with them turned against what they saw as a benighted and corrupt Church that could only persecute dissenters and was incapable of reform. When revolution broke out in 1789 that Church was swept from power and ever since then, progress in France has been identified with secularism.

The Reformation shaped the nations of the British Isles in ways that are still evident. Protestantism triumphed in Scotland, which was then united with England in what has proved to be a long-lasting arrangement, but it failed to make much impression in Ireland, leading to that country's alienation from England that continues to have tragic consequences.

In Germany, the Reformation prevented national unity as the north became mainly Protestant while the south stubbornly remained Catholic. It would not be until the late nineteenth century that Protestant Prussia would forge a kind of national unity, but it did so only by expelling Catholic Austria from its newly minted German Empire.

Beyond Western (Latin) Christendom there is another world, that of so-called Eastern Christianity, represented by a group of churches that we generally label *Orthodox*. These churches are divided among themselves along lines that emerged in the christological debates of the fifth century, but they are united in their rejection of Western Christianity, whether Roman Catholic or Protestant. The Reformation has passed them by, and although occasional attempts have been made in the East to come to terms with it, most Christians of those traditions have gone their separate way.

The religious passions of the sixteenth-century West have largely subsided nowadays, but their effects can still be seen. Martin Luther is a national hero in his native Germany and is also highly regarded in Scandinavia. In contrast, John Calvin is largely ignored in his native France, where the Reformation never caught on, but he is honored in the Netherlands and in the English-speaking world, where his theology has had more influence. The English Reformers enjoy a more restrained, although not insignificant, renown in England, and John Knox is still remembered in Scotland and in the Scottish diaspora, reminding us that Protestant principles and national identities are more closely connected than the modern separation of church and state might lead us to think. For this we must thank (or curse?) the close links between the Reformers and their societies, which in some cases helped them to succeed and in others doomed them to failure, and which continue to shape the way they are perceived in the wider world today.

BECOMING A "SPIRITUAL PERSON"

What would you think if you heard somebody being described as a "spiritual person"? You might find it difficult to produce an exact definition of the term, but it probably suggests to you that the person in question has an outlook on life that transcends the humdrum routine of daily survival, someone who puts moral and intellectual questions ahead of materialistic ones and who thinks in ways that border on the mystical. Such a person need not be a Christian—the Dalai Lama, for instance, is often said to be very spiritual—but in the Western world the chances are that he or she would be attached either to a religious faith or to a philosophical ideal offering a nontheistic alternative "spirituality." Whatever criteria we might use, spiritual people are fairly unusual in our experience and often impressive. We might not want (or be able) to emulate them, but we generally respect and even admire them for their principled and perhaps sacrificial lifestyle.

This modern view is light years away from what medieval people meant by the term, and their attitude toward spiritual persons was very often different from ours. Medieval society was divided into three main groups, or estates—those who prayed (clergy), those who fought (aristocracy), and those who worked (commoners). In a world where everyone (except Jews and a few Muslims) was baptized, the word *Christian* had largely lost its original meaning. It was seldom applied to the aristocracy or to the clergy, who were tiny minorities that were clearly set apart from the mass of the population. It was to that otherwise undefined mass that the word was usually attached, and remnants of that era can still be found today. In Russian, for example, a *krestyanin* is a peasant, a meaning that was once shared by the English word *cretin* (a corruption of French *chrétien*, or "Christian"). As the development of *cretin* suggests, it was frequently used in a derogatory sense, which gives us some idea of how the higher estates regarded ordinary Christians.

An awareness of two types of Christians can be traced back to the New Testament, where the apostle Paul distinguished between members of the church who were *psychikoi* and those who were *pneumatikoi* (1 Cor 2:13-15). The former were unspiritual, living according to the desires of their own minds, whereas the latter were true children of God. As Christianity spread and became the almost universal religion, the number of *psychikoi* increased exponentially, leading to the fear that the *pneumatikoi*, or "true believers" as we would now call them, might be overwhelmed. To counteract this danger, many sincere Christians retreated from everyday life and established monasteries, where they could live in a way that they regarded as a foretaste of heaven.

Pastors and elders, whom Paul had already set apart from ordinary church members by insisting that they should exhibit a higher degree of spirituality than other members of the church, also came under pressure to adopt a similar discipline. Pope Gregory I the Great (590–604) tried to impose a monastic lifestyle on all his clergy, but he was ahead of his time and his project failed. A council held in the imperial palace of Trullum in Constantinople during the winter of 691–692 managed to impose celibacy on bishops but not on the parish clergy, an arrangement that still prevails in the Eastern Orthodox churches, although the canons of that council were never ratified in the West. It was not until the First Lateran Council in 1123 that a serious move was made in the same direction. From then on, priests as well as bishops had to take vows of poverty, chastity, and obedience. In practice that sometimes meant leaving wives and children for a life of celibacy, which became compulsory for everyone in full-time pastoral ministry.

Those in the service of the church constituted a society apart, recognized as such in law. They even had their own law courts, so that if one of their number committed a crime he would be judged by his peers and not by laymen. It was belonging to this society that made one a spiritual person. The term had nothing to do with devotional maturity; it was used exclusively in a legal sense to refer to someone who enjoyed "benefit of clergy," as these privileges were called. Entry into this charmed world was relatively free and easy. Nobody could become a lord or a peasant except by right of birth—those orders were inherited. But the celibacy rule ensured that this could not be the case for the clergy, who were recruited from both the aristocracy and the common people. Relatively few aristocrats entered the priesthood or the cloister, although those who did often founded churches and monasteries with the resources they brought with them. On the whole, the common people provided the clergy, making the spiritual order a form of upward mobility in what was otherwise a static society. A man in holy orders could rise to an important position in the church and might well be able to help members of his family advance their interests, and parents with children to spare were not slow to grasp that fact.

People could become spiritual persons in many ways, but two routes to this status were by far the most common. Parents could dedicate their children to the Lord by enrolling them in a monastery when they were still very young. This often happened with younger sons who could not inherit their father's position or occupation, and with

daughters who could not be provided with a dowry. Sometimes aristocrats would dispose of unwanted family members in this way, although
if an older son were to die, a younger one might be expected to leave the
cloister and take up the vacant inheritance. The monastic life was also
a form of social security, not least for widows who had no other provision. It was not a bad life for those who could adapt to it, and for children
who had grown up in the monastery, it was all they had ever known.

Religious orders also recruited members through conversion.
Adults who had led a sinful life might be struck by the power of God
and decide to devote themselves to a regime of prayer and fasting,
partly to atone for their past sins and partly to contribute something
useful to the society they had previously abused. Some of these converts became famous—for example, Augustine of Hippo (354–430)
and Francis of Assisi (ca. 1181–1226). Martin Luther was also one of
them. Shaken by a fall from his horse that should have killed him, he
attributed his miraculous survival to the providence of God and resolved to dedicate the rest of his life to God's service. Becoming a
spiritual person was the obvious way to fulfill that desire.

Converts, of course, tend to be more zealous than those who have
grown up in a system or entered it against their will, which is one
reason why we often know more about them. Francis of Assisi was
not content with what he saw as the laxity of much monastic observance, so he set up a new kind of religious order—what we now call
the friars.[4] Friars differed from monks by often living in the world,
making their way by begging or offering services for payment. They
were rebels against the established order in a way that monks were
not. Monasteries owned land and were represented in the councils of
the church, to which they often contributed senior members of the
clergy. Friars were outsiders who had no such privileges but were also
free from the obligations that great wealth imposed. Despite these

---

[4]The word is a corruption of the Latin *fratres* (brothers).

differences, the friars followed the monastic disciplines, and by mixing with the wider public they instilled a certain expectation of what a spiritual person should be. A contemporary of Francis, Dominic Guzmán (1170–1221), established an order of preachers who became itinerant evangelists. They appeared at the same time that the universities were being created, and many of them were employed as lecturers, including Thomas Aquinas (1226–1274). The Franciscans ("grey friars") and Dominicans ("black friars") are well known, and others sprang up in imitation of them.[5] One of these was the order of Augustinian canons ("Austin friars"), which appeared slightly later and sought to revive the monastic rule of Augustine of Hippo. Martin Luther joined them in 1505 and remained an Augustinian friar until he was excommunicated in 1520.

Luther's example is a reminder that friars were often closely connected to reform movements within the church. They were not immune to corruption or to a decline of spiritual zeal, but reform was in their blood, and around 1500 it was progressing steadily in some quarters. For example, in the late fifteenth century a suborder of Observant Franciscans emerged that is sometimes credited with heading off the Reformation in places like Ireland, not so much because they opposed what the Reformers wanted but because they were doing the same things already, without breaking their loose ties to the institutional church. It is certainly remarkable that a disproportionate number of early Reformers were ex-friars, attracted by the teaching and ideals of one of their number who appeared to be leading the way when the main body of the church was reluctant or unable to follow him.

Alongside the monks and friars were the ordained clergy, a body of spiritual persons who lived in a different world. Those who were also monks or friars were known as regulars because they lived according to a rule (*regula*), whereas the parish priests were seculars because they

---

[5]The colors reflected the habits they wore.

shared the life of ordinary people. The clergy were subdivided into a number of ranks (called orders), which were cumulative. The top three orders were classified as "holy" and consisted of bishops, priests, and deacons. It was not possible to become a priest without first becoming a deacon, and only a priest could be consecrated as a bishop.[6] Few men remained permanent deacons, and almost all were ordained to the priesthood within a year or so. On rare occasions a man might be elected a bishop before he was ordained to any office in the church, but in that case he would have to be made a deacon and a priest at the same time. This had famously happened to Ambrose of Milan in 374, and it is known as ordination *per saltum* (by leaping). Although ordination *per saltum* was possible, it was very rare and usually regarded as an abuse. It should be noted that there was no correspondence between the religious orders and holy orders—some regulars were ordained but many were not, and it was unusual for a monk or a friar to become a parish priest. What was possible in theory was not particularly common in practice, although exceptions could always be made; our picture is incomplete because no systematic study of the careers of medieval spiritual persons has ever been attempted.

To become a monk or friar, a person needed to submit to the rule of a specific order. Beyond that, there was a great deal of variety. Monks and nuns worked in the monasteries and formed part of the community, but since many had little education, they did not take an active part in the teaching and preaching ministry.

Ordination was different. It required passing an examination, sponsored by a bishop but in most cases administered by his archdeacon, who normally supervised the process. To qualify, a man had to know the Ten Commandments, the Lord's Prayer, and the Apostles' Creed by heart and expound them orally. This pattern covered the three ages of church history—the Old Testament, the Gospels, and

---

[6]Note, however, that all priests were also deacons, and all bishops were both.

the Epistles (since it was believed that the creed had been composed by the apostles) and were also represented in the daily liturgy, in which passages from all three parts of the Bible were normally read. On the theological level, they also covered discipline, devotion, and doctrine, which together formed the basis of the Christian life. The enduring importance of this pattern can be seen in John Calvin's *Institutes of the Christian Religion*, in which he expounded each in detail, a point whose significance is not always appreciated today.[7] The legacy of this tradition was so strong that it can even be seen in Thomas Watson's *A Body of Divinity*, which was published as late as 1691.[8] Watson substituted the Westminster Confession of Faith for the Apostles' Creed but otherwise adhered to the traditional pattern, which he regarded as fundamental for the training of a minister in the church.

How faithfully the official standards were upheld is impossible to say. The Reformers constantly complained about the ignorance of the parish clergy, but how much of that was fact as opposed to rhetoric we do not know. A man could have memorized the required texts and expounded their meaning without being able to read, and the rarity of books might have meant he had little opportunity to exercise that skill if he had once acquired it. His knowledge of Latin may also have been fairly rudimentary and easily lost once he was in the parish, where almost no one could have conversed with him in that language. Until 812 the clergy were expected to preach in Latin, but the futility of this was recognized in that year when Charlemagne gave them permission to address their flocks in the *lingua rustica* (country language), whatever that was.[9]

---

[7]John Calvin, *Institutes of the Christian Religion*, 2 vols., ed. J. T. McNeill, trans. F. L. Battles (Philadelphia, PA: Westminster Press, 1960). His exposition of the Ten Commandments is found in 2.8.10-50, the Lord's Prayer in 3.20.34-49, and the Apostles' Creed in 2.16.5-19 and 4.1.1-3.

[8]Thomas Watson, *A Body of Divinity* (London: Banner of Truth, 1965).

[9]The local dialects were ancestors of the modern European languages, but they were not yet codified as such.

Preaching had been a mainstay of the early church, and men like Augustine and John Chrysostom became famous for it in their own lifetimes. Some of their sermons have been preserved, but it is hard to know how widely read they were or whether they were used as models to be imitated by the parish clergy. Chrysostom was largely unknown in the West until the fifteenth century, but when his homilies were translated into Latin, they caused a sensation. The Reformers were particularly taken with them, often quoting church fathers in their own sermons and writings, using Chrysostom's authority as a father of the early church to bolster their own calling to be preachers of the Word of God. The monastic tradition also produced some notable preachers, such as Bernard of Clairvaux (1090–1153), who was famous for his ability in the pulpit. His eighty-six expository sermons on the Song of Solomon (in which he reached no further than chapter three, verse five) are still in print and were greatly admired by the Reformers.

In the next generation a revived interest in preaching and manuals for its instruction began to appear. A Parisian theologian called Peter the Chanter (d. 1197) is generally credited with writing the first of these, but more influential was Thomas of Chobham's textbook, written sometime around the year 1215. He explained preaching as the art of biblical exposition, which he divided into three parts: *lectio*, *disputatio*, and *exhortatio*. Today we would call them exegesis, exposition, and application, but the basic pattern is the same. The first duty of the preacher was to understand the meaning of his text, which involved intense grammatical study. Those who have tried to read the Bible in a foreign language (as Latin was to Thomas) know that they must pay attention to every word, and that is what Thomas tried to inculcate in his readers. If a preacher did not know what he was reading, there was no point in delivering a sermon on it, since it was almost certain to go wrong.

The second stage was theological argument. To us the word *disputation* sounds negative, but Thomas used it to describe a process of discerning what a particular text meant in the context of the Bible as a whole—how an individual datum related to the overall data. Doing this successfully required a mastery of systematic theology, a discipline that was coming into its own even as Thomas was writing. Finally, and most important, was application. It was not enough for preachers to explain what a text meant—they also had to apply it to the lives of their hearers. Preachers would often resort to typology and even allegory since it might have been hard to find something relevant to convey to the congregation otherwise. The apostle Paul provides precedent for this in 1 Corinthians 9:9, where he quotes Deuteronomy 25:4 ("You shall not muzzle an ox when it is treading out the grain") and applies it to the church's duty to fund its ministers. Thomas recommended this kind of application to the preachers of his own time in an effort to make the Scriptures seem relevant to their hearers.

Thomas is largely forgotten now, but his manual remained in circulation for centuries and his method was used by no less than John Calvin, whose literary legacy can largely be subsumed under the same three categories. Calvin's commentaries are his exegesis, or *lectio*; his *Institutes* are his exposition, or *disputatio*; and his sermons are his application, or *exhortatio*—all of which were designed to model the training of pastors for the Reformed churches. In this way Thomas of Chobham lives on, even though almost nobody today realizes it.

These books and methods intended for preachers existed for three centuries before the Reformation, but how widely were they used? Some priests would have been able to preach, but many could not, nor were they encouraged to learn. It was not just that many pastors would have talked nonsense in the name of expounding a biblical text (a phenomenon that is by no means unknown even now), but there was always the danger that they might use the pulpit for political agitation and spark social unrest in their parishes. That actually happened in England in the late fourteenth and early fifteenth centuries, largely thanks to the ferment caused by John Wyclif and his followers. The upshot was that in 1407 the English clergy were *forbidden* to preach unless they could obtain a license to do so, and we may be sure that anyone who was suspect would not have received one. Those who wanted to hear a sermon could always listen to a visiting friar, and many were sought after for that reason. Little wonder that the Reformation got its greatest support among these people.

In the late Middle Ages, preaching was often seen as a potentially subversive and antiestablishment activity. Friars went out into the streets and spoke to the masses, sometimes with electrifying results. A skillful orator could move the people, as the Dominican friar Girolamo Savonarola (1452–1498) proved when he managed to persuade the citizens of Florence to repent of their sins and turn to an ascetic form of Christian devotion in what became known as "the bonfire of the vanities." When John Wyclif's followers took his message to the streets, it sparked a peasants' revolt, and something similar occurred soon after Luther began his reform movement. Neither man wanted that to happen, but they could do little to stop it. Preaching became and remained the single most important activity of the Protestant clergy, and the Reformers tried to ensure that ministers were properly trained in the principles of the gospel and authorized to convey that message in and through the structures of the church. Their emphasis on a properly ordered preaching ministry must be understood against this background, as must the alarm aroused by unauthorized preachers like John Bunyan, however gifted they may have been.

Putting preaching first was risky, and whether the Reformers realized it or not, this emphasis contributed to a long-term change in the general perception of what constituted a spiritual person. A man had to have something to say when he got up to preach. He could learn the information that had to be conveyed, but ultimately preaching was a gift and not something that could be routinely produced by a process of ordination. The Reformers recognized this because to them preaching was the contemporary manifestation of prophecy. They identified their task with Elijah and Isaiah's, the important difference being that the Reformers were proclaiming a Messiah who had already come. There could certainly be false prophets as in the Old Testament, but real prophets were men filled with the Spirit of God, and the truth of their calling was seen in the fruit produced in the lives of their hearers.

The institutional church did its best to contain preachers within established structures, but the nature of their ministry made that impossible. In the Protestant world a man with the gift of preaching would ideally be ordained and assigned to a pulpit. Unfortunately, as we know, many went through the formalities but either lacked the gift or preached a false doctrine. When that happened, their ministry was discredited—nobody thought that they should be respected and listened to merely because they had been approved by the system. This new dispensation was far from foolproof, but it changed forever the way in which a spiritual person would be defined, and it became the harbinger of a new kind of church.

DEVOTIONAL LIFE

In the Middle Ages the clergy's primary duty was to lead the people in public worship, which was frequent and varied. Preaching was not unknown, but it did not play a significant role in most places. Much more important were the liturgies, composed to a large extent of set prayers and readings from the Bible in Latin, which most people could not understand, and supplemented by a wide range of ritual acts and symbolic gestures that communicated to the worshipers what was supposed to be happening at any particular moment. In the monasteries a daily pattern of prayer was supplemented by the continuous reading of Scripture and the church fathers at mealtimes. Monks were even expected to get up in the middle of the night for prayers so that the apostolic injunction to "pray without ceasing" might be literally honored.[10] Parish churches were inevitably less rigorous, but ideally they would also have morning and evening prayers every day and regular celebrations of the Lord's Supper, especially on Sundays and the numerous "holy days" that commemorated events in the life of Jesus or his mother Mary, such as Christmas, the Epiphany (January 6), the Purification of the Virgin Mary (February 2), and the Annunciation (March 25). Saints' days would also be observed in this way, and there was a wide range to choose from. A few, like the Birth of John the Baptist (June 24) were all but universal, but many honored regional luminaries, like St. David's Day in Wales (March 1) or St. Patrick's Day in Ireland (March 17). The average church might have as many as eighty or ninety such feast days, taking up about a quarter of the entire year.

The content of worship services followed a general pattern, but there were many local variations, and the evidence we have for them is far from complete. The Lord's Supper was central to them all, of course, and its importance was greatly enhanced in the later Middle Ages. This was largely because of the doctrine of transubstantiation, which was first broached by Paschasius Radbertus in the ninth century and subsequently canonized at the Fourth Lateran Council in 1215. Based on the Aristotelian analysis of matter into form and substance, the doctrine claimed that when consecrated, the Communion elements of bread and wine were changed into the body and blood of Christ. This was not a change of form—they continued to look, taste, and feel like bread and wine—but of underlying substance. The communicant would be receiving Christ's body and blood in what only looked and felt like ordinary bread and wine.

Transubstantiation greatly enhanced the status of the priest, who was the only person authorized to perform what was commonly known as "the miracle of the altar." Once the elements were consecrated,

---

[10]1 Thess 5:17. Even the most literalistic modern interpreters do not read this verse in the way their medieval predecessors did.

they had to be consumed or reserved for future use. Over time wine (or "the cup," as it is usually referred to) was withdrawn from the laity and consumed by the priest on their behalf. It is not certain why this was so—some people think it was for reasons of hygiene, but that cannot be proved. In any case, it caused a controversy, and in Bohemia a movement for maintaining Communion "in both kinds" had wide appeal. One of its heroes was Jan Hus (1371–1415), who was actually tried for heresy and burnt at the stake for insisting on it. Hus's "crime" was not doctrinal but disciplinary—he rejected the authority of the papacy, which had authorized Communion in one kind, and therefore had to be taught a lesson. Whether death by fire was the best resolution may be questioned, of course, and the Hus affair remained controversial long after his death. People resurrected Hus's example when Martin Luther broke with the papacy. Luther acknowledged a spiritual affinity with Hus, and we should not be surprised that his followers hid him for three years for fear that he might share his hero's fate.

Unconsumed consecrated bread and wine was put in a box called a tabernacle (after the Old Testament example) and reserved in a part of the church, usually in a side chapel, where it became the object of devotion and might even be paraded around the streets on feast days. There was even a feast of Corpus Christi, which was invented in the thirteenth century in order to legitimize this kind of devotion and spread rapidly after 1300. Once transubstantiation caught on, priests became indispensable; without them there could be no miracle of the altar. They had the power to bring the ascended Christ back down to earth and to feed him directly to his people as a spiritual medicine for their diseased souls. Whether the priest said the words of consecration correctly mattered little since they were in Latin and hardly anyone understood them. But actions spoke louder than words, and everybody knew what was happening when the priest consecrated the elements and elevated them above his head so that everyone could see them—the miracle had occurred. At a moment like that, who but an

academic pedant would have cared what the priest was saying? But in
the late fifteenth century, academic pedants (or scholars, as we would
now call them) were becoming more numerous and vocal, and many
of them were scandalized at what they perceived as nothing more
than popular ignorance and superstition, aided and abetted by clergy
who were little better educated than the people they were expected
to serve.

The Lord's Supper and its central place in Christian worship went
back to New Testament times, but in the Middle Ages it was integrated into a wider sacramental structure of much more recent origin.
The word *sacrament*, which in Latin meant "oath," was taken over
around AD 200 by Tertullian, who used it to describe baptism. As
far as Tertullian was concerned, the church was the Lord's army, and
its members had to vow allegiance to Christ when they were enrolled
in it. This was their profession of faith, which was sealed by the rite
of baptism that had been enjoined by Jesus himself. Later on, and in
a completely independent development, Cyril of Jerusalem (mid-
fourth century) applied the New Testament term *mysterion* to the
Lord's Supper, although the word was not used by the apostles in that
sense. Soon afterward, men like Ambrose of Milan (d. 397) were
using *sacramentum* as the Latin equivalent of *mysterion*, a development that naturally facilitated the combining of baptism with the
Lord's Supper into a single category of sacraments.

There matters rested until the twelfth century, when the urge toward greater systematization of doctrine led to a further elaboration
of this association. A sacrament was defined as a means of grace—in
other words, as a way in which God imparted his grace to his people.
That, of course, was the bedrock of our salvation, which could not
occur otherwise. In earlier times, the gift of grace had not been limited to specific acts; it was generally recognized that God was free to
manifest himself in any way he might choose. But to the Western
theologians of the twelfth century, such open-ended ambiguity was

inadequate. They wanted to tie the matter down, not to restrict the grace of God but to reassure people that participation in certain rites would grant them access to the divine grace necessary for their salvation. Definition, in other words, was intended to bolster people's faith, not to limit the power and sovereignty of God.

It was Hugh of St. Victor (ca. 1096–1141), the first person to write at length on this subject, who picked up and popularized Augustine's statement that a sacrament was an outward and visible sign of an inward and spiritual grace. In other words, the operation of God's grace was proclaimed—and in effect sealed—by a visible sign set aside for that purpose. In baptism, the water was consecrated and then applied to the recipient, either by sprinkling or by immersion; it did not matter which. As Tertullian had claimed, the blessed water was itself charged with the presence of the Holy Spirit, who passed through it into the bodies of those being baptized, cleansing them of their sins. But where Tertullian had advocated delaying baptism as long as possible so as to avoid the possibility that a person would sin again *after* baptism and so lose his salvation, later Christian writers rejected that approach. Instead, following Augustine, they claimed that baptism removed original (or birth) sin, opening the door to a spiritual life that would be strengthened by constant recommitment. If that did not happen, the efficacy of the grace granted in baptism would gradually be lost because the recipient would have shown himself incapable of receiving it properly.

Following Augustine's understanding, baptism was best administered to babies as soon as possible after their birth so that their salvation could be assured before they had a chance to commit actual sins. In the Christian world, baptismal regeneration was more important than physical birth, which usually went unrecorded. Martin Luther was baptized on November 11, 1483, and given the name Martin because that was the feast day of St. Martin of Tours. We assume that this occurred within twenty-four hours of his birth since that was the normal practice at that time, so his birthday is usually said to be November 10. After the Reformation, state authorities began to insist that records of births, marriages, and deaths should be kept, but those who consult these documents today soon realize that what was actually recorded were baptisms, marriages, and burials because they were of more significance. Only occasionally do we know exactly when a person was born or died, and this is usually because he or she was of exceptional importance—a royal or noble personage, for example.

Baptism would normally be administered by a priest in the local church, but that was not necessary. In cases of emergency, of which there were many, anyone could baptize a newly born infant, and midwives frequently did so if it seemed likely that the child would not survive. In order to regularize this situation, a second rite was devised, which we call confirmation. Whether confirmation is a sacrament in its own right or just an extension of baptism has never been finally decided, but in the medieval Western church it gradually acquired a life of its own. In theory it was reserved to the bishop, whose duty it was to ascertain that the recipient had been validly baptized. The sign that sealed it was the oil, or chrism, that bishops regularly consecrated on Maundy Thursday, the day before Good Friday. Priests were expected to go to the bishop and claim some of that oil for their own parishes, which they could then administer to the newly baptized, effectively circumventing the need for a separate ceremony. The chrism was meant to signify the gift of the Holy Spirit, whose presence confirmed the validity of the baptism (see Acts 8:14-17), but the basis for this practice was unclear, to put it mildly. In the end, confirmation probably became a sacrament in its own right because it was needed to make up the number seven, which was held to be the perfect number.

Those who were baptized and confirmed could then receive the other sacraments, of which three (penance, the Lord's Supper, and extreme unction) were intended for everyone and two (matrimony and holy orders) were given only to some. Extreme unction, or the anointing with oil that preceded death, was supposedly based on James 5:14-15, in which the elders of the church were told to anoint the sick. The original purpose was for healing, but that was soon forgotten, not least because in premodern times death rates were very high. The healing was real, but it was interpreted spiritually—the anointed person would be healed in the next life, if not in this one.

Holy matrimony was exceptional in that it was not specifically Christian in origin but had been instituted in the Garden of Eden and was practiced, albeit in different forms, across the whole world. It was therefore a sacrament of creation, not of redemption. The New Testament recognized a link between it and the suffering of Christ (Eph 5:22-30). The early church did not celebrate weddings, and beyond advising people not to marry outside the faith, it had little to do with matrimony of any kind. It was only around the year 1000 that the church began to advocate marriage *in facie ecclesiae* (in front of the church), probably because it was the best way of ensuring that it had actually taken place. By the time of the Reformation, church weddings had become the norm in western Europe and were universally accepted, but the justification for calling matrimony a sacrament remained unclear. The church insisted, however, that those who had received the grace of matrimony were not eligible for the additional grace of holy orders (other than the diaconate). The arbitrariness of that decision was hard to defend yet applied with increasing rigor as time went on. By 1500 the only country where priests were regularly allowed to marry was Ireland, an anomaly that survived until after the Reformation, when Irish priests who remained loyal to Rome were forced to submit to celibacy as a sign of their commitment to Catholicism.

In practice, therefore, the only sacraments that played a part in the everyday life of most Christians were penance and the Lord's Supper, which were closely tied to one another. Following the biblical injunction, someone who had a grievance against another person was expected to reconcile with him or her before coming to the Lord's Table, and that principle was extended to cover everyone all the time.[11] No one was free from sin, and even if a particular person had not offended any other human being, he would certainly have offended God. It was therefore necessary for him to confess that sin before receiving the Lord's body and blood. There was no absolute reason why such a confession had to be made to a priest, but practicalities intervened to make that the accepted norm. To ensure that the confession was sincere, the priest would give the penitent sinner a duty to fulfill, which came to be understood as penance. What was required depended on the gravity of the sin committed, and priests were even given lists of sins with the appropriate penance attached. When the sinner had accomplished what was asked of him, he would return to the priest, be absolved of his sin, and admitted to the Lord's Supper.

It is hardly necessary to say that a system of this kind, however well-intentioned it may have been to begin with, was open to hypocrisy and abuse on a massive scale. Many people confessed trivial sins and did perfunctory penance, leaving their greater crimes unmentioned. Priests swore an oath not to reveal the sins confessed to them, but who could be sure that they would keep their word, especially if the sin was something like murder or rebellion against the secular ruler? The potential for dishonesty and legalism was enormous, and by 1500 penance was often held in disrepute. Worse still was the fact that unconfessed sins would not be paid for in this life, making it doubtful whether those who committed them—virtually everybody—would go to heaven when they died. To deal with that problem, the church invented purgatory, a place where remaining sins could be atoned for after death as a preparation for entering the eternal state of the blessed.[12]

---

[11] See Mt 5:23-24.
[12] See J. Le Goff, *The Birth of Purgatory* (Chicago: University of Chicago Press, 1984).

Purgatory is not mentioned in the Bible and was unknown in ancient times. The Eastern Orthodox churches rejected it, as they still do today. But in western Europe it became central to the church's proclamation of the gospel and was fortified by an extraordinary practice that was theoretically based on Matthew 5:39-41. For example, if the penance demanded for a sin was to walk a mile, the truly penitent would go another mile to show how contrite he was. That extra mile could then be chalked up to his credit as a work of "supererogation" and used to deduct time from his stay in purgatory. In a further development, it became possible to purchase these so-called indulgences, not only for oneself but for loved ones who might even then be enduring the pains that purgatory was imposing. Like today's bookstore gift cards, these indulgences could be used as presents, whether the recipient wanted them or not.

Although this had nothing to do with genuine repentance, and reformers constantly tried to abolish the practice, they met with little success. As long as the alternative was actually doing penance, either in this life or the next, buying indulgences remained popular. At the same time, it is not hard to see why this practice, rather than anything else, provided the spark that set Europe ablaze with the Reformation. The grace of God could not be bought, and the pope had no authority beyond the confines of this life—it was not in his power to determine who could be allowed out of purgatory or on what basis that reprieve might be granted. If limitations of papal jurisdiction were established, it would not be long before the whole system would be questioned and come apart at the seams. The reformation of the church was to a large extent a reformation of its sacramental theology, for even when the practices themselves were retained, they were given a new meaning and set in a new context. That context no longer coincided with the teaching of the late medieval church and was in turn rejected by those who not only wanted to remove recognized abuses but were determined to retain the essence of the traditional structure that they believed was still sound. Very often it was this difference of opinion that determined which side would-be reformers chose. Would they follow Luther, who came to think that only a radical reshaping of the system could bring back the sound teaching of the apostles, or would they prefer the view of someone like Erasmus, who knew that the church had become corrupted in many ways but who believed that the disease was curable and did not require a root-and-branch reformation? The Lutherans became Protestants; the Erasmians on the whole did not.

THE ACADEMIC EXPERIENCE

Beyond the parishes and the monasteries lay the world of the universities, which had emerged in the thirteenth century when newly formed schools of theology, law, and medicine banded together in Bologna and Paris. Later they spread further afield, particularly to Oxford and Cambridge in England. By 1300 they were well established, with further expansion to come over the next two hundred years. At first the universities competed with the monasteries as training centers for the clergy, but their systematic approach and dedication to learning gave them a distinct advantage that increased over time.

Academic study in the fifteenth and sixteenth centuries was fundamentally oral in character. Lecturers would speak in front of a class while their pupils memorized what they said. Students would then be expected to repeat it back to their teachers and expound its meaning. Even after the invention of printing, books were not common in the classroom, and the ancient traditions persisted. We can see this most clearly in some of the writings of Martin Luther, which are in fact lecture notes taken by his students as they listened to his oral presentation. When Luther's famous second set of lectures on Galatians was prepared for publication on the basis of student notes, he was allowed to look over the result before it went to print. Despite a certain skepticism, Luther admitted in his preface that he could hear himself speaking when he read the text—in other words, his students had heard and transcribed him correctly.[13]

Inevitably, this approach to learning produced all kinds of mnemonic devices—short acronyms and rhymes that allowed a student to recall what the subject was without having to look it up. An example of this practice is still seen today when the so-called five points of Calvinism are reduced to TULIP—Total depravity, Unconditional election, Limited atonement, Irresistible grace, and the Perseverance of the saints—even though ULTIP would more accurately reflect the original order. But what happens only occasionally nowadays was standard practice in Martin Luther's time. Students did not write examination papers—their thesis defense resembled an oral presentation in a modern courtroom more than what is normally found in university courses. They had to think on their feet and display an ability to convince their hearers—and of course, they did it all in Latin. To prepare for this, they spent years studying grammar and rhetoric because Latin was a foreign language to them. Stock expressions abound in their works because they were immediately recognized by their readers. Originality was discouraged because it hindered communication and could easily be misunderstood. Something of this tradition lingers today. For example, when we say Luther taught that a Christian is *simul iustus et peccator*, a "justified sinner," the Latin phrase stands out as quintessentially Lutheran, and by using it we can convey a complete theological perspective without actually saying so.[14] This is a remnant of the pre-modern era that we have preserved, perhaps without fully realizing it, but to Luther and his students it would have been completely natural—they did it all the time.

---

[13] Martin Luther, *Luther's Works: American Edition*, ed. J. Pelikan et al. (Philadelphia, PA: Fortress Press, 1957–1975), 27:45 (hereafter *LW*).

[14] It occurs in Luther's second lectures on Gal 3:6. See *LW*, 26:32.

Modern people might think that this method entailed a lot of unnecessary communication, but in fact it did not. The short phrases were meant to assist memory recall and get everyone on the same page, as it were, but they were just the beginning of the discussion. A good student would be expected to elaborate on them, sometimes at great length and taking the subject down all kinds of secondary alleyways before coming to some definite application of the underlying principle(s). In other words, the mnemonics were not an invitation to taciturn brevity, but the very opposite. Particularly notorious in this respect was Martin Bucer, who regularly used Bible verses as opportunities to discourse at length on the subject they addressed, whether his reflections were germane to the context or not. This is one reason why his lectures on Ephesians are now virtually unreadable. When we finally get back to the commentary on the biblical text after so many digressions, we have often lost any sense of where he had started.

The oral nature of this learning and the importance given to rhetoric and thinking on one's feet was obviously very useful for a budding preacher. Someone who combined prophetic inspiration with communication skills was well placed to proclaim the Word of God, and the Reformers were keen on producing an educated ministry. Before the Reformation a university degree was not much of an advantage in securing a pastoral position, and in many cases it was actually a hindrance. One reason was that monasteries had acquired a large number of parishes whose tithes helped to support them, and they naturally preferred to put their own people in charge of them. Another problem was that scholars were ill-suited to rural life. People who knew Greek might not be able to milk a cow, and in the average village the latter skill was required, not the former. Fifteenth-century church records tell of university chancellors begging bishops to find posts for their graduates. Country churches did not want them, and, truth be told, few preachers wanted to go there either. They lived in a different world, and compulsory celibacy, while tolerable in a college environment, looked very different in a small community where everyone except the priest was married.

In the late fifteenth century a candidate for holy orders would normally follow a curriculum that included lectures on the Bible, usually denoted as the "sacred page" (*sacra pagina*), and systematically arranged theological topics. At the end of the course, the successful student would be a professor of sacred theology (*Sacrae Theologiae Professor*), usually abbreviated after his name as STP. An STP who wanted to teach in a university would be expected to write and defend a dissertation on some aspect of Peter Lombard's *Sententiae* (*Sentences*), which was the standard theological textbook of the time. Peter (ca. 1100–1160) had been a teacher in Paris and died there as the city's bishop. He was the first person in western Europe to make a serious attempt at systematizing the church's theology, which he divided into four main categories: the Trinity, creation, the incarnation of Christ, and the sacraments. He wrote a book on each of these in turn, quoting liberally from the Latin fathers of the church, especially Augustine. Peter knew no Greek and so did not quote Greek writers unless they had been translated into Latin. He also cited a number of medieval sources that he believed were from Augustine but (as we now know) were not. Despite such defects, the Lombard's collection became and remained the theological textbook everyone knew and used.[15] To become a university lecturer in theology it was necessary to write a dissertation on some aspect of the *Sentences*, and we now have a vast collection of these.[16] Thomas Aquinas, for example, regarded his massive *Summa Theologiae* as basically an extended

---

[15]Peter Lombard, *Sententiae in IV libris distinctae*, 2 vols. (Grottaferrata: Editiones Collegii S. Bonaventurae ad Claras Aquas, 1971–1981). It is indicative of the eclipse that the *Sententiae* suffered after the Reformation that no translations were produced until the early twenty-first century. See Giulio Silano, trans., *Peter Lombard. The Sentences*, 4 vols. (Toronto: Pontifical Institute of Mediaeval Studies, 2007–2010); and Marc Ozilou, trans., *Pierre Lombard: Les quatre livres des Sentences* (Paris: Cerf, 2012–2015).

[16]See G. R. Evans, ed., *Mediaeval Commentaries on the* Sentences *of Peter Lombard*, 2 vols. (Leiden: Brill, 2002).

commentary on Peter's work. Martin Luther also wrote a dissertation on them, on the strength of which he became not just a professor but a doctor of sacred theology (STD).[17]

This emphasis on Peter Lombard, and the approach taken to his writings, gave medieval theology an identity that transcended local interests and ensured that, however much later theologians might develop their own ideas, they never succeeded in dominating the intellectual life of the church. Today we call it scholasticism because it was the method used in the schools of theology, and in its heyday it raised the standards of education considerably. An STP or an STD had a professional qualification that was recognized across Europe, creating a guild of professional clergy who read and absorbed one another's work. This greatly facilitated the Reformation because men like Luther, Martin Bucer, and Huldrych Zwingli (1484–1531) shared a common world of discourse, even if they sometimes disagreed with one another. Debates of various kinds were by no means excluded from this charmed circle, but they tended to sound esoteric to those who were unfamiliar with the methods being used. For example, a question like "Did Adam have a navel?" sounds odd to the uninitiated, although when you stop to think about it, it is really a debate between creation and evolution.

Unfortunately, like any other educational method, scholasticism eventually reached the limits of its creativity and became increasingly stale as time went on. Theologians repeated worn-out arguments with conventional solutions that surprised nobody. The creative potential of Thomas Aquinas's *Summa* was downplayed because it was regarded as just another commentary on Peter Lombard. Astonishing though it may seem nowadays, John Calvin probably never read it, and certainly did not engage with it, although, like Luther, he had a lot to say about the "Master of the *Sentences*." Nobody in the sixteenth

---

[17]See P. Vignaux, *Luther, commentateur des* Sentences (Paris: Vrin, 1935).

century would have been surprised by this—Peter Lombard was the touchstone of orthodoxy, and compared with him, Aquinas had seemingly little to offer. Shortly before he posted his Ninety-Five Theses on the church door in Wittenberg, Martin Luther produced another ninety-seven in which he attacked many of the premises of scholastic theology, but he did not mention either Lombard or Aquinas. His targets were John Duns Scotus (d. 1308), William of Ockham (ca. 1285–ca. 1347), Pierre d'Ailly (1350–1420), and Gabriel Biel (ca. 1425–1495), the writers whose works he actually read.[18] Of them, Ockham was himself an opponent of traditional scholastic method, and the other three were second-rate thinkers at best. Duns Scotus in particular had a reputation that greatly exceeded his talent, so much so that his followers were called *dunces*, an epithet that was intended to be a byword for stupidity, as it still is.[19]

It was also quite common for university students to study law, which included secular Roman (civil) law and the canon law of the church that was adapted from it.[20] A successful candidate might then become a *doctor civilis iuris*, a *doctor canonici iuris*, or (quite often) a *doctor utriusque iuris* (doctor of both laws) and earn a good living working as an advocate in one of the ecclesiastical courts. Those who attained that level were the church's aristocracy and were usually deeply involved in its administration—the "establishment" as we

---

[18]See Vignaux, *Luther commentateur*, who explores Luther's relationship to these scholastic thinkers in depth. See also Theodor Dieter, "Luther as Late Medieval Theologian," in *The Oxford Handbook of Martin Luther's Theology*, ed. R. Kolb, I. Dingel, and L. Batka (Oxford: Oxford University Press, 2014), 31-48.

[19]See "Disputation Against Scholastic Theology," in *LW*, 31:9-16, reprinted in T. F. Lull, ed., *Martin Luther's Basic Theological Writings*, 2nd ed. (Minneapolis, MN: Fortress Press, 2005), 34-39.

[20]It is noteworthy that Luther quoted from thesis 81 of his "Disputation Against Scholastic Theology" to support his position against the Scholastics. See *Decretum Gratiani*, C. 33, q. 3, d. 5, c. 6, in *Corpus iuris canonici*, ed. E. Freidberg, 2 vols. (Graz: Akademische Druck und Verlagsanstalt, 1955), I, col. 1241. It is unfortunate but sadly typical that there is no chapter in the recent *Oxford Handbook of Martin Luther's Theology* dealing with his use of the canon law, nor is the subject mentioned in the *Dictionary of Luther and the Lutheran Traditions*, ed. T. J. Wengert (Grand Rapids: Baker, 2017).

would call them now—so it is not surprising that they were mostly opposed to any sort of reform and were among Luther's most determined opponents. When Luther submitted his famous Ninety-Five Theses to the canon lawyers of the University of Paris (Sorbonne) for adjudication, they rejected them and virtually condemned Luther as a heretic. For his part, Luther burned the books of canon law in Wittenberg and abolished the teaching of the subject in the university, a pattern that would be followed fifteen years later by King Henry VIII in England. Both men perceived that as long as the canon lawyers could oppose reform, whatever the Reformers wanted to do was ultimately doomed to fail. That was why the power of the canonists had to be broken and why, at the very beginning of the Reformation, the canon law was either secularized (as in Germany and Scandinavia) or put in the hands of lay lawyers who had not been trained in it (as in England and Ireland).

It is important to bear this in mind because before the Reformation the study of canon law and theology often went together and were regarded as two branches of the same discipline. When the Reformers talked about the law and tradition, they had the canon law in mind. Today when we hear these terms, we immediately think of the law of Moses and the interpretations that the Pharisees put on it. The Reformers, however, were primarily concerned with the situation in their own day, which they saw as essentially the same as what Jesus had confronted. They believed that by going to the root of canon law to the original sources of Christianity, they could recover the pure gospel and apply it to the life of the church.

How, then, can we summarize the education of a typical Reformer? First, it was Latin-based. The Reformers not only studied Latin as a subject but spoke and wrote it, sometimes with a fluency greater than what they were capable of in their mother tongues. Great emphasis was placed on oral skills and memorization, and the ability to speak well in public was the hallmark of a truly educated man.

They also studied the classics of Latin literature, especially the works of Virgil and Cicero, which they found impressive more in terms of style than content since these lacked the grace of Christian revelation. Pagan writings could never be embraced wholeheartedly in a Christian world, but despite their obvious defects, the ancient Greeks and Romans were often seen as paragons of virtue whose failure to accept Christ was due to ignorance rather than spiritual blindness or malice. Many were given a status not unlike that of the Old Testament prophets, and in that way they were sanitized for a Christian audience.

Second, students were exposed to the Bible from an early age, much of which they learned by heart (especially the Psalms). They studied it in Latin first, but as time went on the need to add Greek and Hebrew to their repertoire became increasingly pressing. Erasmus established the principle that a biblical scholar had to be a *vir trilinguis* (a man of three languages), a requirement that by 1500 had become all but universal. In the mid-fourteenth century John Wyclif could claim to be a biblical scholar with no knowledge of the original languages of the Scriptures, but that was no longer true in the time of Luther. The new emphasis on linguistic study naturally made people like him sensitive to the nuances of words and to the difficulty of producing accurate translations. The Latin Vulgate Bible's inadequacy was clear to those who studied the original texts, and scholars soon desired to improve on it. Erasmus produced his own Latin version of the New Testament, which he promoted as far superior to Jerome's Vulgate, but others were bolder still. If the Latin was just a translation, what was to stop people from turning the original texts into English or German? Wyclif's followers had already produced two English translations from the Latin: a literal one that was almost impossible to read and a more idiomatic version that can still be understood by educated readers today. Luther's German translation was more successful and set a trend that Reformers all over Europe copied. Their mother tongues, hitherto largely ignored, entered the curriculum and over time established themselves as worthy successors to their ancient classical models.

The Reformers vigorously pursued eloquence in Latin, which they used for university lectures and international communication, and their rigid training in the arts of rhetoric and grammar continued to be useful as they entered the pulpit and started expounding God's Word in their native languages. The spread of printing created a thirst for deeper knowledge of that Word, with all its hidden mysteries and obscure references to long-dead civilizations. Virtually nobody in sixteenth-century Europe had been to Egypt or Babylonia, and almost everything they knew about such places came from the Scriptures, supplemented by a few ancient Greek writers like Herodotus. The Bible became their history textbook, and for many it was thought to speak with comparable authority about all manner of subjects, including biology and astronomy. Whether the biblical writers had any particular knowledge of such things or any interest in them did not matter; what Scripture said was taken to be scientifically true, and anyone who disagreed with that was wrong. Eventually, as we now know, that understanding of Scripture would run into problems that have still not been fully resolved, but the generation of the Reformers remained blissfully ignorant. For them, to build on the principle of the Bible as the sole source of truth was to extend knowledge, not to stifle it, so studying it became central to their concept of education, both secular and religious.

It is not much of an exaggeration to say that education was the key to the Reformation. Long before the sixteenth century the medieval church appreciated the danger that learning presented, and the attempts made to regulate it were usually successful. Neither Wyclif nor Hus had a following like Luther's, probably because printing had not been invented in their time and few people really understood what they were saying. A combination of new technology, increased access to source material, and a general sense that exploration and discovery had opened up a new world made it impossible to hold back change any longer. The church tried to swim against the tide, and succeeded to a degree that seems astonishing to us today, but it could no longer suppress knowledge in the way it had once done. The most it could do was attack those who valued it. Even Erasmus, who had an international reputation and who never officially broke with Rome, was suspected of heresy and was eventually driven to seek refuge in Basel, a Protestant city, where he died in 1536. His followers were progressively shut out of universities in the Catholic world, which ceased to be creative centers of learning. In Protestant countries the traditions of the Renaissance were allowed to develop with greater freedom than was possible elsewhere, although not entirely without censorship.

Although education was a powerful weapon in the Protestant cause, it was neither the only nor the most important one. Protestant preachers knew their subject, but more importantly they knew Jesus Christ as their personal Lord and Savior. Luther was the man he was because his life had been transformed by the power of God, and that, rather than any particular knowledge or brilliance, allowed him to stand head and shoulders above his academic contemporaries and change the course of history. Like his fellow Reformers, he used his learning to the full, but he did so in the service of a gospel that went beyond the limits of human reason and that bore the authentic stamp of the Holy Spirit of God.

Two

The Sources
of Theological Authority

Four Authorities

The pre-Reformation church recognized four distinct sources of authority, each of which had played a part in attempts to reform it over the centuries.[1] The first and most important of these was the Bible, which (if the Old Testament is considered) predated the church by several centuries and remained fundamental as the deposit of the apostolic witness to Jesus. Its supremacy had always been acknowledged (at least in theory), and the other "authorities" all claimed to be secondary and subordinate to it to one degree or another. In practice, however, these subordinate authorities claimed the right to interpret Scripture, which blunted its force in the daily life of the church. In the fourteenth century John Wyclif had tried to liberate God's Word from these authorities by proclaiming that Scripture alone (*sola Scriptura*) should be the criterion for the church's teaching.[2] For a time he succeeded in making Bible reading popular, at least in the rather restricted circles of those who could read and afford to buy books, but the end result of his efforts was that the English church

---

[1] Today the last three of these would probably be grouped together as "tradition."
[2] John Wyclif, *On the Truth of Holy Scripture*, trans. I. C. Levy (Kalamazoo, MI: Medieval Institute Press, 2001).

made translating the Scriptures illegal, and it did what it could to prevent untrained people from gaining access to them.

The second major authority was tradition, originally a disorganized mass of material that had been preserved from ancient church councils, Roman imperial laws, and the orthodox writers or fathers of the early church. The legal texts were collated around the year 1140 by an obscure Italian monk called Gratian, who published them as the *Concordance of Discordant Canons*, or *Decretum* as it was more popularly known. The theological texts of the early fathers were also collected and systematized about the same time by Peter Lombard, who published them as his *Sentences*. Between them, the *Decretum* and the *Sentences* were the chief instruments by which the church brought order out of the chaos of its legal system and its teaching of theology, introducing a uniform standard where none had existed before. That was a major reform in itself, and both books retained their importance into the sixteenth century.

The third authority was the papacy. In theory, this went back to the apostle Peter, who was believed to have been the first bishop of Rome, but it was many centuries before that office assumed the importance it would later have. The papacy as the Reformers knew it was really the product of the eleventh-century reforms spearheaded by the monks of Cluny, a Benedictine monastery in Burgundy. These reforms created the College of Cardinals and established a system for electing the popes, which removed it from the distortions of secular political influence, at least in theory. The power of the popes increased dramatically from about 1050 to 1250, but after that, decay set in, and the fourteenth century was a particularly difficult time. However, the institution weathered the storms that assailed it, and by 1500 it appeared to have regained much of its power and prestige. Whether the papacy would be able to use its power to effect necessary changes in the sixteenth century was an open question. The Protestant reformers gave up on it and broke away, but others

remained faithful to the papacy and did what they could to revitalize
and centralize its authority.

The last great authority was the church councils. The first of these
had met in Jerusalem in the apostles' time and is recorded for us in
the New Testament.[3] Councils were regularly summoned in late
Roman times, but after 870 they ceased to meet until the pope called
one in 1123. From then on, a series of reforming councils laid the
foundations for the medieval church, including such controversial
things as compulsory clerical celibacy. In the late fourteenth and
early fifteenth centuries a massive struggle emerged between those
who advocated a monarchical church government focused on the
pope and those who preferred a conciliar approach. The papacy eventually prevailed and church councils faded out for a time. However,
one was called in 1512 (the Fifth Lateran Council, or Lateran V), and
it managed to produce some reforming measures over the five years it
convened. After the outbreak of Protestantism, many people appealed to a council as the best way of sorting out differences and reuniting the church if at all possible.

Inevitably, the Protestant reformers had to both decide what authority or authorities they would accept and explain why they rejected
the others. Let us take a look at each of them in turn and examine
how the Reformers reacted to them and why.

THE BIBLE

At the heart of the Christian church stands the Bible, the self-
revelation of God without which Christianity would not exist. Its
central role in Christian theology and devotion had been apparent
from the church's beginning. Jesus taught that he had come to fulfill
the Scriptures, by which he meant our Old Testament. The letters of
the apostle Paul are filled with references to it, and the essence of the

---

[3]Acts 15:1-29.

Christian gospel was that the promises made to the Israelites in the law and the prophets had been realized in the life, death, and resurrection of Christ, the Son of God.

The first generation of Christians had no New Testament, of course, but by the time Christian literature began to appear in reasonable quantity, the apostolic writings were accepted as Holy Scripture, supplementing (but not replacing) the revelation that had been given to the Jews. Known respectively as the Hebrew Truth (*hebraica veritas*) and the Christian Truth (*christiana veritas*), the two Testaments were joined together as the "catholic religion" (*catholica religio*), to use the term found in the Athanasian Creed, composed about AD 500. The Hebrew Truth laid the foundations of the church's theology by defining its fundamental monotheism and insisting that the created order is quite distinct from the nature of God. It also established the belief that God is both supreme over the entire universe and the Lord of one small but specially chosen nation on earth. God had established a covenant with the nation of Israel in which he revealed his purposes for them. The law God gave to Moses defined what he expected of his chosen people and held out the promise that one day he would vindicate their faithfulness by fulfilling the provisions of the law in a final and definitive way.

The church never seriously doubted that the Old Testament was the Word of God, but it rejected the literalistic interpretation of it that was favored among the Jews. Without denying its historicity or the validity of the laws given to Moses, Christian interpreters sought to discover the presence of Christ in the text. Initially, this was mainly interpreted as the fulfillment of prophecy, but as time went on, the church began to see the Hebrew Truth as a somewhat opaque revelation of God's purposes in Christ, whose person and work were believed to lie hidden beneath the surface of texts that apparently had nothing to do with him.

The Christian Truth, which we call the New Testament, was read as both the explanation of the fulfillment of prophecy and the key to unlocking the riddles of the Old Testament. It describes how, when the right time had come, God sent his Son into the world to live out the provisions of the Mosaic law in his own life and to sacrifice himself for the salvation of his people. That salvation made much of the Hebrew Truth redundant as far as religious practice was concerned, but this was because its purpose had been accomplished, not because it was bad or inadequate. In fact, the fulfillment of prophecy made it even more important to uncover the hidden meaning of the text so that it would remain relevant for the Christian life and not be discarded as something that was no longer applicable. The two Testaments belonged together in a single whole, centered on and interpreted in the light of the person and work of Christ. This is what we call the Christian faith or the catholic (universal, all-embracing) religion.

Odd though it may seem, the early church never formally defined which books belonged to the Bible. The content of the New Testament had been generally agreed since the fourth century, but the Old Testament was a different story. In principle it continued the Hebrew canon inherited from the Jews, but that was more complicated than it might appear. Very few Christians learned Hebrew, and for the most part the Greek translation made at Alexandria in the centuries before the coming of Christ, occasionally corrected and supplemented by other translations, was accepted as their canon. This was not particularly controversial at the time, because many Jews outside Palestine also used this version, which became known as the Septuagint (from the Latin word for seventy), so called because it was supposedly translated by a team of seventy scholars sent from Jerusalem for the purpose. The Septuagint (abbreviated as LXX) contained all the books of the Hebrew canon plus a number of others, most of which are now extant only in Greek. The status of these extra books was contested by Jerome (ca. 340–420), who said they had no place in the Old

Testament, but they were defended by Augustine, whose view of the matter prevailed in the medieval church.

The controversy lay dormant for several centuries but was revived in the century before the Reformation, along with the renewed interest in Hebrew and Greek. Discrepancies between the original Hebrew and the Greek translation were noticed, and people began to question what the true text was. Logically they should have preferred the Hebrew, and many did, but since the LXX had been translated long before the oldest surviving Hebrew manuscripts were copied, it was not clear that its renderings were necessarily inferior. Jerome's preference for the Hebrew, from which he translated his own Latin version (the so-called Vulgate, the church's standard text), helped to persuade scholars to reject the LXX, but this became a bone of contention between Catholics and Protestants. The Waldensians, who had broken with Rome during the Middle Ages and merged with Protestants in the sixteenth century, sided with Jerome and defined their canon as early as 1530.[4] The Catholic Council of Trent felt obliged to follow suit, which it did by affirming Augustine's position in 1546.[5] The Lutherans seem to have never made any official pronouncement on the canon, although in practice they followed the Waldensians, as did other Protestants.[6]

---

[4] Waldensian Confession 3. The text is in J. T. Dennison, *Reformed Confessions of the Sixteenth and Seventeenth Centuries in English Translation* (Grand Rapids: Reformation Heritage Books, 2008–2014), 1:73.

[5] N. P. Tanner, ed., *Decrees of the Ecumenical Councils* (Washington, DC: Georgetown University Press; London: Sheed and Ward, 1990), 2:663-64. The occasion was the fourth session of the council, held on April 8, 1546. The decree was accompanied by another one, naming the Latin Vulgate as the authoritative text for the church's interpretation.

[6] The Waldensian canon is found in the French Confession of La Rochelle (1559), the Belgic Confession (1561), and the Thirty-Nine Articles of the Church of England. For the Confession of La Rochelle, see J. Pelikan and V. Hotchkiss, eds., *Creeds and Confessions of Faith in the Christian Tradition* (New Haven, CT: Yale University Press, 2003), 2:375-76; and Dennison, *Reformed Confessions*, 2:142. For the Belgic Confession, see Pelikan and Hotchkiss, *Creeds and Confessions*, 2:407-8; and Dennison, *Reformed Confessions*, 2:426. For the Thirty-Nine Articles of the Church of England, see G. L. Bray, ed., *Documents of the English Reformation*, 2nd ed. (Cambridge: James Clarke, 2004), 287-88;

Today, this controversy has largely been resolved because both sides agree that the extra books, known as the Apocrypha, are of lesser authority than the Hebrew ones, but they are an important witness to what we call intertestamental Judaism and thus to the state of the Jewish world in the time of Jesus. But in the sixteenth century the lines were more starkly drawn. To both sides in the Reformation debates, the question was whether the apocryphal books were the Word of God. The Protestant argument, drawn from Jerome, was that if those texts had not been given to ancient Israel as part of their covenant, the answer had to be no. It was not just a matter of language but of recognition by the Jews. They did not hear the voice of God in those texts, and since the process of canonization had been entrusted to them before the coming of Christ, they ought not to be accepted by Christians either. We now know that the early church, although it had the Apocrypha, seldom if ever used it, particularly not in its teaching and preaching ministry. We can tell this from the fact that they did not produce commentaries on it, whereas they did on the Hebrew Old Testament. The Reformers may not have realized that, but their instinct was right and their decision to return to the Hebrew canon was in line not only with Judaism but with the early centuries of the church as well.

The authority of some of the twenty-seven New Testament books we now recognize as canonical was debated in the early church, but a widespread consensus emerged as early as the fourth century that has never been seriously contested. Both Catholics and Protestants accepted it in the sixteenth century, and the position has remained unchanged ever since. The main difference between the two sides in the Reformation was not over the content of the canon but over the priority to be given to the Greek text as opposed to the Latin. The Greek manuscripts used by Erasmus and others dated from late medieval

Pelikan and Hotchkiss, *Creeds and Confessions*, 2:529-30; and Dennison, *Reformed Confessions*, 2:755-56.

times and had suffered from the usual problems of transmission, whereas Jerome had been translating from much earlier Greek sources that in many respects were more accurate. This conflict has since been resolved by the rediscovery of more ancient Greek texts, which sometimes confirm the translation of Jerome and sometimes do not. Both sides in the Reformation debates now admit this, and they also agree that the original Greek must be preferred over the Latin. Convergence in this area has been possible because the dispute is based on historical science and not on theological principles.

On the whole, the Reformers' position has been confirmed by modern research, but in cases where Jerome's version has been vindicated on points of detail, Protestants now accept it on the basis of the evidence. A good example of this is the absence of the doxology to the Lord's Prayer in Jerome's translation of Matthew 6:13, which Erasmus criticized because it was in his Greek manuscripts and he thought that Jerome had omitted it. The Reformers mistakenly followed Erasmus in this, which is why the longer version of the prayer is found in the King James Bible. Modern translations have corrected this mistake, recognizing (on the basis of earlier Greek manuscripts) that Jerome was right. Differences of this kind are few and usually unimportant, but we must accept that the Reformers' desire to read and translate the Bible from the original languages did not always produce the best results, because the manuscript tradition they were following was late in date and occasionally corrupted.

Disputes among Christians about the content of the canon and the best manuscript readings pale in comparison to a more fundamental question—how to interpret the biblical texts correctly. Here Catholics and Protestants were much closer to each other than they were to Jews, as controversy with the latter would show. Jews and Christians shared the same Hebrew Bible but interpreted it in different ways. As Judaism developed, it extended the law's reach to cover aspects of life that the sacred texts do not mention. In the Jewish view, all creation is subject to the law of God and so some extension of revelation is justified. This is especially noticeable in the food laws, which do not mention things like pineapples or potatoes. Are they kosher or not? The rabbis had to find an answer to that kind of question, as they also did to such things as Sabbath observance, which began at sunset. What does a Jew do if he ventures beyond the Arctic Circle, where sunsets do not occur for much of the year? Christians tend to smile when they read about this sort of thing, but it was (and still is) a matter of great seriousness to Jews who take their religion literally, because every eventuality must somehow be covered.

In sharp contrast to this, the early Christians filtered the provisions of the law through the life and teaching of Jesus. That necessitated an interpretation of the texts that put the person and work of Christ at the center. Jesus had taught his disciples that the Scriptures spoke about him, and it was their duty to work out how it did so. Sometimes that seemed to be fairly obvious, as when the prophet Isaiah foretold that a virgin would conceive and bear a son who would be called Emmanuel, "God with us."[7] But few Old Testament texts were as straightforward as that. For the most part, Christians had to resort to a kind of interpretation that we now call typology, which regards the main characters and events recorded in the Old Testament as prefigurations of what Jesus Christ would do for the salvation of his people. Jesus (Joshua in Hebrew) was easily identified as the successor to Moses, who led the chosen people into the Promised Land. The difference between them was that the Old Testament Joshua conquered Canaan and established the Israelites as the dominant people there, whereas Jesus opened the gates of the kingdom of Heaven, the ultimate Promised Land of the saints in glory. Similarly, just as Solomon was the son of David who built the temple in Jerusalem, so Jesus was the greater son of David who identified himself as

---

[7]Is 7:14, quoted in Mt 1:23.

the temple and rose from the dead in order to establish the presence of his atoning sacrifice at the right hand of God.

Typology of this kind easily merged into what we now call allegory, which took this form of interpretation one step further. Typology did not deny the historical reality of the events described in the Old Testament but rather saw them as a fundamental part of God's ongoing self-revelation to his people. Allegory, however, frequently disregarded the historical background and offered an interpretation of the Hebrew texts that aligned them with the body (the literal sense), the soul (the moral sense), the spirit (the spiritual sense), and eschatology (the anagogical sense). The first of these was relatively straightforward, but the others involved varying degrees of conjecture and fantasy. It is hard to say whether the allegorizers believed that the events they were reinterpreting had occurred or not, but that did not matter very much to them. What counted was the spiritual lesson that the texts intended to teach, and that lesson pointed invariably to Christ. The supreme example of this was the Song of Solomon, in which the bridegroom and the bride were understood to mean Christ's relationship either to the church or the individual believer. Read in this way, the Song became one of the most popular books in the Middle Ages and was often preached and commented on as a tale of the Christian life. The same approach was applied to Israel's wilderness journey after their escape from Egypt and to many other things as well.

As time went on, allegorical interpretation became more and more fanciful, and its validity was increasingly doubted. It remained strong in the monasteries, but as universities developed, so too did interest in the literal sense of Scripture. The framers of Christian doctrine had never employed it; rather, they had established their dogmatic beliefs, contained in the ancient creeds of the church, by relying exclusively on the literal sense of the biblical texts. In theory at least, allegory was meant to be a means by which that doctrine could be applied to passages that would otherwise be obscure or even morally repugnant. Essentially it meant that the surface level of difficult Bible passages was given a spiritual meaning that was both universal in scope and applicable to the life of the individual believer.

A good example of this technique can be found in the way that Psalm 137:9 was often understood. It reads: "Blessed shall he be who takes your little ones and dashes them against the rock!" In its historical context, it was the cry of the psalmist who was exiled in Babylon and thirsting for revenge against the nation that had taken his people into captivity. As such, it is perfectly comprehensible as it stands, although we might recoil at the spirit of hatred that it expresses. But for many Christians, the literal meaning was unacceptable, not only for moral reasons but also because it had no practical application to them. So what they did was transpose the text to the level of the human soul. Babylon was interpreted as the power of evil at work in the world, and her children as the temptations to sin that regularly afflict believers. The message is that Christ, operating in and through his Holy Spirit, must put those wicked thoughts to death before they start to grow and gnaw at our ability to resist them. That message is true in itself, of course, and is a valuable commentary on the spiritual warfare that Christians are called to wage against the world, the flesh, and the devil. But is it what the text means? Did the psalmist intend us to think that when reading his words? That is much more doubtful.

Another problem with allegorical interpretation was that, while it might be meaningful for the devotional life of the individual—and the fact that it was largely developed in monasteries by men who were pursuing their own walk with God reminds us of the importance of that perspective—it has less to say to the church in its wider social and institutional context. Typologically speaking, the church was the new Israel, and as time went on and a Christian society developed in western Europe, the laws of ancient Israel were increasingly appealed to as models for its spiritual heirs. This meant that the ministers of the church were likened to the priests and Levites of the Old Testament and that the tithes which the Israelites had paid to them would also be paid by Christians to their clergy. It also meant that the services of worship were increasingly interpreted according to the Mosaic law. This applied especially to the Lord's Supper, which came to be understood as a sacrifice analogous to the one made by the high priest in the temple at Jerusalem. In secular affairs, the rulers of Christendom were often portrayed as latter-day equivalents of the kings of ancient Israel and Judah, and obedience to them as the Lord's anointed ones was insisted, whether they were good or bad in moral and spiritual terms. Church and state remained distinguishable, but they functioned together in much the same way as the monarchy and the priesthood had done in the days of David and Solomon.

Interpreting the Bible in this way made it imperative to concentrate more on the literal sense than had often been the case in the early church, but there were problems with that. The Hebrew priesthood had been a hereditary tribe that was landless because of its special status. Its Christian equivalent, however, was not landless but celibate, an imposition that was regarded as the best way of preventing church property from being alienated by the families of the clergy. The distinct status of both priesthoods was thus maintained, but in different ways, which made direct application of the Old Testament laws more complicated than we might imagine. Also, whereas the ancient temple sacrifices had been a foretaste of what was to come, their Christian equivalents looked back to the sacrifice of Christ on the cross, which he had taken up into heaven when he ascended and which the church now claimed to be "re-presenting" on earth. To put it bluntly, the medieval church appeared to conform to the biblical pattern of worship, but it is more than questionable whether this was required of the new Israel. In many ways the differences between the old and the new were more significant than any perceived similarities, but to admit that was to call into question the applicability of the Old Testament to the Christian life. If imitation, partial though it was, was the wrong approach to take, what should the church do instead?

The problem with the Old Testament also extended to the New, although in a different way. As the revelation of the historical incarnation of the Son of God, the New Testament did not have to be allegorized in the way the Old Testament often was, but the lack of historical perspective that characterized the medieval church could easily lead to false interpretations of the text. Take, for example, the admonition in 1 Timothy 3:2, repeated in Titus 1:6-7, that an *episkopos* (overseer) must be the husband of one wife. On the surface, this appears to be a clear, even a banal, statement. But what does it really mean? Thomas Aquinas, who lectured on both these texts, was aware that the early church saw no appreciable difference between an *episkopos* and a *presbyteros* (elder), but he also knew that things were different in his own time and that his chief duty was to defend current practice on the basis of Scripture, not to seek to change it by returning to the practice of an earlier period. He therefore read *episkopos* as "bishop" and *presbyteros* as "priest" in the medieval sense of the terms. But the bishops and priests of his generation were all celibate, so what did it mean to say that they should be the husbands of one wife? Aquinas solved this difficulty by a curious kind of typology. He said that just as the church was the bride of Christ, so it was the "wife" of the bishop, who stood in Christ's place. In other words, a bishop had to be celibate in human terms because he was married to the church. And because there was no appreciable difference between a bishop and a priest, the same applied to the latter as well! In this way, the practice of the thirteenth century was read back into the first and mistakenly regarded as biblical.

Today we might laugh at this sort of thing, but it was a serious matter for the Reformers who were battling compulsory clerical celibacy as an aberration that lacked biblical support. For them, Aquinas's interpretation had to be wrong; if it was not, their argument against celibacy would have fallen to pieces. The big difference between them and Aquinas was that they had a different sense of historical development. Both confessed that the Bible was the infallible and inerrant Word of God, valid for all time, but whereas Aquinas was primarily concerned to show how its teaching matched the practice of his own age, the Reformers thought of the biblical position as a superior state of affairs from which the church had departed, and they used it to guide the nature of their Reformation. In that sense, their approach to the Bible was not radical but ultra-traditional—they thought it was possible to recover the state of the primitive church by abolishing the corruptions that had crept in over time. Unfortunately, as we know from subsequent events, they could not always agree about what those corruptions were, nor could they forge a common policy about how to get rid of them, resulting in division among themselves. Instead of creating one pure Protestant church based on the Bible, the Reformers ended up with several competing denominations, each of which insisted that its interpretation of Scripture was the only correct one.

Tradition

As the church moved away from a typological or allegorical interpretation of the Bible and started to make more use of its literal sense as a guide to its own administration, it soon became evident that it did not address every question that had to be answered. For example, nowhere did it say at what age a person should be allowed to marry, nor was there any guidance about ordination to holy orders. Myriad complications had to be sorted out regarding such things as the jurisdiction of bishops, the discipline of both the clergy and the laity, and the celebration of public worship, but the Bible said little or nothing about them. In essence, Christians found themselves in a position similar to the Jews, having to find answers to questions that were not dealt with by divine revelation but that had to be decided if the church was to survive as a coherent body that treated all its members alike. To fill in the gaps left by Scripture, church councils, theologians, and bishops produced decrees at different times that were widely regarded as authoritative, if only because nothing else was available. But these decrees were not issued by a single source in a systematic way, and it was never very clear how widely they were meant to be applied. Were they intended only to meet the needs of the immediate situation that had given rise to them, or could they be given a more universal significance?

In a world where the authority of the ancients was highly regarded, this uncertainty could produce contradictory decisions based on equally venerable sources that had no connection with one another. Systematization was needed to make sense of this diversity and provide principles on which the church could resolve the many problems of everyday administration that confronted it. Various scholars did their best to collect as many of these rules, or canons, as they could find and to arrange them in some sort of order, but it was Gratian who finally succeeded in producing a lasting consensus. His *Decretum* was not just a collection of documents but a systematization, rooted in actual case studies, that was designed to educate the budding church lawyers who would operate the newly established system of ecclesiastical courts. It drew on a wide range of sources, including the Bible, the fathers of the early church, and numerous councils held in ancient times. It also included papal pronouncements. We now know that many of Gratian's sources were inaccurate, and even while writing he felt the need to supplement the material with his own commentary. But whatever limitations his work may have had, it met a need and became the foundation of church law for centuries to come.[8] In 1234 it was supplemented by the *Liber Extra*, a series of papal decretals that had been issued since 1140. The *Decretals* were

---

[8]It retained its authority in the Roman Catholic Church until 1917, when it was finally superseded. Most Protestant churches abolished it at the time of the Reformation, but the

arranged in five distinct categories so as to make them easier to use, and that pattern continued until 1500, when the last of these papal collections appeared.

By the time of the Reformation this corpus of canon law (*corpus iuris canonici*) was as large as the *Decretum* and had generated an extensive commentary tradition of its own. The original intention had been to supplement the Bible, but by the fifteenth century the Scriptures were hardly being used, if only because the matters that the lawyers had to resolve were not mentioned in them. Because the canon law was a living thing that changed and adapted according to circumstance, it was more flexible and thus often more useful than the Bible, which remained unchanged and unchangeable. For example, Leviticus 18 decreed what the forbidden degrees of matrimony were in ancient Israel, and the church naturally adopted them. But Leviticus did not cover all cases—for example, could a man marry his godmother? It was also felt in some quarters that the restrictions did not go far enough. This was not so much a problem in Israel, because the law of Moses recognized divorce, but the church did not. It was therefore thought necessary to widen the net of the prohibited degrees mentioned in Leviticus so that many more marriages could be annulled if the need arose.

As a result, it became possible to get out of any relationship within seven degrees of kindred or affinity, although that was later reduced to four. In the village culture of Europe, virtually everybody was related within the prohibited degrees, so if a marriage did not work out, some way of annulling it could usually be found. Needless to say, quarreling couples would use every trick in the book to get what they wanted, and at one point things got so bad that the church had to decree that under no circumstances were the parties in an annulment suit to be believed without corroborating witnesses.

Church of England failed to do so, with the curious result that the medieval canon law continues to enjoy a residual authority in the Anglican world.

As an unfortunate consequence of this system, children of an annulled marriage lost their legitimacy and were unable to inherit from their parents, an injustice that was the natural consequence of trying to avoid divorce (understood as the dissolution of a legal marriage). This sounds cruel to us today, but those who devised and administered these laws believed they were a great blessing. They believed that by developing such a legal tradition, the principles of the New Testament (which forbade divorce in almost all circumstances) and the realities of daily experience could be reconciled. Illegitimate children could always have provisions made for them; what they could not do was claim it as a right.

Tradition also played a significant role in the definition and treatment of heresy. The New Testament is rather vague about this. Discordant voices appeared in the apostolic churches, but what they taught was (and often still is) unclear. The Bible certainly did not contain enough evidence to mount a legal case against any particular heretic. As heresies multiplied in the early Christian centuries, church councils were summoned to deal with them. In the sixth century, Isidore of Seville catalogued the deviations known to him, and his list became the standard one. But over time the ancient heresies died out and were replaced by new ones that had been unknown to Isidore. Also, whereas the ancient heresies had mostly been about the doctrine of God, including the Trinity and Christology, more recent ones tended to be about the church. Was it heretical, for example, to preach against paying tithes to an immoral priest? Medieval reform movements were frequently fueled by corruption within the clergy, but was it right to defy the church for that reason? Did the misbehavior of an individual compromise the institution? This is a very complex question, and even today different answers can be—and are—given to it, but it is easy to see why the medieval church could not allow objections of this kind to escalate to the point that disobedience to its laws would render its administration inoperable.

In the modern world, where change is rapid and few things last for long, tradition is often seen as a clinging to the past. For some people that is a good thing, but for others it is a brake on progress. Either way, it is defined more in terms of resistance to change than anything else. That was not at all how tradition was understood in the later Middle Ages. In that world, it was the Bible that did not (and could not) change. By contrast, tradition was always adapting to meet new needs as they arose. It was a progressive force that was often regarded as God's gift to the church. In 1265 the pope sent one of his cardinals, Ottobuono Fieschi, more usually known to us as Othobon, to the British Isles, where he was charged with restructuring the local churches. Speaking to a synod of the province of Canterbury on April 13, 1268, Othobon had this to say:

> The commandments of God and the law of the Most High were given in ancient times so that the creature who had broken the yoke by turning away from the peace of his God, might live under the observance of the law and commandment as his lamp and light (having been given hope like a shadow in the promises made to the patriarchs) while waiting for the coming of the King of Peace, the high priest who would reconcile the world and restore all things. In the same way, it is the privilege of the adopted children of the bride, and the glory of the sons of holy mother church, to hear from her the commandments of life, so that they may keep their hearts in the beauty of peace, in the purity of chastity and in the discipline of modesty, suppressing their harmful desires by the judgment of reason. In furtherance of this aim, the decrees of the holy fathers, divinely promulgated by their own mouths and containing the principles of justice and the doctrines of fairness, flowed out like broad rivers, and the sacred constitutions of the supreme pontiffs, the legates of his apostolic see and the other prelates of the church, have been circulated to the

entire world like tributaries from the breadth of those rivers. These [canons] have been issued because of the needs of different times and appear as new remedies [corresponding to] the new diseases that have been generated by human frailty.[9]

This speech ought to be much better known than it is because it expresses in a few words how medieval people viewed the role of tradition in the life of the church. The problem, which Othobon probably did not recognize, was that the canons and decrees that made up the church's tradition were held to be just as infallible and unalterable as the Bible itself. Adaptation to circumstances did not mean abolishing what was already there or limiting new decrees to particular situations that might change and make them redundant. It meant adding them to the deposit of faith, giving them an authority that in practice was equal to the sacred texts. If discrepancies existed between the old and the new, then it would probably be argued that the new supplemented the old and in effect superseded it, on the ground that the old had only ever been intended as a temporary arrangement. This was often the way in which compulsory clerical celibacy was reconciled with the evidence that the apostle Peter had a wife. It was explained that Peter lived when things were in transition and was probably married before he was called to follow Jesus. For him to have divorced his wife would have been a sin, so he was allowed to keep her, but now that this situation no longer occurs, we cannot use his example as justification for clerical marriage. There was a progression through time toward the kingdom of heaven, in which there would be no more marriage. The practice of celibacy was therefore a kind of realized eschatology—living the angelic life in this world as a witness of the better things to come in the next.

---

[9]Author's translation of a Latin text found in *Councils and Synods: With Other Documents Relating to the English Church*, ed. C. R. Cheney (Oxford: Clarendon Press, 1964), 2.2, 747-48.

We must understand how tradition was understood in the Middle Ages if we want to appreciate the Reformers' reaction to it. They knew that it was flexible but did not appreciate the advantages that this could bring. Instead, they saw the church as a vast institution staffed by clever lawyers who could make the law mean whatever they wanted it to mean and who were effectively beyond reproach. Fighting such a system is never easy, and when its tentacles reached across the world, it was virtually impossible. As always, money talked, and those with power and influence could usually manipulate the structures to get what they wanted. That is what King Henry VIII of England tried to do when he decided he needed to annul his marriage to Catherine of Aragon, who had failed to provide him with a male heir. He thought he could send an embassy to Rome and bribe the right officials to get his way, and he might have succeeded but for the fact that Catherine's nephew was the Holy Roman emperor. Charles V blamed the corruptions of the papacy for the upheavals caused by Martin Luther, and he wanted the pope to sort things out. So he invaded Rome and made the pope his prisoner, just at the time that Henry's emissaries arrived with their request. Obviously the pope was in no position to grant Henry's wishes, but Henry in turn correctly saw the papal refusal as motivated more by political necessity than anything else. To be sure, the theological rights and wrongs of Henry's case were debated back and forth, but in the end it was a secular consideration that decided the matter. In the words of the (later) Thirty-Nine Articles of Religion, "The bishop of Rome hath no jurisdiction in this realm of England," just as for Luther he had no jurisdiction over souls in purgatory.[10] The Reformers' complaint was that the earthly head of the church was claiming an authority that did not belong to him, and his power grab had to be resisted. As a result, reform within the church developed into Reformation, and a new kind of church was born.

---

[10]Article 37 in Bray, *Documents*, 307-8; Pelikan and Hotchkiss, *Creeds and Confessions*, 2:538-39; and Dennison, *Reformed Confessions*, 3:67.

THE PAPACY

At the apex of the medieval church stood the papacy.[11] As with many other things, its origins could be loosely traced back to the New Testament, in the sense that Peter had originally been the chief of the apostles and quite likely ended his life as a martyr in Rome. Whether he had been the city's first bishop is now disputed, but it was taken as read in medieval times, and the holders of that office were regarded as his rightful successors. At the First Council of Nicaea in 325, a primacy of honor was granted to the three main cities of the Roman Empire—Rome, Alexandria, and Antioch, in that order. This arrangement was soon made redundant, however, because in 330 the Emperor Constantine established a New Rome in the ancient Greek city of Byzantium, which he renamed Constantinople. Before that time, Byzantium had had no bishop and therefore no special place in the Christian hierarchy, but that situation could hardly continue once it became the imperial capital. At the First Council of Constantinople in 381, it was decreed that the new city's bishop would occupy second place in the hierarchy and that the bishop of Jerusalem, the site of the first church, would be added in fifth place. This pentarchy of patriarchates, as these five episcopal sees were known, has continued to endure in some sense, although Rome refused to recognize Constantinople's place in it until 1215.

The main reason for Rome's refusal arose from the fear that it would be relegated to an inferior position once it was no longer the imperial capital. To counteract that, it developed a different theory of primacy. It was not a city's secular importance that should determine its position in the church, its apologists argued, but its apostolic credentials. On that basis, Jerusalem was a natural addition to the list but Constantinople was not. Rome's primacy was spiritually secure because

---

[11]In the broadest sense, the papacy and church councils could be regarded as part of tradition, but they were not understood in that way in the sixteenth century. Tradition was the body of canon law that the papacy and the councils produced.

Peter (and Paul) had been martyred there. Not everybody accepted the logic of this argument, but all were agreed that Rome should occupy first place. In practice, however, this made little difference as long as the Eastern Empire was able to control the city and its bishops. None of the ancient ecumenical councils were held at Rome, but three of the seven met at Constantinople, one at Chalcedon (across the Bosphorus from the capital), and two more at Nicaea, which was only a short journey away. No bishop of Rome attended any of them, although it might be argued that Pope Leo I determined the outcome of the Council of Chalcedon in 451 because his solution to the problem of the person and natures of Christ was the one that the council accepted. It might also be claimed, however, that Leo's victory at Chalcedon split the Eastern church into a Chalcedonian and two non-Chalcedonian branches, all of which exist to this day. It was a mixed triumph.

The Eastern Empire finally lost control of Rome in 751, and after that the popes sought to re-establish a Western Empire that was eventually based in Germany. This Holy Roman Empire was created in 800 and survived until 1806, and it was no accident that the Reformation began within its boundaries. The emperor was elected from among the leading German princes, but by 1500 the post was virtually hereditary in the house of Habsburg. The popes crowned the emperors, and although some epic battles occurred between them in the course of the Middle Ages, most of the time the two powers coexisted by keeping to their different spheres of power and influence. The papacy's reach was always wider than the emperor's because it covered the whole of western Europe. From the mid-eleventh century onward, a series of administrative reforms strengthened the pope's hand, and for two centuries or more he was the most powerful man in the Christian world. It was at his behest that the nobility of Europe went on crusade to deliver the Holy Land from the Muslims, and he asserted the right to exercise jurisdiction over every church in the West, from Sicily to Iceland and from Portugal to Finland.

Rome had such massive power because it was able to assemble a first-class civil service to do its bidding. It even claimed the right to tax church members, although as time went on this was challenged by various secular rulers, who saw their limited resources being sucked away by what appeared to be a kind of spiritual octopus whose grasping tentacles reached out from Rome. Conflict was the inevitable result, and in the fourteenth century the king of France was able to capture the pope and force him to take up residence at Avignon. The city of Rome declined as a result, but the Avignonese papacy was never able to establish its legitimacy in the eyes of the wider world. Back in the late twelfth century, when Emperor Frederick II (1194–1250) had tried to assert his authority over the pope, the Italian mystic Joachim da Fiore (ca. 1135–1202) had called him the Antichrist and predicted that a great pope would arise who would cleanse the church and society generally of its sins and usher in a golden age of spiritual rectitude and prosperity. But by 1350 Joachim's vision had been turned on its head. Now the pope was the Antichrist, and men like Marsilius of Padua (ca. 1275–1342) hoped that a secular ruler would appear to put matters right. The great plague of 1346–1350 killed up to a third of the European population—God's judgment on an evil world that had fallen into the wrong hands. Popular revolts were still localized and generally unsuccessful, but it was only a matter of time before they would gain force and pose a real threat to the established order. The popes were living on borrowed time in Avignon, and in some sense they knew it.

Eventually the papacy went back to Rome where it belonged, but it resulted in what became known as the Great Western Schism. When the pope died, the cardinals elected a successor on the understanding that he would return to Avignon. The cardinals were all French and wanted to go home, but the new pope refused to accede to their wishes, so they deposed him. In his place they elected a rival who did their bidding. From 1378 onward there were two popes, and the different nations of Europe had to choose between them. This they did on purely political grounds. For example, England was at war with France, so it supported Rome. Scotland was frequently at war with England and allied with France, so it chose Avignon.

Many attempts were made to overcome this division, but success was elusive. At one point a compromise candidate was elected, but the two existing popes refused to resign, so for a few years there were actually three rivals competing for the post. The whole mess was eventually sorted out at the Council of Constance (1414–1418), but at a price. In return for re-establishing a single papacy at Rome, the pope had to agree to a new form of church government. Instead of running things himself, he would now be subject to a council that would meet every five years—and not in Rome. Conciliarism, as this compromise was called, never really took off, although it was attempted for a time. In the end, the popes were able to reassert their authority, and the experiment concluded when the council that had been called to meet at Basel in 1431 finally finished in Rome fourteen years later, having passed through Ferrara and Florence along the way.

The pope was able to move the council from Basel to Ferrara because the Eastern Church of Constantinople was prepared to discuss a reunion with the West as long as its council delegates did not venture beyond Italy, where they could remain in close touch with home. It was hard for the conciliarists to resist this opportunity to reunite a divided Christendom, so the majority agreed to the move, even though a remnant resisted and carried on in Basel. Unfortunately, plague broke out in Ferrara and the council moved again, this time to Florence. There the documents reuniting the churches were signed, and so the council has come to be associated with that city, but this apparent triumph proved to be a mirage. The reunion was never accepted in the East, and it collapsed completely when Constantinople fell to the Turks in 1453. In the Western church, however, conciliarism had been crushed and the papacy's jurisdiction was even greater than it had been before.

When Martin Luther was born, the pope was back on his throne and things appeared to have returned to what they had been before the Avignon episode, but the papacy would never be the same again. Secular rulers were much more powerful in the late fifteenth century than they had been two hundred years previously, and the popes were dependent on them to a degree that they had not been before. In Italy, the Renaissance was in full swing, and cities like Florence, Venice, and Genoa easily matched and sometimes eclipsed Rome in power and influence. The popes were part of this movement and wanted their city to shine in the new dispensation just as much as their Italian rivals did. They launched a number of building projects, the most important being the rebuilding of St. Peter's Cathedral. Financing for this could not be raised locally, so it was up to the wider church to contribute, which it did through various fees and exactions that the popes were able to obtain from the many churches under its control. This was not popular, of course. In 1433 the king of France decreed that no money was to be sent to Rome from his country, a prohibition that was not lifted until 1516, only a year before Luther launched his Reformation.

Elsewhere the popes had more success, but Renaissance Rome was far from being a model of Christian purity. It was a corrupt city in which brothels proliferated, often for the convenience of clergy who were theoretically celibate. The popes lived in luxury while pretending to take vows of Christlike poverty. They were patrons of the arts rather than preachers of the gospel, and spirituality was discounted. The situation reached its nadir in 1492 when a Spanish widower named Rodrigo Borja (Borgia) was elected pope as Alexander VI. He promptly promoted his son Cesare to be the effective ruler of Rome, and his daughter Lucrezia became notorious for her often dubious activities. Their careers came to an abrupt end when their father died in 1503, but they left a stench of corruption that proved impossible to eradicate. When Martin Luther visited Rome in 1510–1511, he was overwhelmed by it, and although he could do nothing about it at the time, the memory of his experience remained with him ever after. For him, calling the papacy the "whore of Babylon" was not just a rhetorical expression.

Meanwhile, the theoretical foundations of papal primacy were also being undermined. The papal archivist Lorenzo Valla (1407–1457) demonstrated that the decrees of Constantine, which supposedly gave the popes jurisdiction over the Western Empire when the emperor moved the capital to the East, were forgeries. The discovery made little difference at the time, but as the Renaissance gathered steam, it gained significance. The cry of the humanists was *ad fontes* (to the sources). They wanted to find out the truth by going to the beginning, an exercise that entailed recovering the original text of the Bible but also the historical origins of the various laws and institutions under which they lived. As they discovered that the church's foundations were often the result of misinterpretation, if not outright falsification of the facts, their respect for the institution vanished. It seemed increasingly clear to them that the moral decay of the papacy, which they could observe all around them, had ancient roots and could not be rectified unless and until those roots were dug up and discarded. What would remain standing was anybody's guess.

Corruption seldom causes regimes to collapse. They crumble only when their fundamental legitimacy is called into question. That happened in France in 1789, in China in 1911, and in Russia in 1917. Unlike these examples, the papacy did not disappear altogether, but by 1500 it was approaching a similar existential crisis. No one knew how it would emerge from this plight, but many saw it coming, not least Erasmus, who wrote a condemnation of it called *In Praise of Folly*. That the strongest challenge came from an obscure German friar surprised everyone, but once it began, it proved impossible to stop. The popes would eventually be rescued from destruction, but their spiritual empire would be greatly diminished. Thanks to the upheaval caused by Martin Luther and his disciples, they would cease to play an important part on the political stage of Europe, and their church would be transformed from top to bottom by a thorough Reformation of its own. For all its claims to stand for the permanence of ancient tradition, the Roman Catholic Church would become almost as unlike its pre-Reformation antecedent as any breakaway Protestant church would be.

Martin Luther did not foresee that, of course, nor did he want it to happen. Despite warnings from his friends, he initially believed that if he understood what was at stake and was willing to submit his case to the authorities, the pope would support him. Those friends were right, and Luther had to face the fact that by publishing his theses he had challenged not only the pope's jurisdiction but the institution of the papacy itself. Plenty of people sympathized with him on that point, at least to some extent. Charles V believed that the church's troubles were largely of its own making and that the pope should be responsible for introducing the much needed reforms that Luther and others were advocating. In the past, similar crises had led to the convening of a church council, in which bishops from across the Christian world would convene to resolve disputes and issue decrees putting their decisions into effect.

The problem was deciding where the council should be held and who should preside over it. The emperor was determined that it should meet on territory controlled by him and not in Rome, where the papacy could exert undue influence. He also wanted Luther and his allies to be invited so that it would be a genuine gathering of the Western church and not just of those loyal to Rome. The pope, not surprisingly, resisted this, although he did not object to calling a council in principle. He insisted that it should be held in Italy, where he could get to it without having to cross the Alps. For years this impasse stalled everything, until finally it was agreed to hold the council at Trent, a northern Italian city that was under the emperor's direct rule. The council convened in 1545, only a few months before Luther died, and although the Protestants were initially invited to attend, they refused to do so. They knew they would not have been welcomed and that forces in the Roman church were determined to crush them at the first opportunity.

In the interval between the publication of the Ninety-Five Theses in 1517 and the convocation of the Council of Trent, a new religious order emerged that was determined to shore up the papacy and do all in its power to defeat and eliminate "heretics." This order was the brainchild of a Spanish nobleman, Ignatius of Loyola (1491–1556), who had been a soldier in the army of the king of Spain—the emperor Charles V—until he was invalided out in 1521. While convalescing from his injuries, he had a religious experience and dedicated his life to the service of the church. After making a pilgrimage to Jerusalem, an unusual and difficult undertaking at that time, he returned to Spain, where he dedicated himself to theological study for a decade. In 1534 he moved to Paris, arriving just as the city was convulsing in agitation over the rise of Protestantism. Ironically, that same agitation forced the young and newly converted John Calvin to quit the city and begin his career as a Reformer! Ignatius however, went in a different direction. He gathered a number of like-minded students around him, most of them fellow Spaniards, and together they vowed to dedicate their lives to what they believed was the pope's cause.

It was some years before the papacy was willing to accept this offer of support, but in 1540 the Society of Jesus, as it was called, was given the pope's blessing. This new religious order drew on the monastic traditions of the past in terms of its inner spiritual discipline, but it was not monastic in the traditional sense. Nor could the Jesuits, as members of the Society were called, be regarded as a new order of friars, although they shared similarities as well. They saw themselves as a religious army, determined to do battle with the church's enemies wherever they might be found. Before long, the Jesuits were purging the papal court of cardinals sympathetic to the Reformation as well as strengthening the backbone of those who wanted to combat it. By the time the Council of Trent was summoned, the Jesuits were exerting far more influence than their small numbers and new foundation would seem to warrant, and their outlook would set the council's agenda.

Protestantism was the enemy, of course, and to the Jesuit mind, the way to combat it effectively was to make communion with the pope the essential criterion for membership in the church. What had been an ancient tradition was now transformed into a doctrine. The Roman church was the army of the Lord and the pope was its commander-in-chief. The Jesuits reported only to him, not to local bishops or synods, giving them an authority that others lacked. Boosting the papacy now became a necessary part of their message, since otherwise their role could be questioned and denied by the wider church. This in turn became the defining marker of Catholicism: those who were in communion with the see of Rome were Catholics; others were not, whatever other elements of Catholic doctrine they might have retained. Interestingly, this new approach to the Protestants had a knock-on effect in relations with the Eastern churches, which became more distant and more confrontational. The Eastern churches had always been willing to grant the Roman bishop a primacy of honor in the church, but they never accepted his dictatorship. When the Jesuits insisted that communion with Rome meant unquestioning obedience to the pope, they could not agree, and so a schism that had developed for other reasons became a division that the new exaltation of the papacy could only reinforce.

Protestants and the Eastern churches had similar reactions to these developments. At the very beginning of the Reformation, Luther and his allies were willing to accept the pope as a kind of figurehead over the church, similar to what the East was prepared to do, but they could not defer to him as an absolute monarch. The only head of the church recognized in the Bible was Jesus Christ, and defending "the crown rights of the Redeemer," as his sovereignty was known, became a major and, as time went on, an increasingly important element of Protestantism. After some initial hesitation, Luther himself led the charge: "I believe the pope is the masked and incarnate devil, because he is the Antichrist. As Christ is God incarnate, so the Antichrist is the devil incarnate."[12]

In Protestant eyes, the pope had usurped the place of Christ, which in effect amounted to blasphemy. The view that he was the Antichrist, which up to then had circulated mainly among some sectarian fringe groups, now surfaced in Protestant polemic. Not everybody was happy with this, and the identification retained its radical flavor for a long time, but the image was too attractive to resist, and it gradually found its way into mainstream Reformed thought. When the Geneva Bible was published in 1560, it contained a footnote to the word *Antichrist* pointing out that this term referred to the pope.[13]

That was clearly a misinterpretation of the word *Antichrist*, and it was one reason why King James I insisted that his translation should not contain any footnotes. But the idea lived on. Its classic expression is found in the Westminster Confession of Faith, which reads, "There is no other head of the Church but the Lord Jesus Christ. Nor can the Pope of Rome in any sense be head thereof, but is that Antichrist, that man of sin and son of perdition that exalteth himself in the Church, against Christ and all that is called God."[14]

To their credit, the Westminster divines did not use the New Testament reference to the Antichrist to support their assertion; instead, they relied on Matthew 23:8-10, 2 Thessalonians 2:3-9,

---

[12]Martin Luther, *Luther's Works: American Edition*, ed. J. Pelikan et al. (Philadelphia, PA: Fortress Press, 1957–1975), 54:346. The quotation comes from no. 4487 of his Table Talk and is dated April 11, 1539.
[13]1 Jn 2:18.
[14]See Westminster Confession of Faith 25.6 in Bray, *Documents*, 507; Pelikan and Hotchkiss, *Creeds and Confessions*, 2:639; and Dennison, *Reformed Confessions*, 4:264-65.

and Revelation 13:6, although none of them really proves the point the divines were trying to make. Today we are embarrassed by this, but at the time the mistake was understandable. The claims being made for the papacy were indeed exaggerated, and they would get worse over time, with a move to declare the pope infallible in matters of faith and morals culminating in a decree to that effect in 1870. As a result, the papal claims are now a major stumbling block to reuniting the churches, and it is still not clear whether, or how, the papacy can be reformed without destroying it altogether. What is certain is that being a Protestant soon came to mean rejecting the pope more than anything else, and that perception seems destined to last, even in these days of ecumenical reconciliation.

Identifying Catholicism with the Roman papacy may have been historically and theologically dubious, but it gave opponents of the Protestants a rallying point, and in the long run that probably saved the Roman Catholic Church. Deferring to the judgment of Rome may have been difficult and humiliating for some, but those who accepted papal authority had a sense of stability and unity that would otherwise be lacking. It also cut short serious theological debate. As the expression went, *Roma locuta; causa finita est*—"Rome has spoken; the case is finished," or as we might colloquially put it, "Rome has spoken, and that is that."

The Protestant world rejected the papacy but found no replacement. The Eastern churches had simply transferred the primacy of honor among the bishops to the Patriarch of Constantinople, who still retains it, although he does not have the right to interfere in the workings of individual national churches. Protestants have never produced anything even remotely similar to this. The churches that broke away from Rome huddled under the protecting wings of the secular rulers of whatever state they happened to be in. That was fine as long as the ruler was sympathetic and willing to accept the church's guidance, but that could not be taken for granted. Monarchs in

Protestant countries were often tempted to interfere in church affairs, especially when they threatened to produce disagreements that might split the country apart. Elsewhere, Protestants were forced to organize themselves independently of the state, something that was never welcomed and was often illegal. The passage of time has done much to blur the effects of this in practical terms, and lay Protestants can usually move from one denomination (or country) to another without much problem. But despite many attempts, a truly united Protestantism remains as distant a prospect as ever, and to that extent, the specter of the papacy continues to haunt the churches of the Reformation.

CHURCH COUNCILS

One might think that convening periodic councils to settle points of doctrine and other matters would be a way to keep the church united. This would have been a biblical solution, at least in the sense that the apostles met at Jerusalem (Acts 15) to deal with controversies between Jewish and Gentile Christians, and their example would seem to have divine approval. A number of councils had been held in the early church, and the Reformers were generally content to accept their decisions, particularly in matters of Christology and the Trinity. They knew that after the legalization of Christianity in the Roman Empire, the emperor had summoned a series of ecumenical councils, recognized by most, if not all, of the churches, and for the most part they had little problem with that. They could have supported Charles V in calling a similar council in the sixteenth century (and some of them did), but it was never a high priority, and when the council finally met, the Reformers rejected it because it was so obviously stacked against them.

The reasons for the Reformers' apparent reluctance to adopt a conciliar framework for resolving disputes and uniting the church were complex. Historical research made it plain that even the ancient councils were not as successful at unifying the Christian world as later generations imagined. The fourth ecumenical council, held at Chalcedon in AD 451 and regarded ever since as foundational for Christology, had been rejected in the Middle East, where the great churches of Alexandria and Antioch had split and formed non-Chalcedonian churches that still exist. The Reformers, like the whole of the Western church, sided with the Chalcedonians, but they knew that the council had produced division, not healed it. They also came to believe that as time went on, the councils departed more and more from their biblical moorings. This was especially noticeable in the seventh ecumenical council in 787, the second to have been held at Nicaea, which affirmed the belief that since Christ was a human being, it was lawful for him to be pictured in frescoes, icons, and so on.

In christological terms it was hard to fault the council for that, although an attempt to do so was made as early as the Council of Frankfurt in 794, which maintained that the decision taken at Nicaea violated the second commandment, with its prohibition of idolatry. That was untrue, of course, and the decision taken at Frankfurt was never ratified by anyone else, but subsequent developments gave cause for concern, to put it mildly. By the time of the Reformation, the Eastern churches had a full-blown system of the veneration of icons, which had become central to their worship. The Western churches had never adopted icons to the same extent, but they had statues instead, which played a similar part in popular devotion. Both branches of Christendom also promoted the veneration of relics, most of which were of dubious provenance, to say the least. It is often forgotten nowadays, but when the crusaders captured Constantinople in 1204, one of their main prizes was the hoard of saints' relics that they carted off and sold to credulous buyers in the West.

The Reformers easily saw that this kind of superstition was intolerable, and they began the wholesale removal and then destruction of images and relics in the churches. Unfortunately this extended even to the smashing of stained-glass windows and the senseless vandalizing of decorative statuary in medieval churches, whether those statues had ever been objects of veneration or not. But it would be wrong to put this down to a spontaneous excess of zeal that often occurs in revolutions. That zeal certainly existed, but it was backed up by serious theological arguments, most notably the long tirade against the seventh ecumenical council launched by Heinrich Bullinger (1504–1575) and incorporated almost verbatim into one of the *Homilies* of the Church of England (1563).[15] The veneration of images was thus ascribed to the second council of Nicaea and publicly denounced from the pulpit, something that had the effect not only of condemning the practice but also of discrediting the council that had supposedly authorized it.

Later medieval councils, held only in the West, also provided ample ammunition for the Reformers' attacks on the church. Doctrines like transubstantiation and disciplines like compulsory clerical celibacy had come into the church because of decisions taken at councils. In 1415 the Council of Constance (Konstanz) had been used to condemn John Wyclif's teachings and also to put Jan Hus to death. The conciliar movement of the fifteenth century might have been a good idea at the beginning, but it was too cumbersome to work properly, and it fell apart when the pope manipulated it to his own advantage. There was no reason to think that the same thing would not happen again—as indeed it did. The Council of Trent was a consultation of sorts, but its agenda was clear from the beginning, and Protestants knew only too well that they would be its victims.

When Luther was called to account for his theological views, he took his case not to a church council but to the German parliament, or diet, which met at Worms in 1521. Nine years later, his followers

---

[15]*Second Book of Homilies*, in G. L. Bray, ed., *The Books of Homilies: A Critical Edition* (Cambridge: James Clarke, 2015), 2.

did the same at the Diet of Augsburg, in which they became known as Protestants. For the most part, that was the pattern followed elsewhere. England's break with Rome was ratified by Parliament in 1534, as was Scotland's in 1560. Even in France there was a colloquy convened by the king at Poissy in 1562, which tried unsuccessfully to reconcile Protestants and Catholics within a single church.

How far the state could, or should, intervene in purely church matters was never really resolved among Protestants. In Lutheran countries, the secular ruler came to be regarded as a lay bishop, which gave him powers greater than those found elsewhere, but in practice doctrine was frozen at the time of the Reformation and no further changes were made, at least not by the state. In other Protestant countries, the pattern varied. On the whole, the church authorities were allowed to construct their own doctrinal systems that the state would then ratify as official church teaching. This worked particularly well in Scotland, where the Reformed church established a general assembly that met yearly and enacted provisions that had the force of law. After the union of the crowns with England in 1603, the king occasionally attempted to make the Scottish church fall into line with the English one, but those attempts were generally rebuffed.

In England, however, the Reformation had been a royal enterprise from the beginning, and although the king let his theologians hammer out the church's doctrine, he did not ratify it automatically, and when he objected to something, the church had to give way. A brief window of opportunity opened in the reign of King Edward VI (r. 1547–1553), who was too young to rule the country himself. Church affairs were left to the archbishop of Canterbury, who sat on the regency council and was thus able to secure a number of reforms that introduced a doctrinal Protestantism to complement the formal one engineered by Henry VIII in 1534. But after 1553 the church had to fall back into line, and the final settlement in 1559 was the work of the queen as much as of any of her clergy. It is telling that when religious conflict emerged in England, it was not between the church and the state but between the king and Parliament, two lay authorities that were competing for power in the church.

We know that the English Parliament was victorious, at least in the short term, and that it appointed an assembly of theologians to sort out church affairs. The Westminster Standards that resulted from the assembly's work were eventually approved by Parliament, but they could not be enacted because the army, which held the real power, was commanded by men who did not agree with the proposed solution. The decisions of the Westminster Assembly were eventually made law in Scotland, but not until 1690, and they never gained much traction in England or in Ireland, where conciliar government of the church remained a dead letter until the mid-nineteenth century.

If national Protestant churches had problems like this, we can only imagine how things were on the international scene. Pan-Protestant unity was always a theoretical goal, but practical considerations kept getting in the way. Luther was unable to agree with Zwingli about the nature of the sacraments, so German and Swiss Reformers went their separate ways, despite occasional attempts to bring them back together. Theologians tended to be intransigent on what seemed like obscure points of doctrine to most people, whereas secular rulers were unwilling to accept legislation passed by a foreign or transnational body that they could not control. On only one occasion was an international council of Protestants attempted, and its fate reveals how and why transnational conciliarism never gained a foothold in the Protestant world.

In 1618 the States General (parliament) of Holland invited the Reformed churches to attend a synod held at Dordrecht (Dort) to resolve a conflict over the right interpretation of certain elements of Reformed theology. This conflict had arisen because a number of Dutch leaders followed the revisionist tendencies of Jacobus Arminius (1560–1609) that the theologians of the church mostly rejected.

Since the Netherlands was engaged in a long-running war with Spain over its independence, the country could not afford such a debilitating division, and it had to be resolved. However, the Reformed churches extended well beyond the Netherlands, and an enduring settlement would have to include them as well; hence the invitation to others. The Lutherans refused to come, and they later used the synod's decisions as a benchmark of everything they opposed in Reformed theology. The French Protestants were forbidden from attending by the king, as part of his long-term clampdown on religious dissent. Delegations from various German principalities and Swiss cantons turned up, as did an impressive embassy from Great Britain. The foreign delegates were well treated and exercised considerable influence on the synod's decisions, which the Estates of Holland eventually ratified.[16] But elsewhere the going was more difficult. In countries where the Reformed churches were a minority, the local synods either had to accept the Canons of Dort, which they had not helped in framing, or else run the risk of being excluded from the Reformed community and thus lose support for their own struggle to survive.

In Britain, the canons were generally well received, although some theologians, including a few who had been delegates to the synod, were hesitant about certain aspects of them and tried to articulate a more compromising position. But King James, although he sympathized with the decisions taken by the synod, refused to ratify them or to put them before Parliament, and after he died (in 1625) any chance of ratification disappeared. The Canons of Dort are still widely recognized in Reformed circles as the classic expression of what we now call Calvinism, but only in the Dutch world have they been accorded official status. In the final analysis, church councils, however desirable they may have been in theory, never became an integral part of Protestantism, and the situation remains

---

[16]The Canons of Dort are printed in Bray, *Documents*, 453-78; Pelikan and Hotchkiss, *Creeds and Confessions*, 2:569-600; and Dennison, *Reformed Confessions*, 4:121-53.

essentially unchanged to this day. The World Council of Churches, established in 1948 as an attempt to revive a vision of ecumenical cooperation, was initially welcomed by many and did some constructive work in harmonizing liturgies and the like, but the effects of its theological liberalism and involvement in secular political causes have since discredited it, and it no longer plays a significant role in interchurch affairs.

THE SUFFICIENCY OF SCRIPTURE

The crisis of the medieval church was at bottom a crisis of authority. Where did the truth lie, and who was supposed to proclaim it? The official view was that the Bible was inspired by God and was the ultimate source of all Christian doctrine. Tradition was a gift from God designed to supplement the Bible and interpret it in situations that Scripture did not directly address. This interpretation lay in the hands of the church, and with the defeat of conciliarism, those hands were increasingly the hands of the pope. How much power did he have, or should he have had? In particular, could he (or a church council, for that matter) overrule the teaching of Scripture, as happened in the so-called Utraquist controversy that came to a head in 1415? That arose because a number of Bohemian priests, eventually including the famous Jan Hus, believed that communicants should receive both the bread and the wine. At some point the cup had been withdrawn from lay people, although nobody is sure why. The authorities argued that bodies contain blood, so a person who received only the transubstantiated body of Christ (that is to say, the bread) received the blood automatically and did not need wine in addition. Obviously that runs counter to what the New Testament records, but the church insisted that it had the authority to override the Word of God in matters of that kind. Was it right?

The Reformers argued that it was not. A key element of the Reformation was the belief in "the sufficiency of Scripture." Contrary to some modern interpretations, this did not mean they believed that the Bible was all the church needed to operate properly. They realized that many things, like the conduct of public worship, were not spelled out in Scripture but that the church was obliged to regulate if it was to function coherently. There had to be an agreed structure of discipline, and of what we would now call conflict resolution, and while the New Testament might offer some useful guidelines, it did not provide a complete manual of best practice that could be implemented by anyone who took the trouble to read it. Of course some things, like Communion in both kinds, worship in the language of the people, and clerical marriage, were obviously practiced in the New Testament church and had been forbidden only in recent times (and even then, not in the Eastern churches). To impose rules like that on the church not only had no Scriptural warrant but went against recorded apostolic practice, so the Reformers naturally returned to what they knew was the biblical norm. It was only on matters that were not clear in the Bible that the church had some discretion to act as it saw fit, but when it did so it had to be convinced that it was acting for the sake of common order and not enunciating principles that had the status of divine laws that could not be altered or disregarded.

The "sufficiency of Scripture" is a proposition that can be understood only in the context of the late medieval debate about the sources of doctrinal authority. When the Reformers advocated this notion, they meant that while the Bible did not say everything, it said enough for the gospel message to be clearly understood and accepted by those who heard it. Nothing needed to be added to what it contained, nor did the church have the right to create compulsory doctrine from beliefs not found within Scripture. Popular piety had led to exaggerated claims being made for Mary the mother of Jesus and for a number of prominent Christians who had been canonized as saints, but none of that could form part of the church's fundamental teaching.

An individual Christian might think that Mary had been taken up into heaven in much the same way as the prophet Elijah had been, but no evidence existed for that in the New Testament. The truth of such a belief could not be verified one way or the other, so that while it was hard to say categorically that it was false, it certainly could not be elevated to the level of official church doctrine. Over time, extraneous teachings like this came to be denied by Protestants, but that was a secondary development based as much on the lack of supporting evidence as on the affirmation of Scripture's sufficiency in matters of doctrine.

The early church had never issued a formal statement to the effect that the Scriptures contained everything necessary for Christian belief, but the practice of its leaders and theologians through the centuries shows that this is what most of them believed. To the fathers of the church in particular, all theology was exposition of Scripture in one form or another—it never occurred to them to look anywhere else for the content of their teaching. Augustine's short but significant book *De doctrina christiana* was not a systematic theology, as its name might suggest nowadays, but an essay in biblical hermeneutics, because for him, all theology was biblical theology, and anything else had to be rejected as unchristian.

The privileged place accorded to Holy Scripture continued throughout the Middle Ages, and the highest accolade that anyone could receive was to be recognized as a *doctor in sacra pagina*, a "teacher of the sacred page." It is common among modern Protestants to claim that ordinary churchgoers were denied access to the sacred text, but that is misleading. In most countries, it was quite possible to translate the Bible into the local language, and several such translations were made. Bibles in French or German were rare and expensive, but they existed, and people who had the money were able to buy them without any problem. England was an exception to this, but that was because of the danger posed by the followers of John Wyclif, the so-called Lollards. They had made Bible translation and reading, along with the sufficiency of Scripture for determining matters of doctrine, central to their movement. It was therefore inevitable that those who wanted to suppress Lollardy would place severe restrictions on translating and disseminating copies of the Bible. But the impact of this prohibition in the days before the invention of printing should not be exaggerated. Few people could afford to buy a manuscript Bible, but almost everyone had a general knowledge of its main stories, which were communicated through mystery plays, stained-glass windows, and the like. There was no officially approved English translation, but the Latin text was available for those who were able to read it, and that included almost everyone who could read. It is not as if copies of other books were circulating freely while the Bible was being censored—few people read anything at all, and book buying was confined to people of means and education. The invention of printing and the resulting fall in the price of books made Bible translation a matter of urgency—increasing numbers of people were learning to read books in their own language and wanted to obtain a copy that they could understand.

It must also be said that the early Reformers were naive in their expectations of what the widespread printing and dissemination of the Bible would achieve. William Tyndale, who produced a magnificent English translation of the New Testament and went on to do the Pentateuch as well, thought that if every ploughboy in England were given a Bible, the entire country would be converted to Protestantism because its message would be too obvious to deny. To him the text was perfectly clear; the only problem was that it had to be translated into a language that ordinary people could understand. Today, of course, we realize that things were not quite that simple, even in the sixteenth century. Apart from anything else, most ploughboys were uninterested in reading and would probably not have bought Tyndale's New Testament even if it had been made available to them.

Those who did would have found much in it that they could understand, but they might well have been confused by a lot of it too. The danger that somebody would take a passage out of context, or seek to apply a book like Revelation in a literal way that showed no understanding of its literary genre, was a real one, as the subsequent history of the Reformation would demonstrate. Scripture may have been sufficient in principle, but its meaning was not always transparent and teachers were still needed. In fact, as the Reformation progressed, it was the preachers and expositors of the Bible who popularized it by expounding the text in ways that were favorable to their cause. People who would never have been able to understand the Bible by themselves were directed along the right path by those who knew what it meant, and in that way a thirst for knowing more was gradually created. When ordinary people started reading the Bible in large numbers, it was because they already knew what it said and why that mattered, not because they were adventurers on a voyage of discovery in the hidden pages of an unknown book.

But if the Reformation doctrine of *sola Scriptura* has been romanticized and misunderstood by some of its later advocates, we must not let that obscure the fact that it was an important belief which would have a serious and long-lasting impact on the church. First of all, it established the principle that in matters of faith and doctrine, the teaching of Scripture was the final court of appeal. The immediate effect of this was to discredit a number of doctrines and practices that had crept into the church's devotional life and often dominated popular piety. Protestants allowed that decisions about various matters might still be taken by church bodies or leaders of various kinds, but they were always subject to the scriptural test. If the decisions reached could not be supported by the Word of God, they might still be adopted for pragmatic reasons, but they could not be imposed on the church as a matter of faith, and those who objected to them could not be punished on that account. This was to become especially important in the area of ecclesiastical polity. Should a church be ruled by bishops or not? How autonomous should a congregation be? Who was to exercise discipline and how? These matters were to prove contentious because although the Bible is clear that churches should be governed by responsible people and that their worship should be conducted decently and in order, no fixed pattern was laid down for how those aims would be best achieved.

The first generation of Reformers was not too bothered about this—neither Luther nor Calvin had strong preferences for an episcopal, congregational, or presbyterian system of church government—but somebody had to decide what to do since all three could not coexist in the same church. And because equally sincere people could not agree, the result was often division. There were also arguments about what a preacher should wear. Should he retain the medieval vestments that many people associated with a theology that the Reformation had rejected, or should he dress like a university graduate, which he was supposed to be? Theologically speaking these were trivial matters that did not usually bother educated people, but they were a small minority in the sixteenth-century church. Most worshipers were more attuned to the visual, and things like what the preacher was wearing or where the pulpit was placed in relation to the Communion table meant more to them than they do to most of us. To them, the man in charge was expected to look the part, as we can see from the portraits and engravings of the Reformers that have come down to us.

Real problems did arise, however, when people interpreted *sola Scriptura* in different and mutually incompatible ways. Baptism provides a classic example of this. Before the Reformation, infant baptism was a universal practice, so much so that little or no provision was made for the baptism of adult believers. But the fact that not all baptized people could be said to become fervent Christians in later life led to questions about the validity of this practice. The New

Testament contains many examples of believer's baptism but no clear case of an infant one. Did that mean that infant baptism was unbiblical? Some said yes and others said no. The Bible said nothing either way. In *sola Scriptura* terms, the question could not be resolved, and the Reformed churches divided over it. Something similar happened with the Lord's Supper. What was it exactly? Who should be admitted to it, and (just as important) who should be excluded? How was it best celebrated and who ought to preside at it? These and other questions found ready answers in tradition but little or nothing in Scripture that would influence the arguments in a decisive way. In many Protestant churches the problem was sidelined because the Lord's Supper was itself marginalized as an act of worship. From having been a weekly or even a daily celebration in many places, it came to be featured once every three months or even less often. In the Church of England, for example, a "regular" communicant was defined as someone who received the sacrament three times a year—at Christmas, Easter, and Whitsun (Pentecost)! It was hardly often enough for anyone to worry unduly about its underlying theology.

Another area of controversy concerned the doctrine of the Trinity. Fundamental as this was to Christian orthodoxy, it was hard to see how it was revealed in the Bible. Supposed allusions to it in the Old Testament were generally rejected because they were either based on allegory or were insufficiently explicit. The New Testament made frequent references to the Father, Son, and Holy Spirit, and they were brought together in a few places in what might be seen as a trinitarian formula (cf. Mt 28:19), but the word *Trinity* is nowhere to be found in Scripture. Is it therefore an unbiblical doctrine? Faced with this question, the Reformers were forced to insist that it is not merely what Scripture says directly that counts as biblical teaching but also what may legitimately be implied from it. The New Testament does not explicitly mention a Trinity, but what it says about the three divine persons cannot be squared with its fundamental monotheism in any other way. The word *Trinity* is theological shorthand for a doctrine that is taught in the New Testament, if only in an indirect and subtle way. Belief in it can therefore be insisted because it is scriptural in a deeper sense, and that is basically what the Reformers did.[17] However, it is not difficult to see why their conclusion did not receive universal assent and why anti-trinitarianism got as much traction as it did. The truth is that the clarity of Scripture that William Tyndale took for granted was not equally clear to everyone.

There had always been Jews who rejected trinitarian doctrine, of course, and the Muslims did the same. In Spain and Portugal both groups had been numerous throughout the Middle Ages, but after the Christian reconquest of the peninsula they were forced to leave or else convert to Christianity. The converts, or "new Christians" as they were known, were seldom enthusiastic believers, and it is probable that few were persuaded to accept the Trinity in any heartfelt way. It is perhaps not surprising, therefore, that one of the first people to question the orthodox Christian doctrine was the Spaniard Miguel Servetus (ca. 1511–1553), who fell foul both of the Catholic Church and the Reformers of Geneva, where he was eventually tried and put to death, despite Calvin's objections.[18] More influential were two Italians, Lelio Sozzini or Socinus (1525–1562) and his nephew Fausto (1539–1604), who rejected not only the Trinity but also the belief that Adam had been created righteous and had fallen through his disobedience to the command of God. To the Sozzini, humanity was created morally neutral and acquired virtue through choice and good works. The Trinity made no sense to them, and its apparent absence from the New Testament suited their reductionist interpretation of the Bible.[19] They acquired a considerable following and were

---

[17]John Calvin, *Institutes of the Christian Religion*, ed. J. T. McNeill, trans. F. L. Battles (Philadelphia, PA: Westminster Press, 1960), 1.13.1-3.

[18]Servetus had Jewish ancestry but was not a "new Christian."

[19]For a summary of their beliefs, see Pelikan and Hotchkiss, *Creeds and Confessions*, 2:704-8.

able to establish themselves in parts of Eastern Europe, where the church was unable or unwilling to persecute them. One such place was Raków, Poland, where they established a school that produced the Racovian Catechism, a digest of Socinian beliefs that was widely translated and circulated across Europe.

For much of the seventeenth century, Socinianism was regarded by orthodox theologians as a major heresy that threatened the health of the church, and they combated it without mercy. It is hard to know how much of this antipathy was rhetorical and how much reflected a genuine danger, but denial of the Trinity came to be seen as a hallmark of opposition to the traditional teaching of the church that could claim to have some kind of biblical justification. Socinianism as such declined in the late seventeenth century, but a modified form of it reappeared as unitarianism, which soon became popular among freethinkers who were opposed to any form of divine revelation or ecclesiastical authority. Few people left the mainline churches to become Unitarians, but their theology exerted a powerful influence on eighteenth-century rationalists and soon became the dominant view in academic circles, even if it was seldom officially accepted by any Protestant church.[20]

---

[20]Exceptions would include the English Presbyterians, who opened the door to Unitarianism in 1719 and were soon almost completely taken over by it, and also the Congregationalists of Massachusetts, most of whom had become Unitarians by the time their church was disestablished in 1833.

Three

The Interpretation
of the Bible

One Book or Many?

Should we think of the Bible as a collection of disparate books put
together at different times for reasons that are obscure to us, or should
we see it as a single book made up of different parts? In purely historical terms, the first approach is clearly more faithful to the Bible's origins, and Christians have never denied this. Even today, we can speak
of both "Scripture" in the singular and "the Scriptures" in the plural, a
reminder that we are dealing with a series of texts that retain their
individuality even if they are now incorporated into a wider whole.
The word *Bible* itself began as a plural noun in both Greek and Latin,
but it has now become singular in most modern languages, in recognition of how an originally diverse group of texts has come to be regarded
as a single book. Although the church has always acknowledged the
diverse sources that have gone into making the Bible, it also insists
that these sources have an underlying unity. That unity is theological—
every book of the Bible is the Word of God, transmitted to us by holy
men who were moved by the Spirit to write the texts that we have
today.[1] These texts were eventually put together because the Jews, and
then the Christians, found that they have a common theme, which is

---

[1] 2 Pet 1:21.

the revelation of God's will for his people. Times have changed and the circumstances in which that revelation was originally given have passed away, sometimes beyond recall, but the message the Bible contains remains as living and valid for believers today as it ever was.

The Reformers shared this view, and the fact that they turned to the Bible as their sole authority in matters of faith made it urgent for them to explain why they did this and how they thought its authority ought to be applied in the church. Obviously, the Old Testament presented a particular problem, as Luther was well aware. In the preface to his translation, he tackled this head on:

> There are some who have little regard for the Old Testament. They think of it as a book that was given to the Jewish people only and is now out of date, containing only stories of past times. They think they have enough in the New Testament and assert that only a spiritual sense is to be sought in the Old Testament.[2]

But as Luther pointed out, Jesus told the Jews to "search the Scriptures . . . it is they that bear witness about me."[3] Paul told Timothy to read the Old Testament, and Luke commended the Jews of Berea for their diligence in doing so.[4] The Bereans were especially noteworthy because they were trying to figure out whether Paul's teaching about Jesus was indeed the fulfillment of the prophecies that their Scriptures contained. Luther's conclusion was typically straightforward: "The ground and proof of the New Testament is surely not to be despised, and therefore the Old Testament is to be highly regarded. And what is the New Testament but a public preaching and proclamation of Christ, set forth through the sayings of the Old Testament . . . ?"[5]

---

[2]T. F. Lull, ed., *Martin Luther's Basic Theological Writings*, 2nd ed. (Minneapolis, MN: Fortress Press, 2005), 113; Martin Luther, *Luther's Works: American Edition*, ed. J. Pelikan et al. (Philadelphia, PA: Fortress Press, 1957–1975), 35:235 (hereafter *LW*).

[3]Jn 5:39.

[4]1 Tim 4:13; Acts 17:10-11.

[5]Lull, *Luther's Basic Theological Writings*, 114; *LW*, 35:236.

As Luther understood it, the basic message of the Old Testament was to proclaim the law of God, the standard by which he measured human conduct and found that it falls short of what he requires of us. In contrast to this, the New Testament is a message of grace, by which we learn that our sins have been paid for by the sacrifice of Christ who has now reconciled us to God. Luther realized that this law/grace duality was not watertight; the Old Testament also speaks of divine grace, and the New Testament contains laws for living the Christian life. But in general terms, the categories of law and grace help us to understand what each Testament is about and how they complement each other. In Luther's own words,

> The Old Testament is a book of laws, which teaches what men are to do and not to do—and in addition gives examples and stories of how these laws are kept or broken—just as the New Testament is gospel or book of grace, and teaches where one is to get the power to fulfill the law. Now in the New Testament there are also given, along with the teaching about grace, many other teachings that are laws and commandments for the control of the flesh—since in this life the Spirit is not perfected and grace alone cannot rule. Similarly, in the Old Testament too there are, beside the laws, certain promises and words of grace, by which the holy fathers and prophets under the law were kept, like us, in the faith of Christ. Nevertheless, just as the chief teaching of the New Testament is really the proclamation of grace and peace through the forgiveness of sins in Christ, so the chief teaching of the Old Testament is really the teaching of laws, the showing up of sin, and the demanding of good. You should expect this in the Old Testament.[6]

Luther believed it was necessary for God to reveal his law first because otherwise people would not know what he expects of us, nor

---

[6]Lull, *Luther's Basic Theological Writings*, 114; LW, 35:236-37.

would they realize that they are incapable of measuring up to his standards. Without the law, human reason would have no understanding of sin. It would be able to formulate rules for living an outwardly respectable life, but it would be blind to the evil inclinations of the flesh lurking beneath the surface. Unless and until people understand what sin is, they will not be frightened by it, nor will they do anything to escape from its clutches. It was the task of Moses, as Luther (following the example of both Jesus and Paul) personified the Old Testament law, to make us fully aware of our spiritual predicament so that we shall be ready to seek relief from it. So good was Moses at this task that "he not only gives laws like the Ten Commandments that speak of natural and true sins, but he also makes sins of things that are in their nature not sins."[7] It was in this rather curious way that Luther explained the Jewish food laws and other ritual observances. Eating pork was not a sin in itself, but it became one when God forbade it. Luther said that God did this because he wanted his people to understand that it was not up to them to decide what is right and what is wrong, but also—and more importantly—"that sins might simply become numerous and be heaped up beyond measure."[8] In this way, Luther claimed, the conscience would be so burdened that it would have to recognize its own blindness and inability to save itself. As he put it, "Such blindness must be thus compelled and forced by the law to seek something beyond the law and its own ability, namely, the grace of God promised in the Christ who was to come."[9]

Luther also insisted that the law of Moses had what we would now call built-in obsolescence. According to him, its greatest saying was the promise that the Lord would one day raise up a prophet from among the people, to whom they would listen.[10] He had no doubt

---

[7]Lull, *Luther's Basic Theological Writings*, 118; *LW*, 35:243.
[8]Lull, *Luther's Basic Theological Writings*, 119; *LW*, 35:244.
[9]Lull, *Luther's Basic Theological Writings*, 119; *LW*, 35:244.
[10]Deut 18:15.

that this was Jesus of Nazareth, as the apostles themselves had claimed.[11] Furthermore, the covenant that God established with his people in and through Moses could not last forever, because it was based on human works and not on God's grace. That in itself made it impossible to fulfill, so it had to be replaced by a covenant grounded in God's words and works, not in those of his people.[12]

As far as interpreting the details of the text was concerned, Luther told his readers to apply everything that was said about the high priest (Aaron) directly to Christ. But whereas the sacrifices of the Jewish high priest took away only those sins that were not really sins at all, Christ has taken away real sinfulness—moreover, he has done this once and for all.[13] At the same time, when Moses mentions the high priest's sons, who made daily sacrifices in the tabernacle (and later in the temple), Luther believed that he was referring to us, because as he put it, "Their office of slaughter and sacrifice signifies nothing else than the preaching of the gospel, by which the old man is slain and offered to God, burned and consumed by the fire of love, in the Holy Spirit."[14]

When pressed to say what he found useful in the Old Testament, Luther replied that three main things made it right and proper for Christians to retain it as part of God's Word. First, much of what Moses commanded the Jews to do was sensible, and we can learn a good deal from it. The law itself was binding only on Jews, but when it contains universal principles (as in the Ten Commandments), then it should be followed by everyone. Even things like tithing are useful and can be adopted more widely, not as an obligation imposed on God's people but as a common-sense form of taxation.[15] More importantly, the Old Testament contains God's promises about the coming

---

[11]Acts 3:22; 7:37.
[12]Lull, *Luther's Basic Theological Writings*, 120; LW, 35:246.
[13]Lull, *Luther's Basic Theological Writings*, 121; LW, 35:247.
[14]Lull, *Luther's Basic Theological Writings*, 121; LW, 35:248.
[15]Lull, *Luther's Basic Theological Writings*, 128; LW, 35:166-67.

of Christ, which reassure us as Christians and give us a foundation on which to rest our faith.[16] Finally, the Old Testament provides wonderful examples both of godly people, who are an inspiration to us, and of the ungodly, whose punishment is a warning to everyone who would take God's commandments in vain.[17] This effectively sums up the way Luther interpreted the Old Testament and why he recommended it to Christians despite the fact it had been given to Jews and that much of it had been superseded by the coming of Christ.

When looking at the New Testament, Luther adopted much the same tone as he used for describing the Old. His main concern was to point out that the gospel is the fulfillment of the law and that on no account should Christians try to turn it back into a rule book. As he put it,

> The gospel does not . . . demand works of our own by which we become righteous and are saved; indeed, it condemns such works. Rather the gospel demands faith in Christ: that he has overcome for us sin, death, and hell, and thus gives us righteousness, life and salvation . . . in order that we may avail ourselves of his death and victory as though we had done it ourselves.[18]

Using the criterion of salvation by faith alone, Luther then turned the New Testament over to his readers, inviting them to judge for themselves which of its books were the most important. He himself had no doubts:

> John's Gospel and St Paul's epistles, especially that to the Romans, and St Peter's first epistle are the true kernel and marrow of all the books. They ought properly to be the foremost books, and it would be advisable for every Christian to read them first and most . . . For in them you do not find many

---

[16]Lull, *Luther's Basic Theological Writings*, 129-31; *LW*, 35:168-73.
[17]Lull, *Luther's Basic Theological Writings*, 132; *LW*, 35:273.
[18]Lull, *Luther's Basic Theological Writings*, 110; *LW*, 35:360.

works and miracles of Christ described, but you do find depicted in masterly fashion how faith in Christ overcomes sin, death, and hell, and gives life, righteousness and salvation. This is the real nature of the gospel . . . If I had to do without one or the other—either the works or the preaching of Christ—I would rather do without the works than without his preaching . . . John writes very little about the works of Christ, but very much about his preaching . . . Therefore, John's gospel is the one, fine, true and chief gospel, and is far, far to be preferred over the other three . . . So too, the epistles of St Paul and St Peter far surpass the other three gospels.[19]

It is in line with this that Luther criticized James as "an epistle of straw, compared to these others, for it has nothing of the nature of the gospel about it."[20] Luther did not remove James from his canon, nor did he touch the Synoptic Gospels, but his willingness to divide the New Testament into first- and second-class books is striking and has puzzled readers ever since. He certainly never did anything similar with the Old Testament, perhaps because in his mind it was all second class, and his insistence on what we would now call "a canon within the canon" has been controversial for centuries. In modern times, some scholars have jumped on it and come to their own conclusions, although they are not always the same as Luther's, while others have resisted any suggestion that one New Testament book is somehow superior to the others. They may have been produced in different circumstances, but if they are all God's Word as they claim to be, it is hard to see how one of them can be intrinsically more (or less) important than the others.

Luther was a famous translator of Scripture, but he was not a scholar and was humble enough to admit it. He was quite prepared to

---

[19]Lull, *Luther's Basic Theological Writings*, 111; LW, 35:361-62.
[20]Lull, *Luther's Basic Theological Writings*, 112; LW, 35:362.

believe that others could produce a better translation than his, and he invited them to do it in the conclusion of his preface to the Old Testament.[21] On one point however, he has left his mark. Wondering how to translate the unpronounced Hebrew name of God (written as YHWH), he conformed to standard linguistic practice but with a difference. Instead of writing "Lord," as others did, he put the name in capital letters—LORD—a practice that is still followed by most Bibles today. Few translators, and even fewer scholars, can claim to have had as much impact as that.

The first generation of Reformers was concerned to establish this principle of *sola Scriptura*, by which they meant that whatever could not be proved from the biblical text must not be made a requirement of Christian belief. Perhaps the best statement of what *sola Scriptura* meant to them is the summary given by Thomas Cranmer, the archbishop of Canterbury in the fifth of his Forty-Two Articles of Religion:

> Holy Scripture containeth all things necessary to salvation: so that whatsoever is neither read therein, nor may be proved thereby, although it be sometime received of the faithful, as godly and profitable for an order and comeliness: yet no man ought to be constrained to believe it as an article of the faith, or repute it requisite to the necessity of salvation.[22]

John Calvin went even further than this and gave an extended exposition of the character of Holy Scripture that became, and to a large extent has remained, the standard Reformed teaching on the subject. In Calvin's mind, the Bible was authoritative for two connected reasons. First, it is the Word of God, as the prophets and apostles who wrote it attested. In Calvin's words,

[21]Lull, *Luther's Basic Theological Writings*, 123; *LW*, 35:249-51.
[22]See G. L. Bray, ed., *Documents of the English Reformation*, 2nd ed. (Cambridge: James Clarke, 2004), 287. The article reappears in an abbreviated version as article 6 of the Thirty-Nine Articles of 1563.

The prophets and apostles do not boast either of their keenness
or of anything that obtains credit for them as they speak; nor
do they dwell upon rational proofs. Rather, they bring forward
God's holy name, that by it the whole world may be brought
into obedience to him.[23]

But Calvin also recognized that the truth of this assertion would not
touch people unless God bore witness to his own words by sealing
them in the hearts of the hearers through the inward testimony of
the Holy Spirit:

> Let this point therefore stand, that those whom the Holy Spirit
> has inwardly taught truly rest upon Scripture, and that Scrip-
> ture indeed is self-authenticated; hence, it is not right to subject
> it to proof and reasoning. And the certainty it deserves with us,
> it attains by the testimony of the Spirit. . . . Therefore, illu-
> mined by his power, we believe neither by our own nor by any-
> one else's judgment that Scripture is from God; but above
> human judgment we affirm with utter certainty (just as if we
> were gazing upon the majesty of God himself) that it has flowed
> to us from the very mouth of God by the ministry of men.[24]

When it came to textual criticism, Calvin was largely untroubled
by the doubts and objections that we are familiar with today. As far
as he was concerned, the evidence that Moses not only wrote the Pentateuch but that the miracles and other extraordinary events recorded
in it were a true and accurate reporting of the facts was simply that he
"published all these things before the congregation [of the people]."[25]
Prophecies of things that did not take place until several centuries
afterward were authenticated by comparing them with other events

---

[23]John Calvin, *Institutes of the Christian Religion*, ed. J. T. McNeill, trans. F. L. Battles (Philadelphia, PA: Westminster Press, 1960), 1.8.4.
[24]Calvin, *Institutes* 1.8.5.
[25]Calvin, *Institutes* 1.8.5.

wherein there could be no doubt about the prophetic nature of the
Old Testament witness. For example, when someone objected that
Moses' prophecy that Judah would obtain the preeminent position in
Israel was not a genuine foretelling of events but a gloss (or insertion)
added after it had happened, Calvin countered by citing the prophecy
that one day the Gentiles would be admitted to the Israelite covenant,
which was clearly not fulfilled until long after it was first given.[26] To
get a flavor of Calvin's arguments, consider what he said about the
Isaianic prophecy of the coming of Cyrus:

> More than a hundred years elapsed from the time the prophet
> so prophesied and the time Cyrus was born . . . No one could
> have divined then that there was to be a man named Cyrus who
> would wage war with the Babylonians . . . Does not this bare
> narrative, without any verbal embellishment, plainly show the
> things Isaiah recounts to be undoubted oracles of God, not
> the conjectures of a man?[27]

Here we are a long way from modern textual criticism, whose
exponents either take it for granted that the so-called prophecy was
composed after the event or else that the reference to Cyrus was in-
terpolated after his identity became known. Calvin had no sense of
that and accepted the text at face value. In this respect, he and his
contemporaries were no different from the New Testament writers,
Augustine, and all the generations in between. Their authorities were
literary, not archaeological, and when humanists spoke about "returning to the sources," they were really appealing to tradition, although in this case it was not the tradition of the medieval church but
that of the ancient Israelites and their contemporaries in the Greco-
Roman world. As long as those witnesses were regarded as credible,
Calvin's arguments could hold their own. It would only be in the

---

[26]Calvin, *Institutes* 1.8.7.
[27]Calvin, *Institutes* 1.8.8. See Is 44:28-45:1.

eighteenth century, when they were doubted by Enlightenment rationalists and when other means of discovering "what really happened"
came to be favored, that his line of argument, whatever validity it
might have in some respects, would have to be supplemented by
something more. This is one reason why modern defenders of biblical
authority often find it hard to appeal to the Reformers, despite their
sympathy with what Calvin and others were trying to say. Whether
we like it or not, the world has moved on, and appeals to antiquity
of the kind that Calvin made are no longer as persuasive as they
once were.

When dealing with questions of canon and textual accuracy, the
first generation of Reformers were not breaking new ground but taking sides in a debate that had begun more than a millennium before.
But the second generation, motivated by the appeal to *sola Scriptura*
that had marked the Reformation from the beginning, moved toward
a different conception of what that doctrine meant for their theology.
The first generation had been content to say that the Bible is the
Word of God in written form and that whatever cannot be found in
it must not be imposed on Christians as an article of faith. When it
came to things that the Bible did not speak about, they tolerated diversity. For example, they were prepared to accept different forms of
church government, regarding episcopal, presbyterian, and congregational systems as equally valid. Each local church was free to decide
on the form that best suited them. Even on matters of doctrine the
Reformers could sometimes be flexible. They all believed that
the New Testament taught that the Father is God, the Son is God,
and the Holy Spirit is God, but Calvin admitted that the use of words
like *person* and *Trinity* was a tradition of the church, not part of the
divine revelation, although he regarded the doctrine as true and was
suspicious of those who rejected it for no other reason. He argued
that the traditional expression of the Trinity was the best way to
state what was clearly taught in the Scriptures, but he was prepared to

admit that it did not have the force of revelation itself, which in the context of the time was a relatively liberal position to hold.[28]

Calvin's approach was based on the belief that matters not plainly expressed in the Bible should be classed as *adiaphora* (things indifferent). Much of what had previously been declared orthodox, and therefore compulsory, by an appeal to tradition now came into this category, but it was sometimes difficult to decide whether a particular practice was consonant with the Bible. For example, could devotion to Mary as the mother of God be permitted in a church that was based on the Bible, where such devotion is not recorded? Was the baptism of infants a biblical practice if no clear examples of it are given in the New Testament? Where the principle of *adiaphora* was admitted, differences of this kind could sometimes be accommodated because people were allowed to act according to their own conscience, just as the first Christians were free to follow the Jewish law as long as they did not try to impose it on others. But just as Jewish Christianity died out in the early church, so the principle of *adiaphora* declined over time, as battle lines in the Reformation struggles hardened and things that had previously been left to one side became badges of identity among different groups of Reformers.

The early tolerance of things indifferent did not survive into the next generation, because the basic principles of systematic theology became subtly different. The earliest Reformed confessions had followed the ancient and medieval pattern, beginning with the doctrine of God and moving to the doctrine of Scripture. But in the Second Helvetic (Swiss) Confession of 1566, the doctrine of Scripture was made the first chapter of theological exposition, on the ground that the Bible was the source from which all other Christian doctrines were derived. In theory, this meant that if something was not found in the Bible, it had to be rejected, but that was not always possible

---

[28]Calvin, *Institutes* 1.13.1-3.

in practice. In the matter of church government, for example, Reformed theologians of the second generation were forced to say that the New Testament prescribed one particular order, which they therefore wanted to impose on all the churches. But whether this order was presbyterianism, in which individual churches were part of a wider association represented by a common presbytery, or whether it was congregationalism, in which each local church governed itself, could not be agreed. The result was division, as each side insisted that its view was the only correct one. In this way the flexibility of the original Reformers was lost, and *sola Scriptura* came to be applied in ways that would have been foreign to Luther or Calvin.

The truth is that the second generation of Reformed theologians had no category of *adiaphora*. In their minds, the Bible said everything that needed to be said, and its teaching had to be followed. They defended presbyterianism or congregationalism as compulsory biblical teaching, not as one form of biblically permissible church government. The baptism of infants could not be left to parents' discretion but had to be justified (or rejected) on the basis of biblical evidence, which is unfortunately missing. As a result, both sides in this debate claimed to be following the teaching of Scripture when in fact the Bible does not address the question. Thus, we now have Reformed churches that have divided over matters like these, which most people agree are of secondary importance but which remain powerful barriers to reconciliation within the Protestant world.

The Westminster Confession states that everything necessary for salvation is set out in Scripture, either directly or by implication, and that it needs no further additions. But its content can only be understood by the inner illumination of the Holy Spirit. As it says, "We acknowledge the inward illumination of the Spirit of God to be necessary for the saving understanding of such things as are revealed in the Word."[29] This assertion is vitally important because it is a recognition that mental persuasion of the literal truth of the Bible is not enough for a living faith. The book inspired by the Holy Spirit must also be interpreted by that same Spirit, without whom salvation in Christ is impossible.

The Westminster Confession acknowledges that not everything in Scripture is clear or equally obvious to everyone, but it states that the essential message is plain enough and can be understood by every intelligent human being. That had already been stated a century before by Thomas Cranmer, who wrote, "Although many things in the Scripture be spoken in obscure mysteries, yet there is nothing spoken under dark mysteries in one place but the selfsame thing, in other places, is spoken more familiarly and plainly, to the capacity both of learned and unlearned."[30]

In other words, the difficult parts of Scripture are to be interpreted by the clearer ones, making it unnecessary to appeal to any external authority in the church or the academy. The ultimate authority in matters of interpretation is the Holy Spirit, speaking through the Scriptures themselves, and it is to his authority that the church must defer. In saying this, the Reformers were drawing on ancient tradition but interpreting it in a new way. The difference between the way the church fathers understood the work of the Holy Spirit in the interpretation of Scripture and the approach of Protestant orthodoxy can be seen most clearly in the way that the difficulties of the literal text were treated. In ancient and medieval times, problems of chronology, grammar, and so on were thought to have

---

[29]Westminster Confession of Faith 1.6, in Bray, *Documents*, 488; J. Pelikan and V. Hotchkiss, eds., *Creeds and Confessions of Faith in the Christian Tradition* (New Haven, CT: Yale University Press, 2003), 2:607; and J. T. Dennison, *Reformed Confessions of the Sixteenth and Seventeenth Centuries in English Translation* (Grand Rapids: Reformation Heritage Books, 2008–2014), 4:35.

[30]*First Book of Homilies*, in G. L. Bray, ed., *The Books of Homilies: A Critical Edition* (Cambridge: James Clarke, 2015) 1.2.

been placed there deliberately, as a reminder from God that the Bible is about spiritual things that cannot be understood by rational means alone. The scholars of Protestant orthodoxy agreed with them on this last point but did not resort to allegory in order to explain textual difficulties. Instead, they believed that solutions could be found by rational means—a deeper study of the original languages, closer attention to chronology, and so on. This opened them up to the possibility, and eventually to the probability, that the texts had been redacted by a succession of unknown people who had been empowered by the Holy Spirit to do that. In that way they tried to maintain an essential unity between the human and the divine elements that had gone into producing the Bible in its present form.

The proponents of covenant theology believed that those who understood how the Holy Spirit had guided the historical development of the text would interpret it correctly, so there was no need to go beyond what was written to look for some hidden spiritual meaning. Protestant orthodoxy thus broke with the church's ancient hermeneutical tradition without abandoning its conviction that the Scriptures were inspired by the Holy Spirit. But at the same time, by emphasizing the importance of rational analysis of Scripture's literal sense as the way to understand its true meaning, Protestant orthodoxy also prepared the way for modern critical study of the Bible, in which the appeal to its divine inspiration would cease to have any practical application. By the nineteenth century, academic study of the Bible was becoming a discipline increasingly independent of Christian devotion, while evangelical movements were preaching the gospel in the traditional way and paying little attention to recent critical theories.

Today both of these traditions look to the Reformers as their predecessors in the study of the Bible. In material terms, there can be no doubt that modern scholars have resources for studying the ancient world that men like Luther and Calvin could not have imagined. When we read that Luther, for example, believed that Paul's letter to the

Galatians was relevant to the situation of his own church in Germany because the Galatians were ethnically related to the Germans and therefore shared the same temperament and corresponding problems, we can only smile.[31] But whereas a liberal interpreter of the text might say that Galatians is of no relevance to us today because it was addressed to people in a particular time and place who were quite different from us, conservative interpreters would disagree. To them, it is a message from God to all Christians everywhere, and is just as important today as when it was first written. They reject Luther's speculations about who the Galatians were, not because he was trying to find a meaning in the text that was not there but because his historical understanding was faulty and his application of the text was too narrow. The Galatians were indeed like the Germans of Luther's time, not because they were ethnically related but because they were sinful human beings like all of us and had been saved by grace through faith, just as we are.

If we look at the way the Reformers read and interpreted the Bible, we can accept many of their methods—for example, the appeal to the original languages and the need to establish the correct text. We can regard our modern interest in archaeology and other related disciplines as an extension of their concern for historical accuracy and make full use of the techniques that have been developed in the last five hundred years. Very often we shall be led to different conclusions, but that is because our methods have improved over time, not because they are fundamentally different from the ones the Reformers used. In that sense we are children of the Renaissance just as much as Luther and Calvin were. It is possible to agree that the apostle Paul taught justification by faith alone but not to have had the spiritual experience which that doctrine proclaims. We can accept that the Bible claims to have been inspired by the Holy Spirit yet not know that Spirit at work in our hearts.

---

[31]*LW*, 26:47. He was commenting on Gal 1:6.

This is the real challenge of Reformation hermeneutics today. The Reformers tell us that we must know God in our hearts if we want to understand him in his Word. The Bible reveals its secrets to Christians who have eyes to see and ears to hear its message. The historical details it records are interesting and important, but it is the spiritual message that changes people's lives. The Reformation was not primarily about education, important though that was and still is. It was about transformation—a change that is possible only in and through the working of the Holy Spirit in the hearts and minds of believers. That is the true Reformation hermeneutic, and it is as relevant today as it was five hundred or even two thousand years ago.

Fashioning a Pastoral Hermeneutic

One of Luther's earliest and most devoted disciples was William Tyndale. Moved by a desire to translate the Bible into English, and aware that Luther was doing the same into German, Tyndale went to Wittenberg and enrolled as one of Luther's students. Insofar as he could, he copied Luther's translation methods, adding prefaces to each book of the New Testament as he translated it, plus a general introduction to the whole. The first edition of his New Testament appeared in 1526, but it could not be printed in England, and before long pirated copies were being smuggled into the country. Tyndale lashed out against this in his second edition (1534), by which time he had also produced a translation of the Pentateuch. He managed to complete Joshua and Jonah as well, but he was then arrested in Antwerp and could do no more. The work was completed in 1535 by Miles Coverdale, but although Tyndale was still alive, he was unable to see the finished product and probably died without knowing that it had been published.

What is of particular interest to us is that despite Tyndale's closeness to Luther and his great respect for Luther's example, he did not follow the same interpretive principles, particularly where the law of

Moses was concerned. Instead of positing a law/gospel contrast, Tyndale directed his readers somewhere else altogether. As he put it, "The only way to understand the Scripture unto our salvation, is that we earnestly, and above all thing, search for the profession of our baptism, or covenants made between God and us."[32]

Apparently without any prompting from elsewhere, Tyndale hit on the covenant principle as the key to understanding the Scriptures. In his New Testament he said,

> I have ever noted the covenants in the margins, and also the promises. Moreover, where thou findest a promise and no covenant expressed therewith, there must thou understand a covenant. For all the promises of the mercy and grace that Christ hath purchased for us are made upon the condition that we keep the law.[33]

There is not a word in Tyndale about Moses having added useless laws just so that the people would realize what terrible sinners they were. Nor does he ever suggest that the Old Testament was meant for Jews but not for Christians. For Tyndale, the heart of the law was the Ten Commandments, which are eternally valid and which Jesus summarized as loving God and then loving our neighbor. As Tyndale expressed it,

> He that loveth his neighbor in God and Christ fulfilleth these two, and consequently the ten, and finally all the other. Now if we love our neighbors in God and Christ: that is to wit, if we be loving, kind and merciful to them, because God hath created them unto his likeness, and Christ hath redeemed them and bought them with his blood, then may we be bold to trust in

---

[32]"Tyndale's Preface to the New Testament," para. 4, in Bray, *Documents*, 19; and G. L. Bray, ed., *Translating the Bible from William Tyndale to King James* (London: Latimer Trust, 2010), 29.

[33]"Tyndale's Preface," para. 8, in Bray, *Documents*, 20; and Bray, *Translating the Bible*, 31.

God through Christ and his deserving, for all mercy. For God hath promised and bound himself to us, to show us all mercy and to be a Father Almighty to us.[34]

Tyndale said almost nothing about justification by faith or obtaining the righteousness of God, focusing instead on God's mercy and forgiveness, which he bestows on those who are rightly disposed toward God's law and who trust in Christ as the one who can keep it, and in fact has kept it, on their behalf. He was quite clear that Christ has justified us by his works, not by ours, and that it is he who has made us acceptable in God's presence. But he then went on to explain that those who have been so justified must demonstrate that by loving their neighbors, and he claimed that the law was given for that purpose. Keeping it was therefore not a means of earning eternal salvation but rather the way in which our faith in God is manifested by the love and mercy we show to one another: "Seeing then that faith to God and love and mercifulness to our neighbors is all that the law requireth, therefore of necessity the law must be understood and interpreted by them."[35]

When it came to things like Sabbath observance and the food laws, wherein Jesus criticized the legalism of the scribes and Pharisees, Tyndale understood this to mean that the principle of love had to come first. If loving one's neighbor meant ignoring the letter of the law, then so be it—that was *keeping* the law in its deeper sense, not breaking it. His understanding of the difference between the Old and the New Testaments was that the former was temporal, limited to this life, and the latter eternal. But each has its place and both bear witness to the love and the mercy of God. In his preface to the Pentateuch, Tyndale advised his readers to apply everything to themselves and their own spiritual condition. In evaluating the

---

[34]"Tyndale's Preface," para. 6, in Bray, *Documents*, 20; and Bray, *Translating the Bible*, 30.
[35]"Tyndale's Preface," para. 21, in Bray, *Documents*, 23; and Bray, *Translating the Bible*, 35.

story of Cain and Abel, for example, he reminded them that God looks on the heart and not at the deed; the latter might look good, but if it was done from the wrong motive, it was sinful. In this way, Tyndale walked his readers through the story of Israel, pointing out how at every turn the law of love for God and neighbor was the criterion of interpretation that had to be applied if they were to get a right understanding of it.

Tyndale's essentially pastoral approach to the reading and interpretation of Scripture caught on, at least in England. One of its great promoters was Thomas Cranmer, archbishop of Canterbury from 1533. Although he never had any direct contact with Tyndale, who was an outlaw in English eyes for having translated the New Testament at a time when that was still illegal, Cranmer no doubt shared his basic approach to the text and its interpretation. In 1538 the Church of England received the king's permission to print the Bible in English and was ordered to put a copy in every parish church so that those who wished to read it might do so. In the second edition of this Great Bible, which appeared in 1540, Archbishop Cranmer attached a preface, the main purpose of which was to encourage people to read it. His approach was nothing if not practical:

> As mallets, hammers, saws, chisels, axes and hatchets be the tools of their occupation, so be the books of the prophets and apostles, and all Holy Writ inspired by the Holy Ghost, the instruments of our salvation. Wherefore, let us not stick to buy and provide us the Bible, that is to say, the books of Holy Scripture. And let us think that to be a better jewel in our house than either gold or silver. For like as thieves be loth to assault a house where they know to be good armor and artillery; so wheresoever these holy and ghostly books be occupied, there neither the Devil nor none of his angels dare come near. And they that

occupy them be in much safeguard, and having great consola-
tion, and be the readier unto all goodness, the slower to all evil;
and if they have done anything amiss, anon, even by the sight of
the books, their consciences be admonished, and they wax
sorry and ashamed of the fact.[36]

Cranmer knew that many people would be reluctant to take up
his suggestion, not least because they did not think they were adequate to the intellectual demands that reading God's Word would
make on them. Having been used to a world in which theology was
the preserve of an educated and specialist minority, they thought
they would never understand it. In this, they were not unlike many
people today, who do not attempt to read academic philosophy or
theology for similar reasons. But Cranmer had an answer ready
for them:

> The Holy Ghost hath so ordered and attempered the Scrip-
> tures, that in them as well publicans, fishers and shepherds may
> find their edification, as great doctors their erudition: for these
> books were not made to vainglory, like as were the writings of
> the Gentile philosophers and rhetoricians . . . But the apostles
> and prophets wrote their books so that their special intent and
> purpose might be understanded and perceived of every reader,
> which was nothing but the edification or amendment of the life
> of them that readeth or heareth it.[37]

In this way, Cranmer democratized the Bible, claiming that it had
something for everyone and that no Christian would read it and go
away untouched by its message. Not that he ignored the great teachers of the church or despised their learning. On the contrary, he appealed not only to the witness of the Bible itself but also to the fathers

---

[36]"Cranmer's Preface to the Great Bible," para. 5, in Bray, *Documents*, 237; and Bray, *Translat-ing the Bible*, 82-83.
[37]"Cranmer's Preface," para. 6, in Bray, *Documents*, 237; and Bray, *Translating the Bible*, 83.

of the early church, though with a difference. At a time when virtually everyone quoted Augustine as the main authority from the ancient world, occasionally supplementing him with further testimonies from other Latin writers like Jerome, Tertullian, or Hilary of Poitiers, Cranmer passed over them and went for Greek authors like John Chrysostom and Gregory of Nazianzus instead. He was particularly struck by Gregory's approach to the Bible: "The fear of God must be the first beginning, and as it were an ABC, or an introduction to all them that shall enter to the very true and most fruitful knowledge of Holy Scriptures."[38] What Gregory meant, of course, was that our relationship of obedience to God in faith must take precedence over what Gregory called "matters of high speculation," which could only lead us to fear, but fear of entirely the wrong kind.

Cranmer did this consciously, describing Gregory as one "of whom St Jerome saith, that unto his time the Latin Church had no writer able to be compared and to make an even match with him."[39] In this not altogether subtle way, Cranmer opened up a new dimension of patristic learning, one that had been virtually unknown in the pre-Reformation church and was untouched by the papal traditions against which the Reformers were rebelling.

CREATING A BIBLICAL THEOLOGY
The doctrine of the sufficiency of Scripture forced the Reformers to develop a systematic theology that reflected the inner coherence of God's revelation and could serve as a viable constitution for the church. Systematic theology did not exist as such in ancient times. The first person to write anything like it was John of Damascus (675–ca. 749), and he is usually regarded as the last of the ancient Greek fathers. John's work was translated into Latin several centuries later and formed the inspiration for men like Peter Lombard in

---

[38]Cranmer was quoting Gregory of Nazianzus, *Orations*, 39.8.
[39]"Cranmer's Preface," para. 14, in Bray, *Documents*, 242; and Bray, *Translating the Bible*, 90.

the twelfth century. But as the medieval systematicians demonstrated, their theology was far from being based on Scripture alone. It was a compendium of biblical texts, theological statements, decrees of various popes and councils, and their own reflections. It was conceived as much against a philosophical backdrop as anything else. Both the questions asked and the way they were answered demonstrated a way of thinking that was arguably alien to the biblical writers, even if the content of what they said could be harmonized with the Bible. The fact of the matter is that before the sixteenth century, nobody had ever constructed a systematic theology based on Scripture alone, and it was by no means clear how that should be done.

Martin Luther was not a systematician himself, but he understood that the Bible contained an inner narrative that could be expressed in a theologically coherent way. For him, this was the contrast between the law and the gospel. The law was the objective Word of God revealed to humanity. It was the truth, expressed in a way that only laws can do. But as the apostle Paul so eloquently reminded the Romans, the practical effect of the law was to make sin more obvious and problematic. It was more obvious because the law defined it as any transgression of its requirements. Adam had fallen away from God and transmitted his sinfulness to his posterity, but he was not a sinner merely because he was uncircumcised, for example. That law had not been given in his time, and so he was not guilty of breaking it. But to the Jews of later times, circumcision was essential because the law commanded it, and so to reject it was to sin.

But this way of thinking was also problematic, for two quite different reasons. First, it was hard to believe that failure to keep an external rite like circumcision was a sin in the eyes of God. What difference could circumcision possibly make to him? Outward conformity to such rules could easily lead to hypocrisy and a denial of true faith, and this of course was one of the major themes of Jesus' earthly ministry. But if Jesus could shift the weight of sin from outward observances to inward convictions, sin became more deeply entrenched and harder to deal with. This is clear from the way he expounded the Ten Commandments. Few people have ever killed another human being, so most of us can claim not to have broken the sixth commandment in the literal sense. But when Jesus said that anyone who had a bad thought in his heart toward his neighbor had killed that person already, the number of "murderers" increased exponentially. Worse still, human nature is such that it is almost impossible to avoid sinning in that sense, since evil thoughts occur to us all at some time or other and cannot be dismissed merely by outward acts of penance or contrition. The root of sinfulness is far too deep for that. In his preface to Paul's epistle to the Romans, Luther wrote,

> The little word "law" you must here not take in human fashion as a teaching about what works are to be done or not done. That is the way with human laws; a law is fulfilled by works, even though there is no heart in the doing of them. But God judges according to what is in the depths of the heart. For this reason, his law too makes its demands on the inmost heart; it cannot be satisfied with works, but rather punishes as hypocrisy and lies the works not done from the bottom of the heart. . . . If the law were for the body, it could be satisfied with works. Because it is spiritual, however, no one can satisfy it—unless all that you do is done from the bottom of your heart. But such a heart is given only by God's Spirit.[40]

As both Paul and Luther saw, the only thing that a holy and perfect law can do is to condemn us to destruction because we are

---

[40]Martin Luther, "Preface to the Epistle of St Paul to the Romans," in Lull, *Luther's Basic Theological Writings*, 99; and *LW*, 35:66.

spiritually incapable of keeping it. This is why the grace of the gospel is so important. Right from the beginning, when God expelled Adam and Eve from the Garden of Eden, a note of redemption was sounded. Luther was very clear about that:

> Moses teaches how all creatures were created, and . . . whence sin and death came, namely by Adam's fall, through the devil's wickedness. But immediately thereafter, before the coming of the law of Moses, he teaches whence help is to come for the driving out of sin and death, namely, not by the law or men's own works (since there was no law as yet), but by the "seed of the woman," Christ, promised to Adam and Abraham, in order that throughout the Scriptures from the beginning faith may be praised above all works and laws and merits. Genesis, there-fore, is made up almost entirely of illustrations of faith and un-belief . . . It is an exceedingly evangelical book.[41]

The gospel was a message of deliverance from sin and therefore from the power of the law, which brought that sin to light. But more than that, the gospel was the promise of a new life in Christ that was pleas-ing to God, even though believers remain sinners. In fact, the more we know how sinful we are, the more we shall turn to Christ as our only hope of redemption. Whereas the medieval church had taught that we must improve our behavior in order to draw closer to God, Luther and his followers declared, following the teaching of Paul, that salvation lies in recognizing our own helplessness and turning to God in faith that his promises, worked out in Jesus Christ, will be applied to those who believe in him.

The Bible had been revealed to the church, not just for the pur-pose of showing us why we need salvation and how God has pro-vided it but also for living the Christian life once we have become

---

[41]Martin Luther, "Preface to the Old Testament," in Lull, *Luther's Basic Theological Writings*, 114-15; and *LW*, 35:37.

believers. Luther explained this by saying that Christ is a *gift* from God and also an *example* to believers. The gift comes first, as Luther explained:

> The chief article and foundation of the gospel is that before you take Christ as an example, you accept and recognize him as a gift, as a present that God has given you and that is your own . . . when you have Christ as the foundation and chief blessing of your salvation, then the other part follows: that you take him as your example, giving yourself in service to your neighbor just as you see that Christ has given himself for you. . . . Christ as a gift nourishes your faith and makes you a Christian. But Christ as an example exercises your works. These do not make you a Christian. Actually they come forth from you because you have already been made a Christian. As widely as a gift differs from an example, so widely does faith differ from works, for faith possesses nothing of its own, only the deeds and life of Christ.[42]

Luther was aware that three different kinds of laws existed in the Old Testament. As he put it in the preface to his translation,

> It should be noted that the laws are of three kinds. Some speak only of temporal things, as do our imperial laws. These are established by God chiefly because of the wicked . . . There are some, however, that teach about the external worship of God . . . Over and above these two are the laws about faith and love. All other laws must and ought to be measured by faith and love. That is to say, the other laws are to be kept where their observance does not conflict with faith and love; but where they conflict with faith and love, they should be done away entirely.[43]

---

[42]Martin Luther, "What to Look for and Expect in the Gospels," in Lull, *Luther's Basic Theological Writings*, 95; and *LW*, 35:20.

[43]Luther, "Preface to the Old Testament," in Lull, *Luther's Basic Theological Writings*, 116; and *LW*, 35:40.

Martin Luther's understanding of the relationship between law and gospel in the Old and New Testaments was fleshed out and developed further by Philipp Melanchthon (1497–1560), one of his early disciples and a close collaborator throughout his life. Even as Luther was feeling his way toward a reformation that would break with Rome, Melanchthon was already sketching out what would become the first Protestant attempt at a systematic theology. This was published in 1521 as his *Commonplaces* (*Loci communes*) and it was an immediate bestseller. Luther commended it highly and regarded it as a clear expression of his own teaching. On the relationship between the two Testaments, Melanchthon agreed with the then traditional view that the law could be divided into three parts: judicial (civil), ceremonial, and moral.

But whereas it was generally thought that the first two had been abolished in Christ and that the third reaffirmed and strengthened, Melanchthon insisted, along with Luther, that the entire law had been abrogated by the gospel. For him, the key was that Christ has set us free from the law of sin and death and put his Spirit in our hearts so that we can now do what the law commands:

> Christianity is freedom, because those who do not have the Spirit of Christ cannot in any way perform the law; they are rather subject to the curse of the law. Those who have been renewed by the Spirit of Christ now conform voluntarily even without the law to what the law used to command. The law is the will of God; the Holy Spirit is nothing else than the living will of God and its being in action. Therefore, when we have been regenerated by the Spirit of God, who is the living will of God, we now will spontaneously that very thing which the law used to demand.[44]

---

[44]W. Pauck, ed., *Melanchton and Bucer* (Philadelphia, PA: Westminster Press, 1969), 123.

This principle was already widely accepted with respect to the judicial and ceremonial aspects of the law, which were in no way binding on Christians, although Melanchthon objected to the opinion of Jerome that something like circumcision ought to be forbidden. He pointed out that the apostle Paul made it optional and irrelevant to the question of justification, which could only be by faith, but that he did not forbid it, and in the case of Timothy, he actually insisted on it for practical reasons.[45] Circumcision, and other ceremonies like it, are now matters of indifference. But what about the Ten Commandments? Here the traditional Scholastic theology had insisted that the law was still applicable, but Melanchthon disagreed. In his mind, even the Ten Commandments are no longer in force as law. But this did not mean that it is all right for Christians to kill, steal, and commit adultery. The difference between circumcision, which is optional for Christians, and the commands of the Decalogue, which are compulsory, is not determined by any difference in the law but by the indwelling presence of the Holy Spirit in the heart of the believer:

> Judicial and ceremonial laws are external observances apart from the righteousness of the heart, and they are circumscribed by things, persons, places, and times. Since the Spirit does not necessarily bring these observances with himself, there is no reason why we should do them. The Spirit of God cannot be in the human heart without fulfilling the Decalogue. The Decalogue is therefore observed by necessity. The Spirit of God can be in the human heart even without those external observances. The ceremonial and judicial laws are therefore not observed by necessity.[46]

Melanchthon rounded off his discussion of this subject by making a personal application of the Ten Commandments to the lives of

---

[45]Acts 16:3.
[46]Pauck, *Melanchthon and Bucer*, 127.

individual Christians. They are still necessary for us because we have not yet been made perfect, and the Holy Spirit uses them in order to bring us to maturity as believers:

> For believers, laws are prescribed through which the Spirit mortifies the flesh. For freedom has not yet been consummated in us, but it is being appropriated, both while the Spirit is increasing and while the flesh is being slain. The Decalogue is useful in mortifying the flesh, but the ceremonial and judicial laws are not. So it is that believers need the Decalogue, but not the other laws.[47]

Later on, Luther echoed this, although with an interesting twist. Instead of speaking about three different aspects of the law, Luther said that there were three different kinds of righteousness, with the law of Moses (of which the Ten Commandments was the centerpiece) being the particular concern of the church:

> Righteousness is of many kinds. There is a political righteousness, which the emperor, the princes of this world, philosophers and lawyers consider. There is also a ceremonial righteousness, which human traditions teach, as, for example, the traditions of the pope and other traditions . . . There is another kind of righteousness in addition to these, the righteousness of the Law, or of the Decalogue, which Moses teaches. We, too, teach this, but after the doctrine of faith.[48]

Neither Luther nor Melanchthon ever went any further than this, but in two important respects Melanchthon laid a foundation for future developments in Reformed thinking. First, he abolished the distinction between the different kinds of law that had prevailed until

---

[47]Pauck, *Melanchthon and Bucer*, 130.
[48]Martin Luther, "Lectures on Galatians," in Lull, *Luther's Basic Theological Writings*, 19; and *LW*, 2:4.

his time. The Jews had to keep the whole law, but Christians are set free from that obligation—no exceptions could be made for the moral law, not even for the Ten Commandments. At the same time, what was good and of permanent value in the law is implanted in our hearts by the Holy Spirit, so that in practice we keep the law in a way that is pleasing to God, not relying on our efforts as proof of our justification but on God's mercy and forgiveness in Christ, who makes up for our deficiencies and pleads for us before God the Father on the strength of his righteousness, not ours. Later generations of Reformed theologians would pick up where Melanchthon left off and develop further the continuing relevance and application of the Old Testament law to the Christian life.

This perspective was passed on to John Calvin, who integrated it into a wider hermeneutical framework. Calvin began with creation, which he believed is an open book that reveals God and his purposes to the entire human race.[49] But through a combination of finitude and sinfulness, the human race has failed to grasp the true meaning of this revelation, so it needs something more specific. For that purpose, God chose the Jews and gave them specific instructions about who he is and how we should relate to him:

> He has from the beginning maintained this plan for his church, so that besides these common proofs he also put forth his Word, which is a more direct and more certain mark whereby he is to be recognized. There is no doubt that Adam, Noah, Abraham, and the rest of the patriarchs with this assistance penetrated to the intimate knowledge of him that in a way distinguished them from unbelievers.[50]

Modern readers find Adam and Noah's inclusion in the church somewhat puzzling, but this reflects Calvin's consciousness of the

---

[49]Calvin, *Institutes* 1.5.1-15.
[50]Calvin, *Institutes* 1.6.1.

fact that all those who received divine revelation were members of
God's people. He recognized that the first humans knew about God
only as their Creator, not as their Redeemer, but he insisted that the
message conveyed to them was of saving importance because in order
to understand God's redemptive work it is necessary to begin with
his creative activity. The connection between creation and the law is
clearly spelled out in Psalm 19, which Calvin quoted at length to
demonstrate his point.[51] The Word of God is found in the Old and
the New Testaments, both of which have been inspired by the Holy
Spirit.[52] Christians know this not because they have discovered it by
reading the Bible but because they have been taught by the Holy
Spirit, who dwells in our hearts by faith. Our understanding of Scripture is part and parcel of our relationship with God, without which it
remains a closed book. Calvin extended this principle to his analysis
of the Law of Moses, which is quite different from Luther's. First of
all, Calvin set Moses firmly in the context of the covenant God had
made with Abraham. God had not given Israel a law in order to take
the people away from the promise of Christ but "to hold their minds
in readiness until his coming; even to kindle desire for him, and to
strengthen their expectation, in order that they might not grow faint
by too long delay."[53] Luther had claimed that many of the precepts
decreed by Moses had been given not because they were of any value
in themselves but merely in order to sensitize the Israelites to the
extent of their sinfulness. Without mentioning Luther, Calvin rejected this way of thinking:

> For if something spiritual had not been set forth to which they
> were to direct their course, the Jews would have frittered away
> their effort in these matters, just as the Gentiles did in their

---

[51]Calvin, *Institutes* 1.6.4.
[52]Calvin, *Institutes* 1.6.4.
[53]Calvin, *Institutes* 2.7.1.

trifles. . . . Yet that very type shows that God did not command sacrifices in order to busy his worshipers with earthly exercises. Rather, he did so that he might lift their minds higher.[54]

That higher purpose was to reveal the coming of Christ. Even the prophets knew and proclaimed that God does not want ritualistic worship, but an adoration that is purely spiritual. Moses himself intended this for Israel because he said that it was to be "a kingdom of priests and a holy nation."[55] How could they have fulfilled that calling if they had no awareness of an atonement greater than the one offered through the blood of animals? The entire relationship between God and his chosen people was spiritual in nature, and therefore the signs and ceremonies that marked it were basically spiritual too. The observance of the ceremonial laws taught the people who Christ was and what he would come to do. It was with reference to them that Paul told the Galatians that "the law was our guardian until Christ came."[56] Once he came, it was redundant, but its meaning was clearer than ever. The Jews of Paul's day were guilty, not because they exalted the law but because they were so attached to the outward ceremonies that they refused to abandon them when their spiritual meaning was revealed and fulfilled in Christ. In effect, their persistence in literal observance of those laws was a denial of Christ and therefore an act of disobedience to God, for which they had to be rejected.

Calvin was very insistent that the main purpose of the law was to proclaim Christ, but he recognized that it had other uses as well. One of these was to set limits on the behavior of those who do not know the Spirit of God. Such people are restrained by fear of the punishment that the law will inflict on them, but of course, that is

---

[54]Calvin, *Institutes* 2.7.1.
[55]Ex 19:6.
[56]Gal 3:24.

not to their credit. On the contrary, the more they submit to a law they do not like, the angrier and more resentful of it they are likely to become, and they will do their best to escape from its yoke. But, as Calvin pointed out, society as a whole benefits from this kind of restraint that is placed on what are essentially disordered desires that, if they were allowed to go unchecked, would do great damage to everyone, including God's people. But Calvin also understood that this training in restraint, while hard for the ungodly to bear, was nevertheless a preparation for them in case they should be converted. Someone who becomes a Christian and already knows the law has a head start on those who have never heard of it, and in that sense the law acts as a preparation for the gospel even among those who openly reject it.[57]

But Calvin also taught a third use of the law, and it is for this that Calvinism is now most widely known. In Calvin's eyes, this third use is closely connected to the proclamation of Christ, and as far as Christians are concerned, it is the main function that the law performs nowadays. It may be true that we have the law written on our hearts and that we are motivated by the Holy Spirit to do what it commands, but even those who walk in the light can learn from the written law in two major respects:

> It is the best instrument for enabling them [i.e., Christians] daily to learn with greater truth and certainty what that will of the Lord is which they aspire to follow, and to confirm them in this knowledge . . . Then, because we need not doctrine merely, but exhortation also, the servant of God will derive this further advantage from the law: by frequently meditating upon it, he will be excited to obedience, and confirmed in it, and so drawn away from the slippery paths of sin.[58]

---

[57]Calvin, *Institutes* 2.7.10.
[58]Calvin, *Institutes* 2.7.12.

This is how God's chosen people are brought to maturity in their faith. The law is not a condemnation that curses them and leads them to spiritual death but rather an incitement to shrug off laziness and the fear that even if we do our best we shall still come short of what God requires of us. Instead, we must press on with the commandments that he has given, trusting in Christ to forgive our remaining sinfulness and in his Holy Spirit to empower us for service. As he concludes, "The doctrine of the law has not been infringed by Christ, but remains, that, by teaching, admonishing, rebuking, and correcting, it may fit and prepare us for every good work."[59] In this way, law and grace are seen to be not in opposition to one another but two aspects of the same thing, both pointing us to Christ as he himself taught his disciples they would.[60] In particular, there is no real distinction between the moral and the ceremonial elements of the law. The ceremonies of the Old Testament are no longer practiced because they have been fulfilled in Christ, but we have to understand their meaning and intention if we are to appreciate what it is that Christ has done for us. The moral law, by which Calvin meant the Ten Commandments, remains our ultimate guide to spiritual perfection, and keeping it in a spiritual way is an essential part of Christian obedience, as Jesus himself taught his disciples. Calvin went on to expound the Decalogue in great detail so that no one should be left in any doubt as to what it means.[61]

COVENANT THEOLOGY

Working sometimes separately and sometimes together, the second generation of Reformers inched their way toward a systematic theology based on the principle of covenant. To them, the Bible was essentially a covenant made between God and Israel in which God

---

[59]Calvin, *Institutes* 2.7.14.
[60]Calvin quoted Mt 5:17 in support of this assertion.
[61]Calvin, *Institutes* 2.8.1-58.

declared that he had chosen Israel for salvation. There was no obvious logic to this—Israel had not done anything to deserve the honor and in fact had done a great deal to show just how unworthy of God's favor it was. But God's decision was his alone; it is what we call his election, and it was based on love—the only explanation for it offered by the Bible.[62]

From the Christian standpoint, the covenant that God made with Israel comes in two dispensations. The first is what we call the Old Testament, which to some extent corresponds to the law. With the coming of Christ, that dispensation was abrogated and a new one was instituted in its place. The covenant itself remained the same—those who are saved are saved because they have believed in Jesus Christ, who suffered and died for them. But where the saints of the Old Testament looked forward to his coming, those of the New look back to it. The ultimate reward is the same in both cases, but those who lived before Christ lived in hope in a way that is no longer applicable, although we are still waiting for some of the promises made in Christ to be fulfilled at the end of time.

Over time this basic perspective developed into a systematic covenant theology. It is hard to say who invented it—Calvin never used the term, for example—but by the time we get to the Westminster Confession of Faith (1646) it had become the standard Reformed orthodoxy, and various theologians have been given the credit for its development. It is best to see it as a systematization of the theological scheme already present in the minds of Melanchthon and Calvin, and possibly of Luther as well, that achieved ever greater refinement and definition in the hands of their disciples.

The beauty of covenant theology is that it offers an interpretation of the Bible that does not, and more importantly *cannot*, rely on external sources like Greek philosophy. Everything we know about God's

---

[62]Deut 7:6-8.

covenant is found within its pages, and the concept is flexible enough to be regarded as comprehensive. Furthermore, once we accept the principle that it comes in two dispensations, there is no need to resort to allegory. With a covenant theology it is possible to read the Old Testament in the literal sense while at the same time stating that it is no longer necessary to keep all its rules and regulations, because what was compulsory then has now been abrogated and replaced by something different (and superior).

The adoption of covenant theology as an interpretive principle had the additional effect of shifting the conceptual basis of theology away from philosophical concerns to legal and juridical ones. Instead of debating what God is in himself and how his uncreated nature contrasts with what he has created, covenant theologians shifted their attention to what God has done for his people, and that, after all, is the main theme of the Bible. What Christ *did* for our redemption became more significant than what he *was* (fully God and fully man), although his incarnation remained the necessary precondition for his atoning work. The effects of this on wider theology can be seen from one question that had never been asked before but which now moved to center stage. Did Christ die to atone for the sins of every human being or just for those of the elect? This debate, usually known today as the debate over "limited" or "definite" atonement, is meaningful only when the perspective of covenant theology is taken into account.

The New Testament makes it clear that Christ died for the sins of the whole world and that God wants everyone to be saved. But Reformed theologians then asked why, if that is the case, not everyone is actually saved. Can human beings resist God's will for them? What are we to say about those—the vast majority of human beings at that time and still a significant number today—who have never heard the gospel and could not have chosen it even if they had wanted to?

Put these questions and others like them into a covenant context. Did the high priest of Israel make atonement for the sins of the whole world, or for Israel only? The answer would appear to be the latter, but the question does not end there. Was the sacrifice sufficient to cover the sins of a non-Israelite? Presumably the answer to that would have to be that it was theoretically sufficient to cover any and every sin but that it was not applied to non-Israelites because they did not belong to the covenant people of God. The difference between it and Christ's sacrifice does not lie in its nature but in the extent of the covenant. What had previously been restricted to a single nation was now open to any human being who believed in Christ. This is what the Bible means when it says that God wants "everyone" to be saved—not just Jews but people from every tribe and nation. Although the mission field was now universal, the seed that was sown anywhere and everywhere did not produce good fruit in equal measure. As in ancient Israel, some believed and others did not, because only some had been chosen according to the hidden plan of God. In this way covenant theology managed to resolve what appears to be a contradiction. The universality of the gospel applied to the covenant promises being opened to the entire world, but the number of the elect remained a secret in the mind of God, and it was for them (and for them alone) that Christ had died. The non-elect (or reprobate) might be either Jews or non-Jews, because the basis of election had changed with the new dispensation. But even in the Old Testament it was clear that not all Israel had been preserved down through the centuries, since ten of the original twelve tribes had been lost and many of the rest were far from being exemplary models of their faith. In the end, justification by faith applied to Jews as well as to others—the covenant was, after all, one.

As the Reformers saw it, God had made a covenant with Abraham that was later renewed with Moses and David before finally being fulfilled in Christ. An unbroken history of faith, recounted in part in Hebrews 11, stretched back to the patriarchs of Israel and united Christians to them. That is why some of the Reformers spoke of "the

Old Testament church," a phrase that is not found in the Bible but that served to underline the point that those who believed in the promise of the coming Messiah were just as much part of the people of God as those who came after.

One important consequence of this is that Reformed Christians developed an attitude toward their contemporary Jews that was far more sympathetic than anything that had been known up to that time. Jews had been excluded from full participation in medieval society, and in some countries they had actually been expelled. That had occurred as far back as 1290 in England and as recently as 1492 in Spain and 1494 in Portugal. Martin Luther had a negative view of Jews, much to the embarrassment of modern Lutherans, who have had to endure seeing him quoted in defense of the Holocaust in 1933–1945. Luther fully embraced the Jewishness of Jesus, and his prejudices were unexceptional by sixteenth-century standards, but prejudices they were.[63]

As time went on, however, this negative attitude began to change among Protestants, and covenant theology would play a part in the development of Jewish emancipation. Where once Jews had been seen as "Christ-killers," they came to be viewed more positively as the original chosen people of God, whose current unbelief was tolerated in order for the gospel to be preached among the Gentiles. At the end of time, the remaining Jews would be converted and "all Israel," Jews and Gentiles alike, would be saved.[64] On the whole, the Reformers did not believe that all Jewish people would eventually become Christians, nor did they have a high regard for Judaism as a religion. Nevertheless, it is a fact that Oliver Cromwell (1599–1658) first relaxed the restrictions that had been placed on Jewish settlement in England, and the

---

[63]Martin Luther, "On the Jews and Their Lies," in Lull, *Luther's Basic Theological Writings*, 25-32. The full text is available in *LW*, 47:121-306. See also Gregory Miller, "Luther's Views of the Jews and Turks," in *The Oxford Handbook of Martin Luther's Theology*, ed. R. Kolb, I. Dingel, and L. Batka (Oxford: Oxford University Press, 2014), 427-34.
[64]Rom 11:26.

Netherlands were similarly hospitable to them. They would not acquire civil rights until much later, but they were guaranteed freedom from persecution and came to be integrated into Protestant societies in a way that did not happen elsewhere in Christian Europe.[65]

How Israel, and by extension the Christian church, related to the world at large was another biblical theme that the Reformers expressed in terms of covenant. As they saw it, God had made a covenant of works with Adam, as opposed to the covenant of grace that he made with Abraham. According to this interpretation, Adam would have been saved by his works if he had obeyed God, but his disobedience brought destruction on his descendants. The entire human race has perished in Adam, but in Christ those whom God has chosen for salvation have been brought back to life, and that new life will never end. It is possible to criticize this approach, and many have done so, including some within the Reformed tradition itself. The Bible nowhere speaks about a covenant of works, and the word is first used when God made a covenant with Noah for the preservation of the human race after the flood.[66] In the nineteenth century, Charles Hodge (1797–1878) and Abraham Kuyper (1837–1920) both developed a notion of common grace by which they reinterpreted the covenant that God had made with Adam. It was not a covenant of works, because nobody can be ever saved by works, but of grace, just as much as the covenant made with Abraham was. The difference was one of election—the recipients of the Abrahamic covenant of "special grace" have been chosen for salvation, whereas the recipients of the Adamic covenant of "common grace" have not.

Whether common grace is a truly biblical concept is still a matter of debate among Reformed theologians today, but however we choose to describe God's relationship with the human race beyond Israel, it

---

[65]The Ottoman Empire, which included most of the Balkans (where the majority population was Christian), was strikingly different from this. There Jews were tolerated on the same basis as Christians and other non-Muslim monotheists.

[66]Gen 9:9-17.

is clear from the Bible that the Gentiles come under his sovereign sway just as much as Israel does. His revelation is as relevant to them as it is to the Jews, a point that several Old Testament prophets made in different ways and that has been the foundation for the preaching of the gospel to non-Jews since the coming of Christ. As far as the Reformers were concerned, there was no need to look any further and no merit in the idea that different people could be redeemed according to the principles of their own religions. When it comes to eternal salvation, the revelation of Holy Scripture is exclusive as well as being sufficient and comprehensive for everyone.

The difficulty with covenant theology in the seventeenth century was that those who adopted it believed they had to impose it on society as a whole. In their eyes, a Protestant state was in covenant with God, not just particular individuals within it. Everyone who was subject to that state was a beneficiary of divine election, although (as in ancient Israel), not everyone was in tune with it. Plenty of renegades and reprobates, as well as ignorant people, simply did not understand how blessed they were. Such people could hardly be allowed to have a say in government—the Reformers were not democrats. Instead, power in the state should be entrusted to those who were called to exercise it. On the whole, the Reformers accepted the existing kings, even if their behavior was often unsatisfactory, but they refashioned the aristocracies by which they governed.

Instead of entrusting everything to a hereditary nobility, the Reformers preferred to seek out those who had shown by their enterprise and good faith that they were worthy of high position. It was difficult to examine them spiritually, so property qualifications had to be used instead. A man who owned land or who had made his way in business had demonstrated his social worth, and on the basis of his wealth he would be given the right to vote and to sit in the legislature if his peers elected him to it. This was the beginning of modern parliamentary government, which generations of Protestants fought for and in most cases eventually achieved. When the process was frustrated, as it was in colonial America, there might be rebellion, but once the prize was obtained, things quickly settled down and carried on much as before. As the example of the United States shows, the leaders of the rebellion were not interested in social revolution and did nothing to emancipate women, slaves, or even the poor. On the contrary, their stated aim was to restore the "ancient constitution," which to them meant the rule of the godly class that constituted the "political nation."

Within Protestant societies this pattern worked tolerably well, but it was a different matter when they collided with outsiders. People who did not share their convictions were regarded as inferior and undeserving of any social status. In European countries that meant that Jews and religious dissenters were denied civil rights. In the overseas colonies, things could be much worse, as native peoples were often exterminated or enslaved. Whether we like it or not, it was conservative Protestants, often fortified by a Reformed theology that made them God's chosen people, who established and enforced racial segregation in the American South and apartheid in South Africa. Today, most people accept that this was a perversion of the covenant idea, but whether that is true or not, it was a theological aberration that has left scars which are still a long way from being healed.

PREDESTINATION

Closely tied to the development of a covenant theology, with its focus on election, was belief in predestination. This was logical, and in hindsight we may regard it as having been inevitable, but, odd though it may seem to us, election and predestination had not been tied together in a systematic way before the Reformation. In the New Testament, election (like covenant) is primarily collective—the nation of Israel was God's chosen people, and the Christian church has in some way supplanted it. Within Israel, ten of the original twelve tribes were lost and only Judah, with its younger brother Benjamin, survived to become the Jewish people that we know today. Of them, many were unbelievers and presumably doomed to perish because of that, although the apostle Paul pointed out that the nation was still God's people and that, in the end, all "Israel" would be saved.[67] Unfortunately for subsequent interpreters, he did not specify whether "all Israel" meant everyone who could possibly be regarded as Jewish or merely those individuals within the wider nation who took their religion seriously.[68] In the sixteenth and seventeenth centuries, all Europeans tended to see themselves as specially chosen by God in a way that others were not, even if some of them had a vision for worldwide evangelism. Reformed Protestants in particular often identified with Israel and regarded their nations as elect, independent of the spiritual state of the individuals within them, although this idea could be found among Catholics as well.[69]

The Christian appropriation of the idea of election inevitably led to a doctrine of predestination and greater emphasis on the individual believer. This was because Christianity was not inherited in the way that Judaism was and because Christians looked forward to an eternity in heaven in a way that Jews usually did not. Predestination does not figure much in the Old Testament, even though God sometimes made his purposes for particular individuals clear to them. Jeremiah is a case in point. God called him to become a prophet, saying, "Before I formed you in the womb I knew you, and before you were

---

[67] Rom 11:26.

[68] Ambiguity on this point persists to the present day. The modern state of Israel claims Palestine as its birthright on the basis of the promises made to Abraham, but only a minority of its citizens can be regarded as believing Jews.

[69] The Portuguese were particularly prone to this error, although they were firmly Catholic. That God had chosen them to spread the gospel of Christ was a main theme of Luís de Camões's epic poem "Os Lusíadas," and it inspired the hapless King Sebastian to lead a crusade to Morocco, where he and his army were annihilated in 1578. Even so, Sebastianismo, as this belief in the country's providential destiny was called, survived in different forms until the twentieth century.

born I consecrated you; I appointed you a prophet to the nations."[70]
The apostle Paul was probably thinking of that when he said almost
exactly the same thing about himself in his letter to the Galatians.[71]
But it is in the New Testament that predestination is developed as a
distinct doctrine, tied to the purposes of God for his people. We are
told that God the Father "predestined us for adoption to himself as
sons through Jesus Christ, according to the purpose of his will."[72]
The opening verses of 1 Peter say much the same thing, though in a
more detailed and convoluted way.[73] However we look at it, the first
Christians knew they had been called by God for a purpose and that
this calling was fundamentally to them as individuals, who then
formed a new people of God that was not tied to any ethnic origin.

Predestination was first expounded at great length by Augustine
and was regarded by later generations as characteristic of his theology. To be saved by grace through faith, apart from works or any
form of entitlement due to human inheritance, was possible only by
divine predestination, and the sovereignty of God ensured that what
he planned would actually come to pass. For centuries this belief remained the official teaching of the Western church (Augustine never
had much currency in the East), though it was not emphasized. On
the contrary, as medieval devotional practices developed, predestination was effectively pushed aside in favor of salvation by works, manifested in pilgrimages, penance, and the granting of indulgences. Few
people believed they were going straight to heaven when they died,
even if most hoped to get there eventually, after years of struggle in
purgatory. When predestination was discussed, it was often in an
impersonal way that made it more like determinism. That was the
approach taken by William of Ockham, whose short treatise on the

---

[70]Jer 1:5.
[71]Gal 1:15.
[72]Eph 1:5.
[73]1 Pet 1:3-5.

subject became a medieval classic.[74] From that time onward, predestination and determinism were linked in people's minds, even though the Reformers initially did nothing to encourage that interpretation.

It is easy to see why the Augustinian doctrine of predestination resurfaced alongside the doctrine of justification by faith alone. If a believer was saved through faith, then it was obvious that he was headed for heaven when he died, since otherwise his justification would have no meaning. Martin Luther certainly saw things that way. As far as he was concerned, the preaching of the gospel was evidence that the hearers were elect, since otherwise they would not have received the message. Believing it is the sign and guarantee of predestination, which is the logical and necessary concomitant of faith. Later Lutherans have occasionally speculated about how far this can be read back into the hidden will and purpose of God, but the question has never been central to their church's theology, and those who have preached predestination have usually stayed within the parameters established by Luther himself.[75]

It has been a very different matter among non-Lutheran Reformed Protestants. The doctrine of predestination was already prominent in Zwingli's *Ratio Fidei*, which he presented to the Emperor Charles V at the Diet of Augsburg in 1530.[76] Most remarkably, Archbishop Thomas Cranmer included a long article on the subject in his Forty-Two Articles of 1553, which survived virtually unaltered in the revision ten years later. In its current form it reads:

> Predestination to life is the everlasting purpose of God, whereby before the foundations of the world were laid, he hath constantly decreed by his counsel secret to us, to deliver from curse

---

[74]William of Ockham, *Predestination, God's Foreknowledge, and Future Contingents*, 2nd ed., trans. M. M. Adams and N. Kretzmann (Indianapolis, IN: Hackett, 1983).

[75]See the article on predestination in T. J. Wengert, ed., *Dictionary of Luther and the Lutheran Traditions* (Grand Rapids: Baker, 2017), 613-17.

[76]Dennison, *Reformed Confessions*, 1:116, 118.

and damnation those whom he hath chosen in Christ out of
mankind, and to bring them by Christ to everlasting salvation,
as vessels made to honour.[77]

Furthermore, Cranmer was very clear about the pastoral benefit
that belief in predestination ought to bring to those who believe
in Christ:

> The godly consideration of predestination and our election in
> Christ is full of sweet, pleasant and unspeakable comfort to
> godly persons, and such as feel in themselves the working of the
> Spirit of Christ, mortifying the works of the flesh and their
> earthly members, and drawing up their mind to high and heav-
> enly things, as well because it doth greatly establish and con-
> firm their faith of eternal salvation to be enjoyed through Christ,
> as because it doth fervently kindle their love towards God.[78]

At the same time, Cranmer was also aware that the doctrine of predestination would have a very different impact on those who were not
called and chosen by God, because to them, predestination would be
a message of despair that would plunge them into ungodly living and
damnation. In the end, he concluded that the doctrine should be
taught and maintained in the way in which it is set forth in Scripture,
implying (though not actually stating) that further speculation on
the subject ought to be avoided.

It was only after Cranmer's time that covenant theology began
to develop in a serious way and discussion of predestination increased accordingly. By the end of the sixteenth century the reticence
of the Thirty-Nine Articles had been abandoned, not least by those
who championed them as an expression of Reformed doctrine.

---

[77]Article 17 in Bray, *Documents*, 294; Pelikan and Hotchkiss, *Creeds and Confessions*,
2:532-33; and Dennison, *Reformed Confessions*, 2:759-60.

[78]Bray, *Documents*, 294-95; Pelikan and Hotchkiss, *Creeds and Confessions*, 2:532-33; Dennison, *Reformed Confessions*, 2:759-60.

For example, Archbishop John Whitgift (1530–1604), a noted opponent of Puritanism, had no hesitation on this score, and in 1595 he signed off on the so-called Lambeth Articles, which had been drawn up by William Whitaker (1548–1595), a Cambridge divine of noted Puritan sympathies.[79] Whitgift was unable to persuade Queen Elizabeth I to approve of them, but this was probably due to her innate caution and conservatism rather than to any objection to the articles themselves.[80] There was certainly no mistaking their emphasis, as the very first article stated, "From eternity God has predestined some men to life and condemned others to death."

The second part of this article, the belief in so-called double predestination, would characterize Reformed theology from that time onward and also raise much objection. Serious opposition appeared first in the Netherlands, where Jacobus Arminius (1560–1609) recoiled from the emerging Reformed consensus and tried to moderate it by suggesting that the fall of man was less all-pervasive than the leading Reformers supposed and that it was possible to resist the grace of God. The appeal to a residual form of free will struck a chord among his countrymen, many of whom were independent-minded in any case, and in 1610, shortly after Arminius himself had died, some of them issued a Remonstrance in support of his position, which they presented to the States General of Holland as the true interpretation of the Reformed faith.[81]

The Remonstrance could not go unanswered, and the upshot was the famous Synod of Dort, which met over the winter of 1618–1619

---

[79]Text in Bray, *Documents*, 399-400; Pelikan and Hotchkiss, *Creeds and Confessions*, 2:546; and Dennison, *Reformed Confessions*, 3:46.

[80]That the Lambeth Articles were generally accepted as standard Anglican teaching can be seen from the fact that they were incorporated in the Irish Articles of 1615, which were expressly designed to apply the Thirty-Nine Articles to the Church of Ireland. See Bray, *Documents*, 437-52; Pelikan and Hotchkiss, *Creeds and Confessions*, 2:551-68; and Dennison, *Reformed Confessions*, 4:88-107.

[81]For the five articles of the Remonstrance, see Bray, *Documents*, 453-55; and Pelikan and Hotchkiss, *Creeds and Confessions*, 2:549-50.

and hammered out what Reformed orthodoxy on the subject was and how it would henceforth be expressed. The theologians of Dort stated unequivocally that God's election is unconditional—it cannot be predicted or assumed on the basis of any human qualification or entitlement. Next, they said that the atoning work of Christ was intended only for the elect, not for the entire human race. Third, they reminded the church that fallen human beings had nothing in themselves that could assist them in the work of their salvation—this is the meaning of total depravity. Fourth, they said that the grace of God is irresistible: no human power is strong enough to stand up to him. Finally, they agreed that salvation is permanent and irreversible. However much a believer might suffer from doubt and discouragement, no power in heaven or on earth could separate him from the love of God, and in the end he would be saved.[82]

The Canons of Dort were duly received, and the Remonstrants were expelled from the Dutch churches, although they continue to exist today as a small denomination of their own. Elsewhere the canons were generally received throughout the Reformed world, although there have always been hesitations about the extent of Christ's atonement. These surfaced very soon in the British Isles, where even some staunch defenders of the Reformed position, like James Ussher (1581–1656), came to believe in what is sometimes called hypothetical universalism, which is the idea that Christ died for everyone in principle but that his atoning sacrifice is applied only to the elect in practice. Hypothetical universalism is not logically consistent with the other canons of Dort, because it suggests that human beings have the power to thwart God's will, but it appeals to those who find the pure doctrine of Dort too rigid and unfriendly to the task of

---

[82]See Rom 8:38-39. For the canons, see Bray, *Documents*, 456-78; Pelikan and Hotckhiss, *Creeds and Confessions*, 2:569-600; and Dennison, *Reformed Confessions*, 4:121-53. On the synod, see Aza Goudriaan and Fred Lieburg, eds., *Revisiting the Synod of Dordt (1618–1619)* (Leiden: Brill, 2010).

evangelism since it seems to suggest that the destiny of each human being is already decided and cannot be changed by preaching the gospel. Here an appeal to Luther would soon show that this is a misunderstanding since preaching the Word of God is an integral part of the way in which election and predestination are worked out in human experience, but few people understand that or make the connection, so various forms of hypothetical universalism have enjoyed greater currency than they deserve. Nevertheless, no Reformed confession of faith has ever adopted it, and it cannot be regarded as the official teaching of any Reformed church, however popular it may be at grassroots level.[83]

What can be said with certainty is that the Canons of Dort defined predestination with a degree of clarity that had not been expressed before, and they became the benchmark of orthodoxy among the Reformed, a position they still hold today. Their teaching was repeated in the Westminster Confession of Faith, and from there they have penetrated deep into the English-speaking world and Presbyterianism more generally.[84] Objections to them continue to be raised, and many people are persuaded by these, but to date the canons have not been successfully overturned. They remain not only the standard exposition of predestination but also one of the principal hallmarks of so-called Calvinism. The framers of the canons, as well as the Westminster divines, were careful to express their doctrine in the context of God's will revealed in his Word, and they stressed the effectual calling of believers by the Spirit of Christ "working in due season."[85] Yet it is hard not to think that they also left the door open to a return

---

[83]For a recent defense of the Arminian position on this subject, see David L. Allen, *The Extent of the Atonement: A Historical and Critical Review* (Nashville, TN: Broadman and Holman Academic, 2018).

[84]Westminster Confession of Faith 3, in Bray, *Documents*, 490-91; Pelikan and Hotchkiss, *Creeds and Confessions*, 2:610-11; and Dennison, *Reformed Confessions*, 4:238-39.

[85]Westminster Confession of Faith 3.6, in Bray, *Documents*, 490; Pelikan and Hotchkiss, *Creeds and Confessions*, 2:610-11; and Dennison, *Reformed Confessions*, 4:238-39.

to Ockhamist determinism. Consider the following: "Although God knows whatsoever may or can come to pass upon all supposed conditions, yet hath he not decreed anything because he foresaw it as future, or as that which would come to pass upon such conditions."[86]

It would be wrong to blame the Reformed theologians who composed articles like this one of introducing the impersonal deism that would wreak such havoc in the Protestant world later in the seventeenth century, but we must admit that the groundwork for that was unintentionally laid by people who were convinced that, in their exposition of the divine decree of predestination, they were glorifying God and explaining the mysteries of his mind to the church of their day.

---

[86]Westminster Confession of Faith 3.2, in Bray, *Documents*, 490; Pelikan and Hotchkiss, *Creeds and Confessions*, 2:610; and Dennison, *Reformed Confessions*, 4:38.

Four

THE WORK
OF THE HOLY SPIRIT

THE PERSONS OF THE TRINITY AND THEIR WORK

It is often said that the Protestant reformers made no significant changes to the traditional doctrine of God, which they are supposed to have taken over in its entirety from the medieval Catholic tradition. To the extent that they subscribed to the three classical creeds (the Apostles', the Nicene, and the Athanasian) and to the trinitarian formulations of the ancient church councils, that judgment is undoubtedly correct. But there is more to the doctrine of God than what is expressed in the creeds, and when we probe further, we find that the Reformation marked a new and significant departure in Christian theology.

From the earliest days of the church, Christians had confessed belief in God the Father and in Jesus Christ his Son. What they thought about the Holy Spirit is less obvious, but at key points, his name can be found coupled with those of the other two. All orthodox Christians agree that the trinitarian pattern is fundamental to the New Testament revelation of God. It was not easy to decide how to reconcile that with the monotheism imposed by that same revelation, but after centuries of trial and error, the church reached the point where it expressed its belief as "one God in three persons." Initially it was not clear whether priority should be given to the unity of the divine nature or to the plurality of the persons, although the general tendency was to regard the latter as three different manifestations of the former. But the inadequacy of that approach soon became clear because it failed to recognize the distinctiveness of the persons and effectively reduced them to different aspects (or "modes") of God's being.

There was also a strong temptation to equate the Father with the divine essence itself, reducing the Son and the Holy Spirit to lesser forms of divinity. Those who thought this believed they were protecting monotheism while at the same time allowing for divine intervention in the world, but their proposed solution failed because it made the other persons creatures in opposition to the Father, who alone was the Creator.

To escape from these problems, the Council of Chalcedon in 451 made it clear that the divine persons take priority over the divine nature. The Father, Son, and Holy Spirit all possess the same being but are not simply different manifestations of it. That understanding allowed the person of the Son to acquire a second (human) nature without surrendering his divinity, which enabled the church to proclaim that on the cross, the divine person of the Son of God had suffered and died in his human nature. Chalcedon decreed that in the incarnate Christ, the divine and human natures remain distinct and mutually incompatible but are united in the person of the Son. This solution did not satisfy everyone, and schisms occurred in the Eastern church, wherein large numbers of people were unable to accept so radical a disjunction between the person and natures of Christ. Many of them wanted to say that even after his incarnation, the Son possessed a single nature in which the divine and the human were combined into one, while others saw the person as resulting from a conjunction of two distinct natures rather than as an agent in his own right. The first of these groups we now call Monophysite (or Miaphysite) and the second Nestorian, after Nestorius (ca. 381–ca. 451), who supposedly advocated it. The Western church rallied behind the Chalcedonian definition and regarded it as the touchstone of orthodoxy, a position that is still maintained by both Catholics and Protestants, along with the main Eastern Orthodox churches.

The question of the Holy Spirit's personal divinity proved to be harder to resolve, not least because the Spirit lacks many of the "personal" attributes that obviously inhere in the Father and the Son. Some people thought that the Spirit was the feminine principle in the Godhead, as if there was such a thing, while others wondered whether he was a kind of second Son, an alternative way to the Father that bypassed the incarnation and the atonement. Neither of these solutions was adopted, but it took nearly a thousand years for a stable consensus about the Holy Spirit's identity to emerge, and even then it split the church. The problem was not his personal identity or divinity, on which all were agreed, but his relationship to the Son. Everyone accepted that he was divine because he proceeded from the Father (John 15:26), but did he proceed from the Son as well? The Western church insisted that he did, whereas the Eastern church rejected the idea because it sounded as if there were two principles in the Godhead instead of only one, as their understanding of monotheism would require.

The sixteenth-century Reformers were fully persuaded that the Western doctrine of the so-called double procession of the Holy Spirit was right.[1] They did not engage in polemics to defend this position, because they regarded it as settled, and, on the rare occasions when they mentioned it at all, they unanimously stated that the Eastern churches, both Chalcedonian and non-Chalcedonian, were wrong to reject the Western position.[2] They did, however, insist that the

---

[1] The double procession is frequently referred to as the *filioque* controversy because of the addition of the word, which means "and the Son," to the Latin version of the Niceno-Constantinopolitan Creed. The addition was first made in the sixth century and finally accepted at Rome about 1014.

[2] See Jeffrey G. Silcock, "Luther on the Holy Spirit and His Use of God's Word," in *The Oxford Handbook of Martin Luther's Theology*, ed. R. Kolb, I. Dingel, and L. Batka (Oxford:

reasons for their attitude lay in their exegesis of Scripture and not in
any devotion to papal authority, which many Easterners believed was
the root cause of the Western doctrine. In the Eastern view, the Holy
Spirit created the church on the day of Pentecost, but if the Spirit
proceeded from the Son as well as from the Father, it could be argued
that his creature the church was subject to the pope, who claimed to
be the vicar of Christ on earth.

The Reformers would have agreed with the East if they had accepted the validity of the Eastern logic, but they did not. In their view
no conceptual link existed between papal authority and the double
procession of the Holy Spirit, and they believed it was perfectly possible to reject the one without changing their minds about the other—
a position that the Easterners regarded as inconsistent. Although the
Reformers did not accept the Eastern understanding of this question,
they did develop their own doctrine of the Holy Spirit, which they
saw as fundamental to their experience of God at work in the world.

The main reason why the Reformers did not follow the Eastern
approach, and in many cases did not even understand it, was that the
medieval West had followed a different pathway in its theological
development. In the Western view, the question of the double procession of the Holy Spirit had been settled by Augustine, a generation
before Chalcedon and centuries before the papal claims over the
church were advanced with any seriousness. Augustine saw the matter as an expression of God's love. The Holy Spirit proceeded from
the Father as the love that he had for his Son, but because the Son is
the Father's equal, the Spirit of love must also proceed from him,
since otherwise the love between the Father and the Son would be
unbalanced. Augustine called the Holy Spirit "the bond of love" between the Father and the Son, and the means by which that love is

---

Oxford University Press, 2014), 306, for the evidence regarding Luther. For Calvin and
other Reformed theologians, see Richard A. Muller, *Post-Reformation Reformed Dogmatics*
(Grand Rapids: Baker, 2003), 4:373-76.

communicated to us. It is because the Holy Spirit dwells in our hearts by faith that we participate in the divine love and are integrated into the fellowship of the Trinity, not by natural right but by the grace of adoption.

But the love of God, in particular the mutual love of the Father and the Son, is not just a feeling of empathy that binds the persons together. At its heart stands the cross, which is the supreme manifestation of the divine love, not just between the Father and the Son but also between God and the people he has chosen to save. There can be no authentic experience of the Holy Spirit without the conviction that he brings of sin, of righteousness, and of judgment.[3] The atoning work of Christ is not just one aspect of God's love but its very essence, and unless that is understood, the distinct work of the Holy Spirit will be impossible to appreciate.

When people in the early church wanted to write about the saving work of Christ, they expounded it in terms of his incarnation. As Gregory of Nazianzus famously put it, "What has not been assumed has not been healed."[4] In other words, if Jesus did not have a human soul, then the human soul has not been redeemed. The point of this approach was not to explain the atonement but to define the true extent of the human nature of Christ, which had to be like ours in every respect if it was to be authentic. It was also deeply anti-Platonic. Platonism, like much Greek philosophy, taught that matter was evil, and so neither an incarnation of God nor the redemption of the human body was conceivable. On these key points Christianity contradicted the mainline philosophical tradition, which is precisely what men like Gregory were trying to demonstrate.

This classical approach to the work of Christ was still visible in the eleventh century, but by then the context had changed. When Anselm of Canterbury (1033–1109) discussed the atonement, he called his

---

[3]Jn 16:8.
[4]Gregory of Nazianzus, *Epistula* 101.

book *Cur Deus Homo* (*Why God Man?*).[5] Anselm began with the incarnation, but what mattered to him was not how it had occurred but what it was for. The Son of God became a man, not in order to overcome the gulf between the Creator and his creation nor to demonstrate that it was possible to live a sinless life on earth without appearing to be abnormal, although of course Jesus did both those things. The real reason for the incarnation was that the Son had come into the world in order to pay the price for human sin. It was because as God he could not suffer and die that he acquired a second (human) nature, which made the atoning sacrifice possible. As Anselm understood it, by his death Christ paid the price for every sin ever committed, and when he ascended he took that sacrifice back up to heaven with him. It is now waiting to be applied to our sins specifically, and this is what happens through the sacramental system.

By baptism, penance, and the Lord's Supper, the saving benefits of Christ's death are conveyed to the believer. The work of the Holy Spirit is to consecrate the sacramental elements so that they become the instruments of Christ's saving work in the lives of those who received them in a "state of grace" (i.e., as penitents). This pattern became so deeply ingrained that when Luther revisited the sacramental question shortly after launching the Reformation, he retained these three but not the others. (Only later, and somewhat reluctantly, did he abandon penance, which could not be squared with the new understanding of a sacrament as the proclamation of the gospel.)

Martin Luther modified Anselm's theory in two important ways. First, he said that Christ died for *sinners*, not for *sins*—in other words, for people and not for things. This allowed him to state that it was possible to be a justified sinner—*simul iustus et peccator* in the famous Latin phrase—a concept that many of his contemporaries could not understand, let alone accept. It also led him to stress the penal nature

---

[5]The title is ambiguous because it can mean either "Why did God become a man?" or "Why God became a man" but for our purposes this makes little difference.

of Christ's substitutionary death on the cross. Jesus died, not so much to take our sins away as to pay the price for them, to remove the guilt that they incurred in the sight of God the Father, and to allow us to stand in the presence of Almighty God, still sinners but clothed in a righteousness that is not our own. Speaking of Romans 7, Luther says,

> St Paul still calls himself a sinner; and yet he can say in chapter 8, that there is no condemnation for those who are in Christ, simply because of the incompleteness of the gifts and of the Spirit. Because the flesh is not yet slain, we are still sinners. But because we believe in Christ and have a beginning of the Spirit, God is so favorable and gracious to us that he will not count the sin against us or judge us because of it. Rather he deals with us according to our faith in Christ, until sin is slain.[6]

Today we are familiar with this way of thinking, and Protestants regard it as the great theological breakthrough that produced the Reformation. But if we examine the matter more closely, we shall see that this was possible only because Luther was deeply aware of something else—the work of the Holy Spirit in the life of the believer, which is the second distinguishing mark of Reformation theology. In his words,

> Faith is a living, daring confidence in God's grace, so sure and certain that the believer would stake his life on it a thousand times. This knowledge of and confidence in God's grace makes us glad and bold and happy in dealing with God and with all creatures. And this is the work which the Holy Spirit performs in faith. Because of it, without compulsion, Christians are ready and glad to do good to everyone, to serve everyone, to suffer

---

[6]Martin Luther, "Preface to the Epistle of St Paul to the Romans," in T. F. Lull, ed., *Martin Luther's Basic Theological Writings*, 2nd ed. (Minneapolis, MN: Fortress Press, 2005), 101; and Martin Luther, *Luther's Works: American Edition*, ed. J. Pelikan et al. (Philadelphia, PA: Fortress Press, 1957–1975), 35:370 (hereafter *LW*).

everything, out of love and praise to God who has shown him this grace. Thus it is impossible to separate works from faith, quite as impossible as to separate heat and light from fire.[7]

In the history of the church, the doctrine of the Holy Spirit was late in developing. This was not because the Spirit was unknown or undervalued but because until it was clear who the Father and the Son were and what they had done for the salvation of the human race, it was impossible to expound the doctrine of the Holy Spirit in a coherent and systematic way. Because the Spirit represents the Father and the Son in our hearts and brings their work to bear on our lives, the church had to define the nature and work of the first two persons of the Trinity before it could develop a similarly sophisticated understanding of the third.

In reflecting on the work of the Son, Luther came to see that the way in which his work is applied to our lives very much depends on the complementary work of the Holy Spirit. Luther was not a systematic theologian, so it is necessary to comb his works carefully and pick out what he had to say about the subject in different contexts. Until recently, the absence of an adequate critical edition of his writings made it very difficult to do this, so we should not be surprised that it was seldom attempted. But more importantly, post-Reformation Lutheran theology turned away from any serious interest in the third person of the Trinity. There were no doubt many reasons for this. Theologians in Reformation Germany were horrified by the outbreak of radical movements, whose leaders claimed that the Spirit was guiding them to overturn the established social order. Later on, the growth of rationalism in the eighteenth century created an intellectual climate that was unsympathetic to any work of the Spirit that could not be logically explained, and this contributed to the widespread dismissal of Wesleyan-style revivalism in Lutheran theological circles.

---

[7]Luther, "Preface to Romans," in Lull, *Luther's Basic Theological Writings*, 101; and *LW*, 35:370-71.

It is the tragedy of the Reformation that this truth was subsequently obscured, even among Protestants. Yet we cannot understand the theology of the Reformers unless we appreciate how central the work of the Holy Spirit was to them. It is one of the oddities of modern theology that this question has seldom been discussed in any direct or comprehensive way. So obscure had it become by the mid-twentieth century that the Danish theologian Regin Prenter (1907–1990) felt obliged to write a book, titled *Spiritus Creator*, to explain Luther's teaching on the subject because (as he put it in his introduction) nobody seemed to know what to say about it. Prenter pointed out that although Luther used traditional Augustinian terminology to express his ideas, his own experience of God led him to modify its content considerably. Whereas Augustine had conceived of the Spirit's work in terms of an infusion of divine love (*caritas*) that elicits a corresponding human affection, which the Spirit then leads upward until the believer achieves a perfect union with God, Luther saw the Holy Spirit as the life-giver who enters the believer in order to put the old man to death and give him the indwelling presence of the risen Christ in his heart. In his own words,

> The Spirit, the divine grace, grants strength and power to the heart; indeed, he creates a new man who takes pleasure in God's commandments and who does everything he should do with joy. The [indwelling] Spirit can never be contained in any letter. It cannot be written like the law, with ink, on stone or in books. Instead, it is inscribed only in the heart as a living writing of the Holy Spirit . . . all who believe in Christ receive God's grace and the Holy Spirit, whereby all sins are forgiven, all laws fulfilled, and they become God's children and are eternally blessed.[8]

---

[8]Martin Luther, "Concerning the Letter and the Spirit," in Lull, *Luther's Basic Theological Writings*, 81; and *LW*, 39:182-83.

Prenter's interpretation of Luther's doctrine of the Holy Spirit has been criticized by other Lutherans because Prenter preferred a systematic approach that neglected the historical development of Luther's thought, and unfortunately his thesis has not made much of an impression on Luther studies. But when it has been taken seriously, Prenter's conclusions have been confirmed and his emphasis has been restated. Recent attempts by the Finnish school of Lutheran theology to find a concept of divinization (*theōsis*) in the Reformers have also revived an awareness that Luther and his followers were deeply concerned with the third person of the Trinity.

SACRAMENTAL GRACE?

In the medieval church, when Anselm's theory of atonement was applied to the sacraments, they came to be seen as "means" or channels of God's grace, bringing the saving power of Christ's sacrifice into the lives of those who received them, whether they understood what was happening to them or not. By grace, the water of baptism cleansed the recipient from original sin, and by grace the bread and wine of the Supper became the body and blood of the Savior. As the New Testament makes clear, it is by grace that we are saved through faith, but this meant something different to the early Christians, who, unlike their medieval descendants, did not think of grace as a thing. What they heard Paul saying was: "By God's free will you have been saved through faith." In other words, grace was an action of the mind and will of God, not a kind of medicine that is given to believers in order to cleanse and heal them of their sins. Luther understood Paul's teaching and was quite clear about it. To him, the sacraments were signs and seals of God's *gift* of salvation, not of his grace:

> Between grace and gift there is this difference. Grace actually means God's favor, or the good will which in himself he bears toward us, by which he is disposed to give us Christ and to pour

into us the Holy Spirit with his gifts . . . The gifts and the Spirit increase in us every day, but they are not yet perfect since there remain in us the evil desires and sins that war against the Spirit . . . Nevertheless grace does so much that we are accounted completely righteous before God. For his grace is not divided or parceled out, as are the gifts, but takes us completely into favor for the sake of Christ our Intercessor and Mediator. And because of this, the gifts are begun in us.[9]

In the later Middle Ages, however, grace had come to be regarded as a gift bestowed by God through the mediation of the church, a kind of spiritual medicine that worked to transform its recipients into the kind of people that God wanted them to be in Christ. Grace could be not only objectified but quantified—some people received more grace than others, and some things conveyed more of it than others did. It was even possible for a priest to consecrate bread and wine and then store them for future use or for popular devotional purposes because they had supposedly been transformed by the grace of God.

By laying down the conditions for admission to these sacraments, the church effectively asserted control over the flow of grace from heaven to the believer. This did not matter much as far as baptism was concerned, since that was freely administered to everyone and most of the recipients were infants. For them, baptism was understood as a kind of inoculation against sin that worked even though the recipient was unaware of it. It is true that faith was demanded of the parents and sponsors of the infants being baptized, but that was a secondary consideration and did not affect the validity or the efficacy of the sacrament itself. Moreover, once it had been properly administered in the name of the Trinity, baptism could not be revoked or

---

[9]Luther, "Preface to Romans," in Lull, *Luther's Basic Theological Writings*, 100-101; and *LW*, 35:369-70.

annulled, even if it had been performed by heretics, so nobody could be put out of the church by being "de-baptized."

But the church could impose conditions on the reception of the Lord's Supper, and it did not hesitate to do so when the sins of the prospective communicant appeared to warrant it. Penance was imposed for this purpose, and its nature was determined by what the church thought was appropriate to the gravity of the situation. In extreme cases, a believer could be cut off from grace altogether, or excommunicated, if he or she disobeyed the commands of the church. In theory this was a biblical command, but in practice it was applied rather arbitrarily.[10] A king who disobeyed the pope, for example, might be excommunicated, as were people who failed to pay their tithes. A distinction was even made between the "lesser" excommunication for relatively unimportant infractions and a "greater" one for the more serious cases. The former barred a person from receiving the sacrament; the latter obliged the entire church to shun the unfortunate victim and cut him off from society. There was considerable resistance to the greater excommunication, as we might imagine, but it was a threat hanging over church members and could always be invoked if deemed necessary.

What the sacraments promised the faithful penitent was access to the saving power of God. Sins were canceled not merely in theory but in practice, as divine grace was applied on a regular basis to eliminating the transgressions of the moment. By experiencing the forgiveness of God in this way, a believer could rest assured that he would not be held accountable for the sins that he had confessed and done penance for. Growth in grace was a real possibility as more and more of it flowed into the soul of the penitent. In a few cases, so much grace would be given that the recipients would leave no outstanding debts at death and go straight to heaven as recognized saints. Once there,

---

[10]See 2 Jn 1:10-11.

they would be able to share the grace they had received in order to help others who might petition them for assistance. Some of these saints were even thought to have special areas of interest, and prayers offered to them regarding their specialty would be particularly efficacious. God himself might remain distant and unapproachable in his glorious light, but thanks to these chosen intermediaries, his gift of grace could be brought near and bestowed on those who were most in need of it.

The grace of God was the remedy not only for the effects of sin but for the inherently defective nature of humanity after the fall. As the saying (attributed to Thomas Aquinas) went: "Grace builds on nature and perfects it." This is what was meant by the term *supernatural*, which came into use in the later Middle Ages. Grace was not a product of nature and could not be earned or created, but as a divine gift it was compatible with the created order and could be used to lift it above itself and bring it to perfection. God was the author of both nature and grace, and what was lacking in the one he made up by applying the other. In the Christian life, nature cooperated with grace to achieve sanctification, and that was the sinner's ultimate justification.

The idea that grace could somehow cooperate with nature presupposed that the latter could attract the right amount of grace needed to complement it. This was a difficult subject because grace was a gift that could not be assumed by the eventual recipient as a necessary or just reward for some achievement on his part. That would be what the medieval theologians called condign merit, or a fitting reward for a service rendered. In the sight of God, Jesus Christ is the only person who can claim condign merit because he has paid the price for our sins, which has been accepted and validated by God the Father. Those who believe in the Son must accept what they have been given because it is the prerogative of God to grant or withhold grace as he chooses.

At the same time, God loves his people and has promised to give us more than we could ever ask or think. The grace we receive from him will therefore always be enough—indeed, more than enough—for our needs. Although no limitations can be placed on God's sovereignty, and we know from experience and from the teaching of Scripture that not even the worst sinners are beyond his power of redemption, God loves and honors those who obey his commands and do what they can to please him. To them, he dispenses his grace according to their congruous merit, or what he deems to be appropriate in their case. He is not morally obliged to do this, as he would be if the merit was condign (and therefore earned), which is why congruous merit is always beyond anything we might deserve.

Those who believed in this pattern of grace and who lived according to it did not think they were saving themselves by their works, and to them Protestant accusations along those lines seemed mistaken. This is one reason why Catholic opposition to the Reformation was as strong and successful as it was. Even harder for Catholic apologists to understand was that the Reformers were not questioning the sincerity of those who were trying to do their best, nor were they questioning the fact that God lavishes his grace on those whom he loves. What bothered them was the idea that human acts, however well-intentioned, could never claim any sort of merit. Having done all, said the Reformers, we are still unprofitable servants. Indeed, the closer we come to God, the more aware we are of our own unworthiness to stand before him. The saving grace of God is given to sinners *as sinners*. To grow in grace is to grow in the awareness of just how sinful and needy we really are; it is not to say goodbye to sinfulness and rise to a higher level of sanctification. More important still, the grace of God is given to us in and by the indwelling presence of the Holy Spirit in our hearts. This was very clearly stated by Thomas Cranmer in his Forty-Two Articles of Religion (1553):

The grace of Christ, of the Holy Ghost by him given, doth take away the stony heart and giveth an heart of flesh. And although those that have no will to good things, he maketh them to will, and those that would evil things, he maketh them not to will the same; yet nevertheless he enforceth not the will.[11]

The grace of God is seen in a transformed heart and mind, brought about by the working of the Holy Spirit and not by the application of a consecrated substance. Once that principle was grasped, the sacramental theology that dominated the later Middle Ages was bound to be modified, as we can see when we look at the two gospel sacraments specifically.

THE LORD'S SUPPER

In the medieval church, discussion of the atoning work of Christ had been closely tied to the sacrament of the Lord's Supper, in which the celebrant was said to have transubstantiated bread and wine into Christ's body and blood. In the course of the liturgy the Holy Spirit was thought to descend on the elements and to change their inner substance into the saving body and blood of Christ, so that whoever received them also received the gift of salvation that his atoning death brought. The solemnity of the Supper had been a recurring theme in patristic literature, and the belief that the Holy Spirit descended on the consecrated elements in what is technically known as the *epiclesis* was of ancient origin. But there was little real discussion of the sacrament for many centuries, and different views of it coexisted. This is apparent from the "controversy" between Ratramnus of Corbie (d. 868) and his monastic brother Paschasius Radbertus (d. 860). Paschasius claimed that the historic, incarnate body and blood of Christ were really present in the Lord's Supper, whereas Ratramnus believed

---

[11]Article 10. See G. L. Bray, ed., *Documents of the English Reformation*, 2nd ed. (Cambridge: James Clarke, 2004), 291. The article was dropped in the 1563 revision.

that the bread and wine represented them in a purely spiritual way.[12] There is no record of any dispute between them, and it seems that both opinions coexisted for several centuries without controversy. The first sign of trouble over this came in the mid-eleventh century, when Berengar of Tours (d. 1088) supported Ratramnus's position and developed it in a way that insisted that Christ was present in the sacrament in a spiritual but not in a physical sense. For this, he was condemned by Pope Leo IX in 1050 and forced to sign a series of recantations at periodic intervals for the rest of his life.[13]

It was only in the twelfth and thirteenth centuries that a detailed doctrine of the consecrated elements was worked out. It was based on the Aristotelian distinction between substance and accidents, which supposedly applied to all material things. Bread, for example, was a substance, but it appeared in many different shapes and sizes, all of which are basically accidental. What happened in the consecration is that these accidents—the taste, shape, color, and so on—remained the same, but the inner substance was transformed from being bread to being the body of Christ, and by a similar process, the wine became his blood. To those who elaborated this doctrine, it seemed to solve the problem of how Christ could be "really present" in the Supper (in his invisible substance) without falling into the absurdity of suggesting that every consecrated piece of bread was his physical body. The accidents appeared in time and space, but the substance reflected the eternal dimension that lay behind them. It was on this basis that transubstantiation was first mentioned at the Fourth Lateran Council in 1215, although what it really meant was still undefined.[14]

---

[12]Ratramnus of Corbie, *Christ's Body and Blood*, 10; and Paschasius Radbertus, *The Lord's Body and Blood*, 1. Both are found in G. E. McCracken, *Early Medieval Theology*, Library of Christian Classics, 9 (Philadelphia, PA: Westminster Press, 1957), 94-96, 120.

[13]See G. Macy, "The Medieval Inheritance," in *A Companion to the Eucharist in the Reformation* (Leiden: Brill, 2014), 23-25.

[14]N. P. Tanner, ed., *Decrees of the Ecumenical Councils* (Washington, DC: Georgetown University Press; London: Sheed and Ward, 1990), 1:30.

Thomas Aquinas would work out the details, and by the end of the thirteenth century the doctrine of transubstantiation was firmly established in the church, although formal recognition of that had to wait until 1551.[15] In the meantime, Aquinas's definition was contested by a number of theologians, not least by John Wyclif, who seems to have believed in what some would now call consubstantiation. This is the theory that Christ was spiritually present alongside the elements of the Lord's Supper but that the bread and wine remained what they always were. Wyclif's view was close to what would later become Lutheran orthodoxy, which explains why the latter is often referred to as consubstantiation, even though Lutherans themselves seldom (if ever) use that term and it is now falling into disuse.[16]

Reception of the consecrated elements was always meant to take place in the context of faith, but the doctrine of transubstantiation made them independent of that. Any properly ordained person, using the correct formula of words, could produce the "miracle of the altar" regardless of his own spiritual state. The Holy Spirit was believed to operate externally on things, by means of a laying on of hands or some other act of consecration that had the same effect. Once transubstantiation had occurred, the elements of bread and wine had a spiritual power that applied the benefits of the atoning work of Christ to believers whenever and wherever they received them. If an unbeliever ate and drank the consecrated elements, he condemned himself and would be consigned to hell on the day of judgment. Nor could the celebrating priest leave the consecrated bread unattended, because in

---

[15]Thomas Aquinas, *Summa theologiae* 3.75.4, available online at www.newadvent.org /summa. The official proclamation of transubstantiation as Catholic doctrine occurred at the thirteenth session of the Council of Trent, October 11, 1551. See Tanner, *Decrees*, 2:95.

[16]Wyclif's treatise *De eucharistia* was written about 1380 but has never been translated into English. It was edited by Johann Loserth and published for the Wyclif Society (London: Trübner, 1892). See Ian C. Levy, *John Wyclif: Scriptural Logic, Real Presence and the Parameters of Orthodoxy* (Milwaukee, WI: Marquette University Press, 2003). Wyclif's doctrine was condemned at the fifteenth session of the Council of Constance (July 6, 1415). See Tanner, *Decrees*, 1:22.

its transubstantiated state it could be stolen and used for magical purposes quite alien to the gospel. The "real presence" of Christ, as it came to be called, was such that a whole array of devotions was constructed to surround the consecrated elements, which were adored quite independently of the liturgical celebration of the Supper. Furthermore, it was in this context that the withdrawal of the cup from the laity was justified; Christ's body contained blood, which was therefore present in the consecrated bread, making the separate consumption of the wine unnecessary.

This was the situation that confronted Martin Luther. It was relatively easy for him to reject Communion in one kind, as the withdrawal of the cup was known, and transubstantiation was such an improbable theory that he could reject that too without much difficulty. He was also able to distance himself from the idea that the consecration of the eucharistic elements was a meritorious spiritual work on the part of the priest, since that was no more than a pious opinion and, even if it were true, benefited only the clergy. But denying the real presence of Christ in the Lord's Supper was a more difficult matter, not least because it touched directly on popular belief in the applicability of his atonement for sin to the penitent believer. Those who received the consecrated elements in faith needed to be assured that their sins had been forgiven and that they had been put right with God, and most people were persuaded by the conviction that divine grace was present in the bread and wine.

Luther never rejected the real presence of Christ in the sacrament, but he reinterpreted it in light of his overall understanding of what the sacrament was for. To his mind, transubstantiation was wrong because it made the consecration an independent act, divorced from any context, which destroyed its sacramental character. God had not instituted the Lord's Supper for its own sake but as a comfort and aid to believers, who could benefit from it only if they approached it in faith. That way they would discern the presence of the Lord in the sacrament and be strengthened in their own walk with him.[17] To bolster this, Luther began to insist that the celebration of the Lord's Supper must take place within the context of the preaching of God's Word. It would be in response to the Word that the communicant would be moved to receive the consecrated elements in faith, because in the final analysis, it was the Word, not the actions of the celebrant, that guaranteed the presence of Christ in the sacrament.[18]

Luther reached this understanding of the Lord's Supper through his own reflection on the relationship between the signs of bread and wine and the things they signified—the body and blood of Christ, a relationship that was guaranteed by the promises of God's Word and sealed by the faith of those who received it. But it was not long before he was faced with opposition, not only from traditional Catholics but from others who claimed to be Reformers just as much as he was. Three in particular stood out—Andreas Karlstadt (1486–1541), Huldrych Zwingli, and Johannes Oecolampadius (1482–1531)— whom Luther lumped together as a kind of three-headed monster. With slightly different emphases, all three rejected the real presence of Christ in favor of something much closer to the teaching of Berengar of Tours. Karlstadt insisted that if Christ were present in the Supper, the uniqueness of his sacrifice on Calvary would be compromised. Similarly, Zwingli believed that the Supper was a public affirmation of a divine grace that had already been given once for all on the cross, and Oecolampadius translated Christ's words of institution ("This is my body") symbolically as "This is a sign of my body."[19]

To Luther's mind, their way of thinking bordered on the heretical because it denied (or appeared to deny) the union of the divine and the human in the incarnate Christ. He believed that when Jesus

---

[17]Martin Luther, "The Babylonian Captivity of the Church," in *LW*, 35:11.

[18]Martin Luther, "Concerning the Order of Public Worship," in *LW*, 53:13.

[19]See B. C. Brewer, *Martin Luther and the Seven Sacraments: A Contemporary Protestant Reappraisal* (Grand Rapids: Baker Academic, 2017), 209-14.

ascended into heaven he took his body with him, integrating it somehow into the realm of the divine. That transformed body could now appear wherever Christ was—in the heart of the believer just as much as in the consecrated elements of the Lord's Supper.[20] As he saw it, salvation is both physical and spiritual, so to separate the two is to deny the fullness of the grace of God in the gospel. Counterarguments that appealed to logic, such as saying that a body is finite by nature and therefore incapable of being in more than one place at once, were lost on Luther. To him the real presence of Christ in the Lord's Supper was a divine mystery that could be received only by faith, and no amount of opposition could ever sway him from that judgment.

Luther could not come to terms with his Reformed opponents, because he believed that they had a spirit that was different from his, and in a sense he was right. For him, the Lord's Supper was the means by which God made the atoning sacrifice of Christ real in the life of the believer. For his opponents, the death of Christ was a historical fact, a once-for-all revelation of divine grace that the Supper now helps us to remember and appropriate to ourselves. It is not a means of grace in its own right but rather a sign that points us to the grace that had already been given. Nowadays God does not act by a representation of the Son's sacrifice, as medieval theology had insisted, but by the indwelling presence of his Holy Spirit. It is in and by the Spirit that believers partake of Christ in the Supper, with the result that those who do not have that Spirit dwelling in them do not consume the body or blood of Christ in any form whatsoever.

Not surprisingly, given their roots in Zwinglian Zurich, the Anabaptists tended to follow Zwingli's logic on this point, although it can be argued that they placed a greater emphasis on the Supper as a fellowship meal, designed to draw believers closer together. That may

---

[20]This is known as belief in the "ubiquity" of Christ's body.

have been so, but it was a secondary emphasis, as can be seen from the wording of the Schleitheim Confession of 1527: "All those who wish to break one bread in remembrance of the broken body of Christ, and all who wish to drink of one drink as a remembrance of the shed blood of Christ, shall be united beforehand by baptism in one body of Christ."[21]

The Anabaptists were saying that participation in the Lord's Supper should be restricted to true believers, a position that was (theoretically at least) no different from that of the Catholic Church. The difference, if any, was one of discipline, not of principle. Catholics (and other Protestants) might well take people at their word, without any serious investigation of their faith, whereas the early Anabaptists were certain to examine partakers of the Supper much more conscientiously. In practice they excluded anyone who did not share their view that baptism should be administered only to professing believers and who had not been so baptized (or rebaptized) themselves.

Somewhere in the middle of all this was the teaching of John Calvin. He was basically closer to Zwingli and to Luther's other opponents than he was to Luther, but he was sufficiently independent of them to be able to draw on many different strands of eucharistic thinking. Unlike Luther, he rejected any notion of a real presence of Christ in the elements and stressed the Holy Spirit's work in the heart of the believer as the key to understanding the sacrament's efficacy. At the same time, he resisted the idea that the Supper was no more than a symbolic memorial of a historical event. Like Luther, he stressed the power of the Word of God and the commandment of Christ that we should break bread in remembrance of him. The reason for this, said Calvin, echoing Luther once more, was not that the bread contained

---

[21]See "The Schleitheim Confession," in J. Pelikan and V. Hotchkiss, eds., *Creeds and Confessions of Faith in the Christian Tradition* (New Haven, CT: Yale University Press, 2003), 2:694-703; and W. L. Lumpkin and B. J. Leonard, eds., *Baptist Confessions of Faith*, 2nd ed. (Valley Forge, PA: Judson Press, 2011), 26.

any spiritual power of its own but that the Word of God speaks to the whole man, body and soul. The message is spiritual, but it must be appropriated by the flesh as well because our faith touches every aspect of our lives. By eating the consecrated bread and drinking the consecrated wine, believers commit themselves to a total submission to Christ, whose Spirit works in us at every level of our being. In the final analysis, like Luther, Calvin confessed that he could not define how this happened; he could only experience it. The work of the Holy Spirit is ultimately a mystery that surpasses human understanding and can truly be known only by surrendering to his superior wisdom and embracing the reality of his ongoing work in our lives.

As a result of this, the Protestant world adopted a number of different eucharistic beliefs, many of which overlapped but did not coincide sufficiently for intercommunion among the various denominations to be a matter of course. Today it would be fair to say that most Protestants have come to something approaching a common mind, but that mind is closer to Zwingli's than to either Luther's or Calvin's. Our scientifically sensitive approach recoils from the notion that material things can be vehicles for spiritual realities, and we are likely to be more impressed by the active faith of the communicants than by the credentials claimed by the minister or the words of the rites of consecration.

That this emphasis was known and indeed taught by the Reformers themselves can be seen from the language of the Anglican Book of Common Prayer. In the rite of Holy Communion, the intending communicant is invited to "draw near *with faith*" and receive the sacrament to his comfort. When consuming the bread, he is reminded to "take and eat this in remembrance that Christ died for thee, and feed on him in thy heart *by faith* with thanksgiving." Finally, one of the post-Communion prayers reminds us that the bread and wine that we have just received are "the spiritual food of the most precious body and blood of thy Son our Saviour Jesus Christ," and we are assured thereby that "we are very members incorporate in the mystical

body of thy Son, which is the blessed company of all *faithful* people."
On this, Lutherans, Calvinists, Anabaptists, and Anglicans can all
agree. Not only the sacrament but the church itself is a spiritual fellowship of those who live by faith, not just a gathering of those who
have been baptized and enrolled as members of an earthly institution
that purports to follow Christ and his teachings whether they themselves are active participants in it or not.

BAPTISM

What was true of the Lord's Supper was also true of baptism, which at
least from the second century (if not before) was believed to wash away
original sin. Because sin was regarded as a stain on the soul, and the
baptismal water was consecrated, spiritual cleansing was the inevitable
result of water baptism. What the recipient thought about it was irrelevant, and since almost everyone was baptized in infancy, that question was impossible to ask. Baptismal regeneration—the belief that by
being baptized a person was born again—was simply taken for granted.
It is true that men like Augustine also emphasized the importance of
faith for the efficacy of baptism, but how this was supposed to apply to
infants was never properly clarified, as can be seen from the following:

> The cleansing [of baptism] . . . would on no account be attrib-
> uted to the fleeting and perishable element [of water], were it
> not for that which is added, "by the word" [Eph 5:26]. This
> word of faith possesses such power in the Church of God, that
> through the one who believes, presents, blesses and baptizes,
> [it] cleanses even a tiny infant, although itself unable as yet with
> the heart to believe unto righteousness, and to make confession
> with the mouth unto salvation. All this is done through the
> word, whereof the Lord said: "Now you are clean through
> the word that I have spoken to you." [Jn 15:3].[22]

---

[22]Augustine, *Tractates on the Gospel of John* 80.3.

Augustine lived in a world where it was assumed that children would follow their parents, and he placed faith and the power of the divine Word in the context of the church, wherein an infant's parents and others would teach it what to believe. But he also assured his hearers that the efficacy of the sacrament did not depend on the worthiness of the minister, so that heretical baptism, while hardly desirable, was not invalid. That inevitably placed great weight on the rite itself, which would do its work if it were properly administered. In the Middle Ages, belief that baptism as a means of grace cleanses its recipients from original sin was the standard view, and blanket coverage of the entire population was taken for granted.

The Reformers had great difficulty with this understanding of the sacrament because they could not dissociate it from the recipients' need for faith. As early as 1519, Martin Luther wrote a treatise on baptism in which he reaffirmed the traditional doctrine that it was a cleansing from sin, although he was careful to add that it was only the beginning of a lifelong struggle for spiritual purity that would not be finally accomplished until death.[23] Baptism was made effective not by any innate power that it possessed but by the faith that accompanied it. Without that, the rite alone could accomplish nothing. Given the universal practice of infant baptism in his time, Luther had to explain where this essential ingredient of faith came from. Initially, he seems to have adopted a view not unlike that of Augustine, relying on parents and other adults to supply what the child could not provide for itself.[24] Unfortunately, that did not square with his insistence elsewhere that it was impossible for one person to stand proxy for another when it came to questions of faith—each individual had to make his own profession for it to be valid.[25] That left the defenders of infant baptism in an untenable position and, much to Luther's

[23]"The Holy and Blessed Sacrament of Baptism," in *LW*, 35:30-43.
[24]See Brewer, *Martin Luther*, 172-79.
[25]Luther, "Babylonian Captivity," in *LW*, 36:48.

discomfort, provided ammunition for those like the Anabaptists who subsequently rejected it.[26]

To counter this unintended consequence of his teaching, Luther was forced to develop a doctrine of infant faith, according to which the child possessed what was needed for it to receive baptism, although naturally that was unverifiable.[27] He did his best to justify this assertion by referring to Scripture passages that speak of the faith of a little child, but his arguments smack of special pleading and are not very convincing, even to those who accept the validity of infant baptism. Ultimately however, whether a child had faith did not determine Luther's position, because he did not believe that human faith, even if it was a gift of God, validated the divine act of baptism. Still less did he think that the consecration of water or the words of the celebrating priest could manufacture a regenerated spirit. For him, the focus of baptism and the foundation of its efficacy did not lie in the spiritual state of the recipient, or in the power of consecrated water, but in the promise of the God who instituted it:

> We . . . know that baptism is a God-given thing, instituted and commanded by God himself . . . We find baptism in itself to be a holy, blessed, glorious and heavenly thing, to be held in honor with fear and trembling, just as it is reasonable and right to hold any other ordinance and command of God. It is not the fault of baptism that many people abuse it. It would be as wrong to call the gospel a vain babbling because there are many who abuse it . . . the Word of God is greater and more important than faith, since faith builds and is founded on the Word of God, rather than God's Word on faith.[28]

---

[26]Brewer, *Martin Luther*, 179-82.

[27]Martin Luther, "Concerning Rebaptism," in Lull, *Luther's Basic Theological Writings*, 246-49; and *LW*, 40:241-46.

[28]Luther, "Concerning Rebaptism," in Lull, *Luther's Basic Theological Writings*, 257; and *LW*, 40:259-60.

In other words, the validity of baptism lay in the commandment of God, whether the sacrament was rightly received or not. In saying this, Luther was trying to answer the objections of those who rejected the baptism of infants. For these Anabaptists, baptism was not a divine gift to be received in faith but rather the expression of a faith already professed, making the rite itself spiritually redundant. Some of them took comfort in Luther's words about the need for a profession of faith before receiving the sacrament, but in fact they were closer to Huldrych Zwingli in Zurich, which is one of the more important places where Anabaptism began. Zwingli did not accept that any material substance could contain or transmit a spiritual reality, and so the idea that water, however consecrated, could produce a spiritual effect was alien to him. Of course, if that is the case, the question arises as to what baptism signifies, and to Zwingli it was mainly a sign that the recipient desired to follow Christ. It is then hard to see what difference the time and manner of its administration would make, although Zwingli himself adhered to the practice of infant baptism and opposed Anabaptists like Balthasar Hubmaier (1480–1528) and Conrad Grebel (1498–1526), who took his views to what they believed were their logical conclusion.

The problem for the Anabaptists was not so much that the sacrament was being given to the uncomprehending children of ignorant parents; rather, since it made no difference to the spiritual state of the recipient, its very existence was hard to explain. The Anabaptists knew that Christ had commanded baptism, but they did not know why it was necessary, since what it expressed had already taken place in the life of the believer. In faithfulness to this viewpoint, they considered their own baptism as infants to be invalid and insisted on being baptized again, which is what the word *Anabaptist* means. To them it was not rebaptism but true baptism for the first time, but the unfortunate effect of this conviction was that all other Christians, including those who shared their other beliefs, were disqualified from being members of the true church because they were not properly baptized.

The second generation of Anabaptists was in a somewhat different position to the first since it had not been baptized in infancy and was therefore not repudiating anything. Other churches could accept believer's baptism as long as the recipient had not been baptized as an infant, so from their point of view the practice was less divisive theologically, but this willingness to accept adult baptism was not (and in fairness could not have been) reciprocated on the other side with respect to infant baptism. Anyone joining an Anabaptist church had to be baptized according to its criteria—an insistence that continues to divide them from other Protestants to this day. By rejecting infant baptism, the Anabaptists created a new kind of church, one that was "gathered" out of the world and not institutionalized in the way that other churches tended to be. Of course, they brought their children up in their faith, but the children had to decide for themselves when they reached a certain age, and they were not regarded as Christians until they made their own profession of faith. Most of them did, and Anabaptist groups quickly propagated themselves more from within their own ranks than from converting others to their point of view.

It is one of the great ironies of church history that a movement that attempted to break with the notion of an inherited Christianity ended up creating the closest thing the Christian world has to Judaism. One of the pioneers of this movement was Jacob Hutter (1500–1536), whose communities still survive today, but the most prominent exponent of this approach, and in many respects the refounder of Anabaptism, who put it on a solid foundation and ensured its long-term survival, was Menno Simons (1496–1561), a converted Roman Catholic priest. Mennonites, Hutterites, and later the Amish, a breakaway group led by Jakob Ammann (1644–ca. 1730), became semi-nations of their own, and the more conservative among them remain that way even now. Their children still have to choose to be baptized, and although some depart from their communities when they reach adulthood, the retention rate among Anabaptists is surprisingly high and their communities continue to survive, mainly by self-propagation.

Traditional Anabaptists are only tangentially related to the wider Baptist movement with which we are familiar nowadays. That movement did not emerge until the early seventeenth century, when some English dissenters who had fled to Holland met some local Mennonite Anabaptists and were persuaded to reject infant baptism. But these English Baptists did not become Mennonites. For the most part they remained anchored in their erstwhile Reformed faith, modifying it only in terms of their baptismal doctrine and practice. Apart from that, it is fair to say that most Baptists today are more like other Reformed Christians and that they have no more in common with the original Anabaptists than other Protestants do.[29] Yet it is also true that the growing secularization of modern society has persuaded many people who previously accepted infant baptism that the practice is no longer effective or particularly meaningful. Although relatively few of them would actively seek a second (adult) baptism, many prefer not to baptize their children in infancy but rather to wait until they are old enough to decide for themselves. In that respect, the Anabaptist legacy is more widely accepted and more favorably viewed today than their relatively low official numbers might suggest.

In between these extremes was the view put forward by John Calvin and later regarded outside Lutheran circles as the standard Reformed position. According to Calvin and his followers, baptism was not a sacrament of regeneration (as the Catholics taught) but a proclamation of the gospel that every human being, of whatever age, needed to receive in order to be saved. But the moment at which the gospel promise becomes a reality in the life of an individual is not decided either by the

---

[29]For an explanation of this, see Lumpkin and Leonard, *Baptist Confessions*, 75-77.

minister of the sacrament or by the recipient. It is a sovereign work of the Holy Spirit, who convicts those whom God has chosen for salvation of the truth of Christ's atoning work, which baptism represents. The sacrament is an extension of the preaching of the Word of God, which is given to many but received only by those whom the Spirit enlightens by the gift of faith. How and when that happens is decided by God and cannot be manipulated by human acts or desires:

> In baptism, the Lord promises forgiveness of sins: receive it and be secure. I have no intention, however, to detract from the power of baptism. I would only add to the sign the substance and reality, inasmuch as God works by external means. But from this sacrament, as from all others, we gain nothing, unless in so far as we receive in faith. If faith is wanting, it will be an evidence of our ingratitude, by which we are proved guilty before God, for not believing the promise there given. In so far as it is a sign of our confession, we ought thereby to testify that we confide in the mercy of God, and are pure, through the forgiveness of sins which Christ Jesus has procured for us; that we have entered into the Church of God, that with one consent of faith and love we may live in concord with all believers.[30]

This reconstruction of the sacrament separated the external sign from the inward and spiritual grace that it represented, allowing that the sign would probably be given to more people than the grace. It was not necessarily so, of course, since a person could profess faith in Christ without having received the sacrament or even, in special circumstances, without having sat under the preaching of the Word either.[31] The sovereignty of God cannot be restricted by human

---

[30]John Calvin, *Institutes of the Christian Religion*, ed. J. T. McNeill, trans. F. L. Battles (Philadelphia, PA: Westminster Press, 1960), 4.15.15.

[31]Calvin admitted this, especially with respect to infants who died without being baptized. See Calvin *Institutes* 4.15.22.

constructions, however well-intended they may be. What Calvin and others in the Reformed tradition were describing when laying down a pattern for the administration of baptism was the normal pattern of events that the ministers of the Word could expect to see in their churches rather than something that had to occur because it was prefigured in an external act or else could not happen because that act had not taken place. Spiritual regeneration was possible even for someone who had not been baptized because, in Calvin's words, "a sort of seal is added to the sacrament, not to confer efficacy upon God's promise, as if it were invalid of itself, but only to confirm it to us."[32] As Jesus said to Nicodemus, "The wind blows where it wishes . . . but you do not know where it comes from or where it goes. So it is with everyone who is born of the Spirit."[33]

The differences of opinion among Protestants were so great that they divided the Reformation movement in ways that had previously been unknown in the church. At the heart of the matter was the relationship between the sacramental rites and the grace of God that they were supposed to represent. At one extreme were the Lutherans, who wanted to insist on the objective character of the rites, which conveyed divine grace to those who received them whether they wanted it or not. At the other extreme were the Anabaptists and the Zwinglians, who rejected any notion of sacramental grace and saw the rites as symbolizing a faith that was already present in the recipients. Somewhere in the middle were the Reformed followers of Calvin, who wanted to preserve the idea that the Holy Spirit operates through the ordinance of baptism without suggesting that his regenerating work can be guaranteed by the mere performance of a sacramental rite. The Anglican Book of Common Prayer, for example, although it claims the promise of spiritual rebirth for those who have been baptized, including small children, nevertheless prays that the

---

[32]Calvin, *Institutes* 4.15.22.
[33]Jn 3:8.

newly baptized person "may crucify the old man, and utterly abolish the whole body of sin: and that, as he is made partaker of the death of thy Son, he may also be partaker of his resurrection; so that finally, with the residue of thy holy Church, he may be an inheritor of thine everlasting kingdom." In other words, baptism is a good start, but it is not a guarantee that the new life it proclaims will be realized in those who receive it.

No one view has ever been able to impose itself on the Protestant world generally, although, as in the case of the Lord's Supper, it is probably fair to say that the Zwinglian or Anabaptist model is nearer to the mindset of most modern Protestants than either the Lutheran or the Calvinist position is, if only because most people today put more weight on personal spiritual experience than on "objective" theological presuppositions. Few Protestants nowadays are likely to be impressed by claims made about the rite of baptism, whatever those claims might be and however sincerely thy may be held. What matters to most of them is the evidence of the transformed life that baptism represents, and if that evidence is lacking, then no theory of the efficacy of a baptismal rite is likely to carry much conviction.

Perhaps the fairest judgment on the different ways in which Protestants absorbed the concept of sacramental grace is to say that the Reformers were confronted with a challenge that was too great for them to appreciate and confront as they should have done. They had inherited centuries of teaching on the subject that they could not simply dismiss, even though they recognized that it had often gone wrong. They wanted to develop a theology based on Scripture alone, but the problem was that although the New Testament authorizes both baptism and the Lord's Supper, it has no overarching concept of sacrament to tie them together, nor does it contain a doctrine of grace in the sense that this was understood in the later Middle Ages. In their different ways, each of the major Reformers tried to make their devotional practices conform to their theological principles, but they

were unable to escape from the sacramental framework they had inherited. Eventually the implications of their doctrine of the Holy
Spirit's work would filter down to the grassroots level, but by then
confessional lines had been drawn and theologians found themselves
committed to upholding traditions that it might have been better to
abandon, or at least to recast in significant ways. The Pietists and
evangelicals of the eighteenth century saw themselves in this light,
and their promotion of a nondenominational Protestantism can be
understood as an attempt to emphasize the work of the Holy Spirit
contra nonbiblical concepts of sacramental grace. It would be too
much to claim that they have succeeded in relativizing the sacraments completely, but it is fair to say that different understandings of
them no longer impede fellowship in the gospel in the way that they
did in the sixteenth century.

JUSTIFICATION BY FAITH

What Martin Luther realized, and what became the heart of his Reformation, was that we can stand before God, not because we have
somehow been improved and made "righteous" by divine grace but
because God has reached out to us in his Son, paid the price for our
sins (and for our sinfulness), and counted Christ's righteousness as
ours because of our faith in him. Saving faith is a divine gift, not a
human work. Nobody can believe in Christ except through God's
revelation.[34] This revelation is not simply knowledge, but conviction.
The difference can be seen in the New Testament. Plenty of people
heard about what Christ had done but did not accept the message,
even if they found it persuasive—the chief example being King
Agrippa II, who was "almost persuaded" to become a Christian.[35]
True conversion is demonstrated by the experience of the apostle
Paul, the man who preached to Agrippa. Paul did not want to become

---

[34]Mt 16:17.
[35]Acts 26:28-29.

a believer and was certainly not persuaded by any drawn-out, rational argument. On the contrary, he was overwhelmed by the presence of Christ, who drew him into his fellowship, even though Paul had little or no idea what was happening to him at the time. This is the action of God without any human input, and it is paradigmatic of Christian experience.

If we are saved by God's grace through faith, and if faith is a gift from him, how is it given? It is a work of the Holy Spirit, who bestows God's gifts as he chooses. As Luther put it in his preface to the epistle to the Romans,

> Faith is not the human notion and dream that some people call faith . . . Faith is a divine work in us which changes us and makes us to be born anew of God. It kills the old Adam and makes us altogether different men, in heart and spirit and mind and powers; and it brings with it the Holy Spirit.[36]

The Reformers all recognized that it is possible to be baptized in water but not in the Spirit, just as it is possible to receive the consecrated elements of bread and wine in the Lord's Supper without partaking of Christ. Material things and human rituals cannot by themselves guarantee the presence or action of God in a person's life, and to imagine that they can is to misrepresent the spiritual character of our relationship with God. The idea that divine grace can be manufactured and distributed to people, even without their knowledge or consent, is a travesty of the gospel, according to which the Holy Spirit bears witness with our spirit that we are children of God.[37]

The transformation that the gospel brings to a person is not a gradual improvement over time that may still be unaccomplished when that person dies, necessitating a spell in purgatory, but a sudden and

---

[36]Luther, "Preface to Romans," in Lull, *Luther's Basic Theological Writings*, 101; and *LW*, 35:70.
[37]Rom 8:16.

complete change that the Bible calls a new birth. The Holy Spirit is never only partially present in someone's life—either he is there or he is not. The change that others see in us when he is present is not the result of our efforts but of his power at work within us. "I have been crucified with Christ," said the apostle Paul, "It is no longer I who live, but Christ who lives in me."[38] The Son of God came into the world to pay the price of sin, but this was not a business transaction—he came to save sinners who were incapable of doing anything to save themselves.

This assertion lies at the very heart of the Protestant doctrine of justification by faith. We have to realize this if we want to appreciate the real difference between Protestantism and Catholicism. For example, if a Protestant questions a Roman Catholic about justification by faith, he is likely to meet with either agreement or incomprehension. Agreement will come from the tiny minority of theologically informed Catholics, and incomprehension from everyone else. In fairness, it must be said that most Protestants are equally mystified by this doctrine, which they may have heard of but cannot explain in any depth. Debates about justification are the preserve of theological specialists and therefore are not very useful for explaining to nonspecialists why the Reformation was so important. If we want to see why Protestants and Catholics do not agree with each other, the best approach is to start with the simple question: "Where am I going when I die?" Protestants will answer that they are going to heaven. Catholics will say that they hope to go to heaven but will probably end up in purgatory because they will not be good enough to join the saints in glory. They do not have the assurance of salvation that Protestants proclaim as fundamental to our experience of God. To Protestants, Catholics are trapped in a system that denies them peace with God. To Catholics, Protestants are arrogant people who think they are going to heaven even though they are not perfect.

---

[38]Gal 2:20.

This is where the theological differences between the two halves of Western Christianity become clear. For a Catholic, a saint is someone who has attained moral and spiritual perfection, a feat which is possible in this life but extremely rare. For a Protestant, that kind of perfection is impossible, unnecessary, and ultimately a denial of the work of Christ. We have been saved by him in spite of ourselves. But how, the good Catholic will ask, can someone who is imperfect stand in the presence of God? The answer to that was clearly explained by John Calvin, who spoke about the Holy Spirit as the Spirit of adoption:

> He is called the Spirit of adoption because he is the witness to us of the free benevolence of God with which God the Father has embraced us in his beloved only-begotten Son to become a Father to us.[39]

An adopted child does not share the nature of his parents and has no physical claim on them. Such a child has been taken into the family by personal choice and identified with his new parents not by blood, but by love. So it is with believers. We are not children of God by nature and have no inherent right to spend eternity in the kingdom of heaven, even if we could somehow attain moral and spiritual perfection. We are heirs through hope of the kingdom of God because we have been adopted—that is the seal and the assurance of our salvation. This adoption is the work of the Holy Spirit, who comes into our hearts and cries "Abba! Father!"[40]

It is generally agreed that Luther said the church stands if it preaches the doctrine of justification by faith alone, or falls if it does not. Although this was a prominent theme as early as his first series of lectures on Galatians (1519), it did not become the center of his teaching until some time later. In the Augsburg Confession of 1530,

---

[39]Calvin, *Institutes* 3.1.3.
[40]Gal 4:6.

for example, which became the defining statement of (Lutheran) Protestantism, the doctrine of justification was treated quite briefly:

> Men cannot be justified before God by their own strength, merits or works, but are justified freely by faith on account of Christ, when they believe that they have been received into grace and that their sins have been forgiven on account of Christ, who by his death has made satisfaction for our sins. God reckons this faith as righteousness in his sight (Romans 3:4).[41]

There is no further elaboration of the theme and, in particular, no discussion of the place of good works *after* justification. It was only in Luther's magisterial second series of lectures on Galatians in 1535 that the subject would get a full airing, after which it would occupy a more significant place in the confessions of the Protestant churches. This development can be seen from the confession of faith resulting from the negotiations between the Wittenberg theologians and the ambassadors of King Henry VIII of England in 1535–1536, where justification was treated at much greater length than it had been before.

In these so-called Wittenberg Articles, justification by faith was placed in the context of the three consecutive parts of penitence: contrition, faith, and the new obedience in Christ.[42] Contrition was defined as a conviction of sin so deep that it drives the sinner to despair of finding salvation by his own efforts. It is at that point that the gospel message comes to rescue and restore him:

> By this faith [in Christ] terrified consciences are lifted up and hearts are made peaceful and set free from the terrors of sin and

---

[41] Augsburg Confession 4, in Bray, *Documents*, 607; for the full text of the Augsburg Confession, see Robert Kolb and Timothy J. Wengert, ed., *The Book of Concord: The Confessions of the Evangelical Lutheran Church* (Minneapolis, MN: Fortress Press, 2000), 27-105; and Pelikan and Hotchkiss, *Creeds and Confessions*, 2:49-118.

[42] Bray, *Documents*, 118-61.

death, as Paul says: "Being justified by faith we have peace with God" (Romans 5:1). For if, to God's judgment against sin, we were to oppose our worthiness and our merits as a satisfaction for sin, the promise of reconciliation would become uncertain for us and our consciences would be driven to despair, as Paul says: "The law works wrath" (Romans 4:15). What ought to be offered for sin is Christ's merit and the free promise of mercy which is given for his sake.[43]

The articles then go on to add,

> This faith, which comforts terrified hearts, is engendered and strengthened by the gospel and by absolution, which applies the promises of grace to individuals. . . . Therefore justification, which comes about through faith in the manner described, is renewal and regeneration.[44]

Having dealt with the first two parts of penitence, the Wittenberg Articles then expound what Luther called the "new obedience" of the Christian—that is to say, the place and value of good works in the life of the believer. After stating at great length that not even the most devout saints can earn God's favor by their behavior, the articles continue in this vein:

> Since renewal occurs in justification, this new life is obedience to God. Therefore justification cannot be retained unless this incipient obedience is retained . . . the value of this incipient obedience is great, for although it is imperfect, nevertheless, because the people concerned are in Christ, this obedience is reckoned to be a kind of fulfilment of the law and is righteousness, as Scripture often calls it . . . This should not be understood as if we obtain remission of sins and reconciliation on account

---

[43]Wittenberg Articles 4, in Bray, *Documents*, 125.
[44]Wittenberg Articles 4, in Bray, *Documents*, 125-66.

of our works, but that both righteousnesses are necessary. First, faith is necessary, for by it we are justified before God . . . and then another righteousness is necessary and owed, the righteousness of works and of a good conscience.[45]

Here we find another theme that was prominent in Luther's teaching— the existence of two kinds of righteousness, which Luther distinguished as *passive* and *active*. Passive righteousness could be received only by faith in Christ, and so it was unique to believers. Active righteousness came from human works and was by its nature restricted to the affairs of this world, although it could also be obtained by unbelievers, who would inevitably want to use it to justify themselves. As Luther expressed in his preface to his second series of lectures on Galatians, which he delivered in 1531 and which was published around the time that the Wittenberg Articles were being composed,

> This is our theology, by which we teach a precise distinction between these two kinds of righteousness, the active and the passive, so that morality and faith, works and grace, secular society and religion may not be confused. Both are necessary, but both must be kept within their limits. Christian righteousness applies to the new person and the righteousness of the law applies to the old person, who is born of flesh and blood. . . . In a Christian, the law must not exceed its limits but should have its dominion only over the flesh, which is subjected to it and remains under it. When this is the case, the law remains within its limits.[46]

It was passive righteousness that validated its active equivalent, because only a righteousness received from Christ could have justifying power. From beginning to end, Luther's constant refrain was that we

---

[45]Wittenberg Articles 5, in Bray, *Documents*, 135.
[46]Martin Luther, "Second Lectures on Galatians," in *LW*, 26:7, 11; and Lull, *Luther's Basic Theological Writings*, 21-23.

can do nothing to save ourselves; we must be united to Christ so that his righteousness can be extended to cover us by imputation. But active righteousness is valid only insofar as we are united to Christ and his righteousness is at work in us, because even after we have been justified we are still sinners.

The importance of the work of the Holy Spirit in justification becomes clearer when we realize that for Luther, the Christian is not a person who has ceased from sinning, which is impossible in this life, but someone who has been made to realize what his true spiritual state is and who trusts in Christ's righteousness for his salvation. Luther made that point forcefully in his comments on Galatians 3:6, which summarize his teaching nicely: "The Christian is righteous and a sinner at the same time (*simul iustus et peccator*), holy and profane, an enemy of God and a child of God. Only those who understand the true meaning of justification will understand this apparent paradox."[47]

"The true meaning of justification" was to be the battleground and the cause of irreparable division between the followers of Luther and those who remained loyal to Rome. Sixteenth-century Protestants came in different shapes and sizes, but on this point they were all agreed. When the Roman authorities finally got together to decide what to do about them, justification was one of the first subjects to which they turned their attention, thereby lending additional credibility to Luther's claim that this doctrine would make or break the church. At its sixth session (January 13, 1547), held nearly a year after Luther's death, the Council of Trent issued a long statement on justification, making its position vis-à-vis the Protestants abundantly clear.[48]

In some respects, the Council of Trent agreed with Luther. It anathematized anyone who said that it was possible to be justified by

---

[47]Luther, "Second Lectures on Galatians," in *LW*, 26:232-33 (not in Lull).
[48]Tanner, *Decrees*, 2:671-81. The canons start on p. 79.

his own works, or who claimed that people could choose to be saved
or to love God without the help of God's grace (canons 1-3). But having said that, it then denied the key elements of Luther's teaching.
The council claimed that God's grace was given to enable a person
to exercise his free will by cooperating with God in order to obtain
justification, and it specifically rejected the concept of passive righteousness (canon 4). It went on to reject the bondage of the will and
the Protestant belief that good works done before justification are by
nature sinful (canons 5, 7). The idea that faith alone justified the
wicked was condemned, as was Luther's assertion that we can be justified only by Christ's righteousness (canons 9-14). The council further denied that anyone could have assurance of salvation based on
justification by faith alone, and it rejected Luther's contention that
even those who are justified and in a state of grace cannot fulfill the
commandments of God (canons 15-18).

On occasion, it is clear that the fathers of the council misunderstood Protestant teaching, as when they gave the impression that
Luther had taught that the Ten Commandments do not apply to
Christians, which was manifestly false (canon 19). They seem to
have had no idea of the new obedience, or of its importance in Protestant teaching, because many of the remaining canons were directed against those who thought that good works performed *after*
justification were unnecessary or harmful (canon 21-26), and
it seems from the context that this was the council's understanding of Protestant teaching. This condemnation is summed up in
canon 32:

> If anyone says that the good works of a justified person are the
> gifts of God in such a way that they are not also the good merits
> of the one justified; or that the justified person does not, by
> the good works done by him through the grace of God and the
> merit of Jesus Christ (whose living member he is), truly merit

an increase in grace, eternal life and (so long as he dies in grace) the acquisition of his own eternal life and also an increase in glory: let him be anathema.[49]

From the standpoint of the Council of Trent, to be united to Christ was not to be saved outright but to be set free to cooperate with him in working off the penalties incurred for sin both before and after the reception of grace. In this way, the council validated and reinforced the traditional penitential system that had come under such strong attack from the Protestants, thus closing the door to any reform of the church that would take it in a Lutheran direction. Luther understood that to change the doctrine of justification by faith would be to change the church along with it, which at first he did not want to do and did not think was necessary. For some time he continued to believe that the Roman church was the body of Christ, who worked in and through it, and it was only slowly that he and his followers came to realize that Christ's body was not to be found in the church of Rome as it then existed.

Luther died just as the Council of Trent was starting, so he never had the chance to respond to it. It was a different matter with the next generation, and in John Calvin's works we find the whole question of justification set out in a clear, concise, and logical way. He made a clear distinction between the work of Christ, accomplished for the salvation of the elect by the sacrifice that he presented to the Father, and the work of the Holy Spirit, by whom believers are united to Christ. In particular, Calvin stressed that the Holy Spirit comes to believers in and through Christ, to whom he has been given in his office as Mediator of the new covenant. In other words, the Holy Spirit comes to believers not just as the Spirit of the Son of God but also as the Spirit of the man Jesus Christ, in whom he dwells "in a special way; that is, to separate us from the world and to gather us unto the

---

[49]Tanner, *Decrees*, 2:81.

hope of the eternal inheritance."[50] Calvin stated this quite explicitly
when he wrote,

> [The Spirit] is called the Spirit of Christ, not only because
> Christ, as eternal Word of God, is joined in the same Spirit
> with the Father, but also from his character as the Mediator.
> For he would have come to us in vain if he had not been fur-
> nished with this power.[51]

Calvin went on to say that giving faith to believers was the Spirit's
first and most important work. Quoting a number of New Testament
passages that support this view, he culminated his exposition by a
short discussion of Christ's words to his disciples before his crucifix-
ion, when he promised to send them "the Spirit of truth, whom the
world cannot receive."[52] As Calvin explained,

> As the proper office of the Spirit, he [Christ] assigned the task of
> bringing to mind what he had taught by mouth. For light would
> be given the sightless in vain had the Spirit of discernment not
> opened the eyes of the mind. Consequently, he may rightly be
> called the key that unlocks for us the treasures of the kingdom
> of heaven; and his illumination the keenness of our insight.[53]

After discoursing at great length on the nature of faith as a divine
gift and refuting a number of errors that had crept into the teaching
of the medieval church, Calvin finally came to the central question of
justification. In eight substantial chapters, followed by a further one
on Christian liberty, Calvin expounded the doctrine of justification
by faith alone, ignoring the objections raised against Luther's teaching
by the Council of Trent but concentrating instead on the false teaching of Andreas Osiander (1498–1552), a Lutheran theologian who, in

---

[50]Calvin, *Institutes* 3.1.2.
[51]Calvin, *Institutes* 3.1.2.
[52]Jn 14:17.
[53]Calvin, *Institutes* 3.1.4.

Calvin's words, taught "that we are not justified by the grace of the Mediator alone, nor is righteousness simply or completely offered to us in his person, but that we are made partakers in God's righteousness when God is united to us in essence."[54] Calvin, along with Melanchthon and other Lutheran theologians, opposed Osiander on the ground that he misrepresented what the New Testament taught about the work of the Holy Spirit in the life of the believer. Using the image of the sun, which is both light and heat, Calvin argued that just as we cannot say that the earth is warmed by the sun's light or illuminated by its heat, so we cannot confuse the two aspects of God's grace at work in our lives. Justification and sanctification are inseparable, but they are not identical. The Father accepts us into his presence thanks to the intercession of the Son our Mediator, but he then gives us his Spirit of adoption so that we may be re-formed in his image.[55]

This distinction is often referred to as the "double grace" that comes from the believer's union with Christ. As long as Luther was alive, controversy over this was avoided, but after his death (February 18, 1546) his followers advanced different interpretations of his teaching on the subject of justification and sanctification. Osiander was one of the first to take a public position on the matter, and he was perceived by most of his fellow Lutherans as an extremist. He regarded justification by faith alone as a declaration by the Father that the elect have been accepted in and by the sacrifice of the Son for their sins. In his mind, sanctification was the inevitable consequence of that, and it was signified especially in the Eucharist, wherein the believer partook of the body and blood of Christ that were present "in, with and under" the forms of bread and wine. It was Christ's divine nature, not his human one, that made the believer righteous,

---

[54]Calvin, *Institutes* 3.11.5. Osiander had been one of Luther's closest colleagues, and his niece married Thomas Cranmer, the future archbishop of Canterbury, so the disagreement between him and his fellow Reformers struck at the very heart of the Protestant movement.

[55]Calvin, *Institutes* 3.11.6.

because only his divine nature possessed that quality in a pure and objective sense. Luther's teaching that the body of Christ was "ubiquitous" made Osiander's interpretation possible because the ascended and glorified Christ could be present, along with his human nature, wherever he chose, but that was not Luther's teaching.

Osiander took a one-sided view of Luther's doctrine, and to the consternation of his fellow Lutherans, he taught that in the Eucharist (and more generally in union with Christ), the believer is essentially one with the Son of God, partaking of his nature in a real and direct way. There was a strong reaction in Lutheran circles to Osiander's lopsidedness, which occasionally went to the opposite extreme, denying that believers had any direct contact with Christ's divine nature in the Lord's Supper. In the end, the Formula of Concord (1577) reached a mediating position, insisting that the communicant partakes of *both* the divine and the human nature of Christ, and that each nature conveys his righteousness to believers.[56]

Ironically, some people perceived Calvin to be very close to Osiander in his teaching because he too proclaimed a real union with Christ that was not just a forensic declaration of righteousness but a genuine transformation of the believer. The difference was that Calvin insisted that this transformation did not come about by a union of natures (or essences) between God and man but by the indwelling of the Holy Spirit, who made the believer a child of God and opened up the way to his receiving all the benefits that accompanied that status. For that reason, it was not Christ who was present "in, with and under" the species of bread and wine, but the Holy Spirit, who used those material things to enter into spiritual communion with those who received them by faith.

Osiander's error, as Calvin saw it, was due to a wrong understanding of faith. Properly understood, faith is the designated means to

---

[56]See R. Kolb and C. R. Trueman, *Between Wittenberg and Geneva: Lutheran and Reformed Theology in Conversation* (Grand Rapids: Baker, 2017), 130-31.

achieving union with Christ, but it is not to be mistaken for the end itself. Calvin compared faith to a jar of clay in which gold (justification) is deposited—it is not the faith, which is always weak and inadequate, that counts but rather the gift that it brings which is our real treasure and salvation.[57] The clay jar in which this treasure is enclosed stands, first of all, for the human nature of the incarnate Son and, secondly, for us who share that human nature. Jesus was made righteous for us not because of his divinity but because his human nature was transformed by the indwelling presence of God. If he were righteous only by virtue of his divine nature, he would not be our Savior, because we would be incapable of sharing that righteousness in any way. But just as the divine righteousness was imputed to his human nature, so it is also imputed to us by the indwelling presence of the Holy Spirit. We remain jars of clay and can never be anything other than that, but the divine Spirit inside those jars works his regenerating power in us so that we become by grace something that we could never be (or become) by nature. After a lengthy discussion of this subject, Calvin summarized it as follows:

> We confess that while through the intercession of Christ's righteousness God reconciles us to himself, and by free remission of sins accounts us righteous, his beneficence is at the same time joined with such a mercy that through his Holy Spirit he dwells in us and by his power the lusts of our flesh are each day more and more mortified; we are indeed sanctified, that is, consecrated to the Lord in true purity of life, with our hearts formed to obedience to the law.[58]

Calvin contrasted this with the teaching of the medieval Scholastics, whom he grouped together as one. He began by saying that there was no difference at all between them and the Reformed as far as the basic principle was concerned, since they both agreed that sinners are

---

[57]Calvin, *Institutes* 3.11.7.
[58]Calvin, *Institutes* 3.14.9.

freely delivered from condemnation and receive justification by the forgiveness of their sins. But he went on to point out that

> [the Scholastics] include under the term "justification" a renewal, by which through the Spirit of God we are remade to obedience to the law. Indeed, they so describe the righteousness of the regenerated man that a man once for all reconciled to God through faith in Christ may be reckoned righteous before God by good works, and be accepted by the merit of them.[59]

The idea that good works could earn merit with God was anathema to all the Reformers, and to that extent their teaching was diametrically opposed to that of the Scholastics. Modern observers might remark that the difference is more theoretical than real since Protestants emphasize the need to live in accordance with God's commandments just as much as Catholics do, but the theological understanding that undergirds their behavior is quite different and leads Protestants to claim an assurance of salvation that Catholics find alien and incomprehensible. To understand why, we must look more closely at what the Reformers taught about living the Christian life and how this differed from the traditional teaching of the medieval church.

THE CHRISTIAN LIFE

For the Reformers, the Christian life was lived only and entirely in and by the grace of God, with no human merit of any kind attached. Luther, never one to mince his words, was particularly emphatic about this: "Do we do nothing and work nothing to obtain this righteousness? I reply; Nothing at all. For this righteousness means to do nothing, to hear nothing, and to know nothing about the Law or about works."[60]

---

[59]Calvin, *Institutes* 3.14.11.

[60]Luther, "Second Lectures on Galatians," in *LW*, 26:8; and Lull, *Luther's Basic Theological Writings*, 21.

One of the principal effects of this was the radical way in which the Reformers separated the concept of justification from that of sanctification. Previously, sanctification had been the goal that believers were expected to achieve, and if they succeeded they were justified in the sight of God. Luther turned that on its head. To be justified was an act of God's undeserved grace, and sanctification was its inevitable result. This raised the question of what sanctification actually is, and it must be said that Protestants have not always understood the radical implications of the gospel on this point. To be sanctified is not to be or to become a "better" person but to be a child of God by adoption and to live according to a pattern that is not ours by nature.

Luther is famous for having told his associate Philipp Melanchthon to "sin boldly" because it would not affect his salvation, but his somewhat ironic comment has frequently been misunderstood.[61] Many have supposed that Luther was indifferent to sin as long as a person confessed faith in Christ, but nothing could be further from the truth. What bothered Luther was that people had grown accustomed to being overly scrupulous about keeping certain rules of the church, particularly ones concerning things like fasting, and that they did not fully understand what it meant to be sinful. Whether we commit actual sins or not, we are still sinners in need of the grace of God. Faith in Christ is a life-transforming thing because it enables us to live without guilt or fear of losing our salvation. It does not justify wrongdoing but rather frees us to live for God in the way he originally intended for us to live. The truth is that Protestants are much more likely to have a reputation for clean living, bordering on puritanism, than they are for licentiousness, and it would be hard to find anyone in a Protestant church who thinks that it is perfectly fine to do whatever they want as long as they have "faith" in Christ. As the New

---

[61]Martin Luther, Letter 99.13, August 1, 1521, in *LW*, 48:232 (not in Lull).

Testament makes plain, saints are not perfect or even morally superior people, but men and women who have been changed by the power of God at work in their lives. They are far from perfect, but because they have been united to Christ in the Holy Spirit, their sins are not held against them. Such people are not proud or boastful of their achievements but rather are humble and reticent to claim anything for themselves. They are hesitant to accept praise from others because they know that if there is any good thing in what they have done it has come from God and not from them.

More common among Protestants has been the belief that sanctification is a gradual process following justification that is practically synonymous with Christian growth. According to this view, after making a profession of faith, the believer is gradually transformed by the indwelling presence of the Holy Spirit and turned into a more Christlike individual. In some ways, this is similar to what was advocated by the pre-Reformation church, but there is a key difference. The medieval church understood Christian growth as something that contributes to our eventual justification, not as the inevitable result of being justified by faith. The Reformers understood that in the New Testament, all God's people were saints by virtue of their election in Christ. It was because they were *already* holy that the apostle Paul wrote to encourage them to work out their salvation in fear and trembling, as he put it, and not to quench the gift that was in them.[62] They were not required to *become* holy but to *manifest* the true nature of the holiness that was theirs by the indwelling presence of the Holy Spirit.

Some might be tempted to think that this was no more than the pre-Reformation way of sanctification by another name, but the Protestant conception is rule-free. Those who are trying to earn their sanctification are almost bound to do so by adopting a series of rules

---

[62]Phil 2:12; 1 Thess 5:19.

that serve as benchmarks of progress. These rules will vary from time to time and from place to place, but the pattern is the same. Those who would be "holy" must behave in a certain way, usually by abstaining from various activities or habits—no smoking, no drinking, no dancing, and so on. The forms of abstinence may be good in themselves, but they are not meritorious in the sight of God, nor do they count toward our salvation in Christ. As Jesus demonstrated to his disciples, there are no fixed rules that must be obeyed at all costs. If someone needs help on the Sabbath day, it is wrong to use the excuse of divinely appointed rest as a way to avoid helping them. The criterion for true sanctification is not "keep the rules" but "love your neighbors," a deeper principle that may be expressed by but also transcends keeping the law. Only the guidance given by the indwelling presence of the Holy Spirit can help us discern which approach is required on any given occasion, and only he can give us the wisdom and the will to respond accordingly.

Obviously there will always be margin for error here—we may show what we think is love to other people only to discover that our kindness has been misplaced or was not as disinterested as we thought it was. We are sinful human beings, after all, and even if we get it right we have nothing to boast about. Just as we live by the grace of God, so we are forgiven for our mistakes and failures by that same grace. We cannot lose our sanctification (as some people like to put it) by misbehavior any more than we can earn it by doing the right thing.

The key to understanding this lies in our relationship with God in Christ. If we are focused on him and living by faith in his power, then we do not have to worry about our inadequacies—God will make up for our deficiencies and bring his good out of our chaos. When we sin we discover again the greatness of his mercy and love for us as we are brought to repentance and restored to newness of life in Christ. We shall sin again, that is for sure, but God's grace will never fail us as long as we have faith in him and in his promises.

FIVE

THE GODLY COMMONWEALTH

CHURCH AND STATE

Whether, or in what way, the grace of God was extended to nonbelievers was not a question that concerned the Reformers very much. With their strong emphasis on faith, unbelief was not something they could easily come to terms with, and they were usually more ready to denounce those who rejected the gospel and to warn them of their impending fate than to see them as instruments of God's mercy and loving kindness. Nevertheless, they knew that certain places in the Bible describe unbelievers as instruments of God's grace. In particular, the Reformers were well aware that Paul had told the Romans that their pagan secular authorities were set over them for their own good and that they must honor that by praying for their rulers, paying their taxes, and obeying the laws.[1] They were to be obeyed because they were put there by God and operated according to his will, even if they persecuted the church. The Reformers held the same view, although their rulers were at least nominally Christian. Protestants were encouraged to obey them even if they did not share the same form of Christianity—obedience to a Catholic king was just as obligatory as obedience to a Protestant one. That stood in sharp contrast to the position often advocated by the Roman Catholic Church, which declared war on heretics and urged its members to defy them

---

[1]Rom 13:1-7.

whenever possible. The most outrageous case of this occurred in 1570, when the pope excommunicated Queen Elizabeth I of England and called on loyal Catholics to remove her—by assassination if necessary. That was an extreme position even then, and many Catholics rejected it, but it reveals a distinct difference in mentality between the two halves of a divided Western Christendom. For Catholics, salvation could be found only within the bosom of the Roman church, and there was little respect for anyone outside it—particularly not for those who had left it deliberately. Protestants thought differently. However much they may have insisted on the rightness of their own theology and tried to persuade others to accept it, their understanding of God's sovereignty meant that they could see his gracious hand at work in the most unlikely places, even Rome.

We must not exaggerate this willingness, of course. Religious toleration was not a virtue in the sixteenth century, and little of it was seen anywhere. Protestants usually tried to impose their form of Christianity within the territories they controlled, and they could persecute their opponents with as much zeal as the Catholics. But at least the Reformers did not think of themselves as vicars of Christ on earth who were entitled to pass divine judgment on those who disagreed with them. Foreigners in particular were often granted special exemptions and allowed to practice their form of Protestantism, even if it differed from the one officially sanctioned. There were so-called stranger churches in London, Rotterdam, and elsewhere that operated outside the structures of the local church but with its blessing. Despite their narrow outlook, most Protestants remained open to the idea that the grace of God was at work beyond the confines of their own congregations, and in time that awareness would help to encourage a form of tolerance that has now become all but universal, at least in the Western world.

All Reformed theologians agreed that the ceremonial parts of the law had been made redundant by the coming of Christ. He is the great high priest; his sacrifice is the final and complete atonement for sin; his body (to which we are united by the Holy Spirit) is the temple. We can read what the Old Testament says about those things and learn the full dimensions of what Christ's life and death mean for us, but we cannot replicate them in the way that the medieval church had done. Indeed, to do that would be a form of blasphemy and a denial of the once-for-all sufficiency of Christ's sacrifice. The depth of feeling on this point among the Reformers can be gauged from the words of the Anglican Book of Common Prayer, in which the prayer of consecration (of the bread and wine used in the Lord's Supper) goes as follows:

> Almighty God, our heavenly Father, who of thy tender mercy didst give thine only Son Jesus Christ to suffer death upon the Cross for our redemption; who made there (by his one oblation of himself once offered) a full, perfect, and sufficient sacrifice, oblation, and satisfaction, for the sins of the whole world.

It would be hard to make the uniqueness and comprehensiveness of Christ's atonement any more explicit. But if the Reformers believed that the ceremonial aspects of the Mosaic law had been made redundant, they retained its moral commands in full, saying that now they were implanted in the hearts of believers by the Holy Spirit. Christians could not claim the right to kill, steal, or commit adultery on the ground that the law had been abolished, although some Catholic polemicists tried to say that that was what Protestant teaching amounted to. The real difficulty for the Reformers came with the civil law, the principles that governed the life of the state. To what extent and in what way could they still be applied in a Christian context?

Some of the more radical Reformers preached a kind of anarchy and engaged in rebellion against the established order, but most of them repudiated anything of that kind. They insisted that Christians must obey the authorities set over them, whether they agreed with them or not. The Roman Empire had persecuted the church, but the apostles had valued the peace, order, and good government that it provided, and the Reformers believed that sixteenth-century Protestants should have the same attitude. Of course, if a ruler was Protestant, more could be hoped for. Protestant kings were expected to be supporters of the church, applying its teachings in their laws and seeking to order public life in ways that honored God. Education, justice, and financial support for godly preachers all came into this category. So too did the public worship of God, which was expected to be theologically orthodox in content and universally imposed on the ruler's subjects, who were obliged to attend services regularly and conform to the Christian "rites of passage"—baptism, marriage, and burial—which were now systematically registered and recorded for the first time. Sunday was set aside as a day of rest, and among the more dedicated Protestants it was strictly observed, a practice that continued for centuries and has only weakened in recent years under pressure from secularism and the strains of modern life.

Leaving the state church was not a viable option for most people, partly because those who refused to conform were regarded as outlaws who deserved to be coerced into submission and partly because there was no choice of denominations in the modern sense. This is hard for us to appreciate because we are used to individual religious freedom and plurality, but those concepts were alien in the sixteenth and seventeenth centuries. Just as people today who do not vaccinate their children or send them to school are regarded as undesirable oddities and are sometimes made to suffer for it, religious nonconformists in the days of the Reformation were considered to be antisocial and potentially dangerous, especially if their opting out of the state church weakened the community's ability to defend itself against outside aggressors, who were always lurking in the background.

The Protestant Reformation could not have happened without the involvement of the secular states. In almost every case, a country's ruler decided that it would become Protestant, and the majority of his or her subjects acquiesced. Conversely, where the ruler remained Catholic, so did the people. Individuals who did not agree with their ruler's decision were either punished, often quite brutally, or expelled. In the Holy Roman Empire this became the law in 1555, when a peace agreement between Protestants and Catholics, signed at Augsburg, stipulated that the secular ruler would decide the religion of his territory (the famous principle known in Latin as *cuius regio, eius religio*) and provided for population exchanges in order to eliminate dissenting minorities. This may sound harsh to us, but Germany was subdivided into many small states, so most people did not have to travel very far to find one that suited their preferences, and that was much better than taking legal action against dissenters.[2]

The two major exceptions to this rule demonstrate the importance of state involvement. One was the northern Netherlands, centered on the province of Holland, which revolted against its Spanish overlords and after eighty years of intermittent fighting secured its independence. Three things should be noted about this. First, only half of the Netherlands broke away and became Protestant. The southern part of the country (what we now call Belgium) remained Catholic and under Spanish control. Second, the country was ruled by a foreign king who sent a deputy to exercise authority on his behalf. In other words, it was more like a colony than an independent country in its own right. Third, it took eighty years for the war of independence to succeed, despite the widespread support of the population and neighboring states.

The second exception was Ireland. Like the Netherlands, it too was ruled by a foreign king through lieutenants who were rotated on a

---

[2]Population exchanges for religious reasons reappeared in the early twentieth century, when the Ottoman Empire was dismantled following the First World War. Christians of all denominations were expelled to Greece and Muslims to Turkey, regardless of their language or ethnic affinity. It was a harsh solution to an intractable problem, but it worked.

regular basis, but unlike the Netherlands, Ireland was only partially conquered. Most of the country was outside of the king's control in the sixteenth century, and Catholicism could flourish there unmolested. The island needed to be conquered politically if the Reformation was to be introduced and the island Protestantized successfully, but that did not happen, and the result was a Protestant state with a largely Catholic population—a situation that managed to survive for three centuries but left a bitterness that is still remembered today.

Elsewhere, populations followed the desires of their rulers. In France, the grassroots movement for Reformation was held back because the Protestants were never able to gain control of the state, although they came close to doing so at one point. They were numerous and influential enough to obtain a limited degree of toleration in 1598, but that was soon curtailed, and in 1685 their remaining rights were abolished. In Great Britain, England went back and forth for a few years before finally settling on a moderate form of Protestantism in 1559. There were martyrs on both sides, but they were relatively few in number, and most people just complied with the prevailing sentiment. Scotland adopted Protestantism in 1560, with a more thoroughgoing Reformation that was voted in by the country's parliament and so could claim a popular mandate that later events confirmed as genuine. Even so, Protestantism triumphed mainly because the Scottish monarchy was too weak to resist and it was strongly supported by the English government.

Elsewhere, the Scandinavian countries accepted Lutheranism, and about half the Swiss cantons became Protestant. Parts of Poland and Hungary also turned to the Reformation, but in these two highly decentralized countries the major landowners were largely responsible for this change. With greater state centralization in the seventeenth century came less tolerance. Poland eventually managed to eliminate Protestantism almost entirely, but the Muslim presence in much of Hungary allowed it to survive "behind enemy lines" as it were. Portugal and Spain remained solidly Catholic because they took a hostile line toward any form of "heresy" and punished it severely. The rich Italian city-states regarded Rome as a rival and enjoyed asserting their independence from it whenever they could, but they were too vulnerable to external attack to break with its spiritual hegemony. For them, staying Catholic was prudent politics as much as anything else, and their citizens generally remained loyal to that policy, with the few exceptions emigrating north to more congenial spiritual climes. Venice was unusually tolerant in that it allowed the Eastern Orthodox to worship freely and admitted Protestants to the University of Padua, where many northern Europeans went to study, but citizenship of the mercantile republic was reserved for Catholics.

Religious minorities were present in most countries, to a greater or lesser degree, and their fate largely depended on their numbers. Where there were large minorities, as in France, they were usually tolerated, if somewhat grudgingly and only for a time. Where they were few they were either allowed to leave, as happened in Germany, or were persecuted out of existence, as in Spain. On the whole, Catholics were better off in Protestant countries than the other way around. In Catholic eyes, Protestants were heretics and could be dealt with by the church under existing legislation against them. Catholics in Protestant lands were harder to classify in this way because they were mostly traditionalists who rejected change rather than heretics or enemies of the state.

To understand how Catholics were treated in a Protestant country like England, it is perhaps best to look at what happens today when a government tries to engineer social control. Not so long ago, smoking tobacco was an acceptable habit that was even encouraged by advertising and the like. But once its health risks became too obvious to ignore, campaigns to end it started to proliferate. Smokers were taxed and inconvenienced in any number of petty ways. Points of sale were restricted, and minors were forbidden to buy tobacco products. Every discouragement short of outright banning was employed, with considerable (though not total) success. Interestingly, it was only when smoking rates reached a low level that outright banning was considered and implemented in a number of places like hotels, schools, hospitals and so on. Smoking is now almost an act of social rebellion, policed not merely by the state but by any number of concerned citizens who do not hesitate to rebuke smokers for their habit.

Now transpose this scenario to religious practice in Protestant states of the late sixteenth century. Catholicism had until recently been generally accepted by the population, even if devotion to it had been waning. Forbidding it proceeded by stages, with priority being given to teaching the new faith rather than disturbing traditional customs, which were modified or suppressed more gradually. As the process gathered pace, so did intolerance of the old religion. This was especially obvious in England, where a Puritan movement grew more influential even as traditional Catholicism went into virtually terminal decline. Strange as it may seem, religious tolerance often became less common as the need for it diminished. There were exceptions of course, but the overall trend is unmistakable, and by 1700, when the Reformation was virtually over, religious minorities were dwindling everywhere, even in England, where dissenting Protestants were granted official toleration in 1689. In one respect, England was an innovator in dealing with nonconformists—it exported them. Beginning as early as 1620, Puritans who were unhappy with the religious situation at home sailed away to found the different colonies of New England, and this later became official government policy. William Penn was given land to establish a Quaker settlement, and religious toleration was actually introduced into the Carolinas, whose original constitution was written by the liberal John Locke (1632–1704). But this apparently enlightened policy must not be overidealized. The founders of Massachusetts liked to think that they were proclaiming religious freedom, but they neglected to add that it was freedom for them, not for anyone else.[3]

To understand why the Reformation worked out this way, we must look carefully at the nature of church-state relations in the sixteenth century and the policies that the Reformers adopted toward them. Before 1500 most of western Europe had been united by the Roman church for more than a millennium. Following the collapse of the Roman Empire, the church was left as the only functioning social institution. As barbarian kingdoms came into existence, they were heavily dependent on the church for their administrative personnel, a situation that became more serious as they expanded and consolidated the embryonic states that we know today. Furthermore, the church was universal in the way that the old empire had been, but none of the successor states exerted the same influence. Most people identified as Christians first and as subjects of whoever's territory they lived in second. Secular rulers came and went, but the church remained the same as it always had been, especially at the local level. Even the papal schism in the late fourteenth century did little to change that. Schools, hospitals, and government remained in clerical hands, as the dual meaning of the word *clerical* indicates. The man who sat in the office handling the paperwork was probably ordained, and most priests functioned as notaries, registrars, and the like, wherever they happened to be.

As an institution, the church had its own legal system and operated as independently of the secular authorities as it could. The special status of the clergy was reinforced by compulsory celibacy, a monastic discipline that gradually spread to the parish priests as well. Celibacy set them apart from the people and prevented church property from being alienated in the form of dowries and inheritances. It was also intended to represent the life of heaven, because the clergy

---

[3]It ended up with its own state church, which survived the Revolution and was not finally disestablished until 1833.

were a superior caste who witnessed to the eschatological dimension of the faith that they professed and proclaimed. This ideal may have been honored as much in the breach as in the observance, but it was deeply rooted in the popular mind and admired more than its critics care to admit. To enter the ministry of the church was to sacrifice the pleasures of this world, and those who did so sincerely generally earned the respect of their less devout contemporaries.

Church and state had their own spheres of influence, but they had to live together in a common Christian society. Sometimes this could get quite complicated. For example, only the church could ordain a priest, but the right to appoint a priest to a particular parish lay with whoever owned the local church, and that could easily be the landowner whose ancestor had originally built it. The advowson, or right of presentation, as this was called, was private property and could be sold or donated to anybody at all, even to non-Christians. The law governing this was secular, not religious, and many church people, especially would-be reformers, found this situation deeply unsatisfactory. Opposition to it was one of the main causes for the growth of puritanism in England, where convinced Protestant preachers were often kept out of parishes by lay patrons who preferred to appoint men who would be subservient to them—like their younger sons, for example. Disentangling this kind of mixed-up relationship was essential if the church was ever to reform itself, but vested interests stood in the way.[4] The church's saving grace was that its offices were non-hereditary and therefore at least theoretically open to talent, but the landed interests were passed on from one generation to the next. In other words, they had staying power that the church's officials lacked.

Throughout the Middle Ages the relative strength of the church and the secular authorities varied over time. When Charlemagne was

---

[4]The sale of advowsons in England was not made illegal until 1925.

king of the Franks (ca. 742–814), he forced the pope to crown him
Holy Roman emperor (in 800) and basically did as he liked with the
church. Two and half centuries later, the papacy was greatly strengthened by sweeping reforms, and by 1095 the pope was able to summon
the rulers of western Europe to go on crusade. Two centuries further
on, the crusades had run out of steam and the secular states were
demanding the right to tax church property. People did not realize it
at the time, but the papacy was in a long-term decline, partly because
of internal dissension and partly because there was a growing sense
that the secular world did not need clerics to run it. As more laymen
became educated, they could (and did) take government posts that
had previously been occupied by churchmen, or had not existed at all,
and these laymen saw no need to defer to the clergy.

Throughout the fifteenth and early sixteenth centuries the growing tension between these two worlds was kept under control, but
when Luther questioned the secular authority of the papacy, a significant body of support in the secular establishment protected him
and made the Reformation politically feasible. In their different ways,
both Luther and the papacy were made to understand that they
needed secular support in order to survive, and they acquiesced in it.
Both Luther and the popes probably thought they were strong
enough to get what they wanted from their supporters, and perhaps
they were—for a time. But the Augsburg settlement of 1555 was imposed by the state on the warring factions of the church, not the other
way around, and after that there was no doubt as to who was in control. The state was in charge of the church, and both the popes and
the Reformers had to come to terms with that situation.

This does not mean that they desired it, of course. The more radical Reformers, like the Anabaptists, rejected it but paid the price by
being marginalized and persecuted. Calvin managed to secure some
independence for the church in Geneva, but he did not dominate the
city government to anything like the extent of popular legend,

and Geneva was too small to be a model for Protestant countries elsewhere. John Knox tried to copy it in Scotland and succeeded for a while, but only because the civil government was too weak to resist him. Once it recovered its strength, Knox's successors were gradually put back in their place, although it would not be until the eighteenth century that the Scottish church's independence would be completely extinguished.

However we look at it, the Reformation did not bring about religious freedom in the modern sense, nor did it achieve any real separation of church and state. That would be the work of the late eighteenth-century Enlightenment, which would result in the marginalization of the church and is separation from the state. These states would also determine the degree of freedom from outside interference that the churches would be allowed to enjoy. To appreciate what that could mean, we have only to look at the Quaker colony of Pennsylvania. When it was established in 1681, its constitution included Quaker ideals such as pacifism. But in 1775 the Continental Congress revoked that because, in its opinion, all loyal Americans had to take up arms (on its side, of course), whether they were pacifists or not. Congress won and Pennsylvania lost out. The secular state determined what would and would not count as religious freedom or conscientious objection, and the poor Quakers just had to put up with it. So it has been ever since in what was once the world of Christendom.

The Social Impact of the Reformation

The Protestant reformers could not do much to change the nature of the church-state relationship. The Reformation accelerated the process of secularization that was already under way, but this probably would have happened even quicker if the Reformers had dismantled the medieval church completely. We know this because of the reforms that they successfully incorporated within the parts of the church that they controlled. The first and one of the most successful things they did was to get rid of the traditional clerical caste. The celibacy rule was abolished, removing the most obvious distinction between the clergy and the laity and creating a whole new social phenomenon—legitimate clergy wives and children, who had to be provided for. This was trickier than it might seem, for two reasons. In the sixteenth century it was still usual for sons to follow their father's profession, but could this apply to the clergy? In many cases it did, and great clerical dynasties were founded as one generation succeeded the other in the pulpit. Clergy wives and daughters were another story. To what social class did they belong?

This does not matter very much today, but five hundred years ago it was all-important. Could a clergyman marry above his social station, and (more important) could he marry his daughter to someone from high society? Given that the Reformers wanted their clergy to be university graduates (a restricted social privilege), it was probably inevitable that the clergy would find their own niche on the social hierarchy—below the aristocracy and the wealthy gentry but well above the peasants or the urban working class. Before the Reformation, a priest might easily fraternize with the peasants, especially if he was one himself, but afterward this became much less common. As a graduate he was not their type, and he would not have wanted his daughters to fall in love with men who could not keep them in the style to which they had grown accustomed. We have only to look at the novels of Jane Austen and the Brontë sisters to appreciate the nature of this difficulty. It was a problem that has persisted into modern times, when the "middle-class captivity" of the clergy remains a factor to be reckoned with in almost every Protestant denomination.

The place of women in the Reformed churches was another issue that was little discussed at the time but has attracted more attention in recent years. In the Middle Ages, women could enter the religious life on the same basis as men—they could become celibates in convents, as female monasteries are usually called. A mother superior of such a convent could become a powerful figure, and several women distinguished themselves as writers, especially in the realm of mystical theology. During the Reformation these convents were dissolved and the women in them were either married or pensioned off. The Reformers saw this as a liberation, and it was not unusual for previously celibate clergy to marry a former nun, as Martin Luther himself did. These women could be powerful forces in their own right, but unless they were exceptionally privileged, they operated behind the scenes. A woman who tried to preach or teach publicly might easily be accused of witchcraft, and no Protestant church employed them as ministers in their own right. But women in high positions could be very influential by choosing the men they patronized. Jeanne d'Albret, for example, and her mother Marguerite d'Angoulême were queens of the small Pyrenean kingdom of Navarre and members of the French royal family, who adopted the Reformation and turned Navarre into a Protestant state. More famous still were the half sisters Mary I and Elizabeth I of England. The former reversed the Reformation of her father Henry VIII and brother Edward VI by taking the country back to Rome, and the latter was largely responsible for establishing the moderate Protestantism that came to characterize the Church of England. Less fortunate was Mary, Queen of Scots, who was a weak ruler and could not withstand the Protestantism of John Knox, who eventually drove her out of the country, but she was the exception that proved the rule. Women in positions of power were an anomaly in the sixteenth century, but they could achieve a lot, and in England's case at least, their achievements would prove lasting.

After the Reformation, there was still a difference between laymen and clergy in Protestant churches, but it was one of function rather than of status or being. Only a properly ordained man was allowed to preach or administer the sacrament of the Lord's Supper (there was more flexibility concerning baptism, mainly because of the high rate of infant mortality). He usually continued to enjoy certain privileges related to his office that were denied to ordinary people, but if so, these were governed by secular and not by spiritual criteria. For example, an ordained man might be exempt from jury duty because passing judgment in a secular court could be incompatible with his ministry, but provisions of that kind were not important enough to make the clergy a separate social caste. It is true that much of the aura that surrounded the medieval priest was transferred to the Protestant pastor, and remnants of that can still be seen today, but this was (and is) the legacy of social convention, not the official teaching of the church.

The secularization of the parish clergy was accompanied by the dissolution of the monasteries. The Reformers might not have objected in principle to the idea of withdrawing from society in order to live a life dedicated to prayer, but monasticism had long since developed into something else. Monasteries were often farms or businesses competing for trade, and many of them were quite wealthy. The spirituality of many monks was often called into question, not least by men who wanted to bring them back to their primitive ideals. To the Reformers the challenge of monastic spirituality was clear. If the monks were right, then what they practiced in the cloister ought to be the norm for Christians everywhere. Prayer and Bible reading should not be the activities of a privileged few who were a cut above the ordinary but rather the daily diet of every Christian. The New Testament portrayed a church in which these and other spiritual activities flourished in the world, not apart from it.

What the Reformers wanted was a godly society in which families, not monasteries, would be the bedrock of the spiritual life. The head of the household was responsible for instructing its members in the way of the Lord. Women were expected to bring up their children in the faith. Everybody was assumed to have a vocation—a word that would soon change its meaning. Before the Reformation, a vocation was a call to the priesthood or to the so-called religious life, but afterward it became a calling to any legitimate activity. A tinker or a chimney sweep was just as much a child of God as a bishop or a king, and he was just as accountable for the right performance of his duties. The ungodly were the slackers—the layabouts and good-for-nothings who tried to live off the charity of others when they ought to be fending for themselves. It would be wrong to say that the Reformers had no interest in poor relief. On the contrary, they were often in the forefront of such social action. But such charity had a purpose. Those who had fallen on hard times must be helped, but helped to get back on their feet and become useful members of society, not allowed to become permanent burdens on the church or on the state treasury.

With this end in view, the Reformers put a special premium on education. Young people (boys in particular) were expected to learn a trade or pursue academic study with a view to entering one of the professions. Ideally, all children would receive an education, and public schools were set up in as many places as possible to achieve this goal. It was not a perfect system, and universal, compulsory, free education had to wait until the late nineteenth century, but the desire for it was evident and the Reformers realized this goal to the extent that their resources allowed.

As a result, Protestant countries witnessed the emergence of a new social class that gradually became dominant to the point of near universality. The old world of aristocrats and peasants gave way to a society in which what we now call the middle class became the norm. The peasantry was gradually absorbed into it, and the old aristocracy, never very numerous, retreated into irrelevance. More and more, a man of natural talent could rise to the top and fulfill his ambitions in life. The same people also began to demand political representation to a degree that had never before been possible. In England, for example, the lower house of Parliament, in which the new middle class was represented, became more assertive and eventually more powerful than the House of Lords, which represented the bishops and the nobility.

This process can be traced from the Reformation Parliament of 1529, when the king appealed to the House of Commons for support in his battle to annul his marriage, to 1689, when parliamentary sovereignty (and not the divine right of kings) became the acknowledged basis of government. In between those dates a protracted struggle for power resulted in a civil war and the almost fatal weakening of the old social order.

On the whole this process was gradual and incremental, depending as much on the vagaries of politics as on any concrete plan. But remarkably at least one major Protestant theological treatise was written about the right ordering of secular government and has retained its interest into modern times. Its author was Martin Bucer, one of Martin Luther's earliest disciples, who is credited with introducing the Reformation to what was then the German city of Strasbourg. Bucer is in many respects the forgotten "missing link" of the Reformation. An early Lutheran, he also had great sympathy for the Swiss Reformers and welcomed John Calvin to his city when he was expelled from Geneva in 1538. Bucer was also interested in English developments, and when Strasbourg fell to Catholic forces in 1548 he was invited to take refuge in England, which he did in the following year. Before long he was involving himself in English church affairs, and in 1550 wrote a book called *De regno Christi*, in which he outlined his vision for a truly Reformed society.[5]

The book was not published until 1557 (in Basel), but its original intention was not forgotten. Nearly a century later it was still being

---

[5]The text is available in a modern critical edition, *Martini Buceri Opera Latina XV: De Regno Christi*, ed. F. Wendel (Paris: Presses Universitaires de France and Gütersloh: C. Bertelsmann Verlag, 1955). There is no complete English translation. Most of it appeared in W. Pauck, ed., *Melanchthon and Bucer* (Philadelphia, PA: Westminster Press, 1969), 174-394, but the key section on divorce (book 2, chapters 22-46) was omitted because this part of the text had already been translated by John Milton in his *Judgment of Martin Bucer Concerning Divorce* (London: Matthew Simmons, 1644). It is now readily available in any edition of Milton's prose works. On this subject, see H. J. Selderhuis, *Marriage and Divorce in the Thought of Martin Bucer* (Kirksville, MO: Thomas Jefferson University Press, 1999).

read by English Puritans, some of whom used it as a blueprint for the reforms they wanted to introduce. Bucer was never as influential in England as he wanted to be, and his treatise cannot be read as a guide to what actually occurred in the English Reformation, but it remained as an ideal of what a leading Reformer thought should happen. In that respect it remains the most valuable witness we have concerning what a truly Reformed state might look like.

The work is divided into two books. The first contains fourteen chapters, the first five of which explain the history of the church as the kingdom of Christ. From there Bucer discussed how the church should administer its discipline and sacraments. On the whole, he denounced those who would impose particular disciplines as essential for the spiritual health of the church, but he recognized that in most cases traditional practices should be retained, as long as nobody tried to rely on them for their salvation. Typical of his approach is the way he addressed the question of fasting, which the medieval church had fixed for the period of Lent, forty days before Easter. Should this custom be retained? Bucer rejected that as a matter of principle, but he added,

> However, since the Lord himself and his apostles so highly recommended fasting to the churches, certainly they who observe no fasting at all cannot glory in the spirit and sovereignty of Christ. It is necessary, therefore, for those who wish to see the Kingdom of Christ solidly restored to retrieve the discipline of fasting, at least on some days of the year.[6]

Most modern Protestants would find Bucer's advice strange, to say the least, but it was taken seriously in post-Reformation England, where fast days were periodically proclaimed as late as 1857.[7]

---

[6]Pauck, *Melanchthon and Bucer*, 254.
[7]For a complete list of them, see N. Mears et al., eds., *National Prayers: Special Worship Since the Reformation* (Woodbridge, UK: Boydell and Brewer, 2013–2017), 1.cxiii-cxlvii. To mention but one example, the British government enjoined fasting on the nation no fewer than six occasions during the American War of Independence.

Of particular interest is Bucer's insistence on the establishment of
regular poor relief, another injunction that was taken more seriously
than most modern people imagine.[8] The first comprehensive Poor
Law in England was enacted in 1563 and went through several revisions, each of which was intended to make the system work better.[9]

In Bucer's second volume he devoted his attention to the reformation of society outside of the immediate confines of the institutional
church. In sixty-one chapters he covered everything from the preaching of the gospel to prison reform. Bucer realized that unless people
were persuaded of the need to reform society, nothing much would
be done about it, and so he gave priority to preaching and evangelism,
devoting no fewer than eight chapters to the subject. He then went
on to introduce what he called fourteen laws, starting with the education of children and moving to the conduct of public worship, the care
of church buildings, the provision of a regular ministry, the proper
administration of church resources, and—once again—poor relief.
Most of these things were subsequently incorporated into the *Second
Book of Homilies*, which was produced in 1563 and which the clergy
were expected to use in teaching their congregations.[10]

Extraordinarily, at least from a modern point of view, Bucer devoted no fewer than thirty-two chapters to questions of marriage and
divorce. Bucer upheld the sanctity of marriage, but he also wanted to
introduce civil divorce, which had not previously existed. This was
not because he wanted to encourage it but because he recognized that
a system that permitted only separation or annulment (in which latter case the children were illegitimate and therefore disinherited) led
to even worse abuses. It must be said, however, that Bucer's views,
while common enough nowadays, caused great disquiet at the time,

---

[8]Pauck, *Melanchthon and Bucer*, 256-59.
[9]It remained in force until 1948, when the modern welfare state replaced it.
[10]See G. L. Bray, ed., *The Books of Homilies: A Critical Edition* (Cambridge: James Clarke,
2015).

and the chapters dealing with the subject were sometimes omitted from printed editions—and certainly never given much of an airing. It was left to the Puritan poet John Milton (1608–1674) to resurrect them, largely because he had an unhappy marriage himself, but he failed to persuade his contemporaries of the justice of Bucer's proposals, and they did not resurface until the nineteenth century.

The eighth of Bucer's laws, to which he devoted seven chapters, is also of particular interest. It covered the provision of education for young people, which Bucer thought should be geared to teaching boys a trade and establishing them in profitable labor. As part of that, idleness was to be reproved, public inns were to be monitored, and leisure activities, which for Bucer included not only sports in the modern sense but also theatrical performances and hunting, ought to be strictly regulated. His opinion is worth quoting:

> In charge of these sports . . . there should always be men singularly experienced in the field involved, men of universal wisdom most zealous for all piety and virtue, who are admired and therefore have the authority and power to relate and to adapt all youthful sport to a zeal for and practice of the virtues, which is the one goal of all sports among Christians; for we have been created for the praise of God and the glory of his name and we have been redeemed by the blood of the Son of God in order to obtain the salvation of our neighbors and not in order to be destroyed in pernicious buffoonery and empty vanity.[11]

Bucer's approach was controversial at the time and was generally resisted by the state authorities, but it became part of the Puritan program and was one of the main causes of their disaffection in the early seventeenth century. Hard as it may be to believe now, fulfilling this vision was one of the main reasons for the Pilgrim Fathers

---

[11]Pauck, *Melanchthon and Bucer*, 253.

to leave England and set out to found a New England across the
Atlantic, where they could be free to ban such evils as football and
dancing—which they lost no time in doing.[12]

Bucer's ninth law envisaged strict controls on luxury goods and
what he called "harmful expenses," a theme that had preoccupied
pre-Reformation preachers and that would continue into modern
times. Basically, Christians should dress and behave modestly and
without extravagance, something that in the sixteenth century was as
common among fashionable men as it was among women. Paintings
of the period show Reformed worthies dressed in black and with a
generally somber demeanor, which is what Bucer was trying to encourage. It is probably fair to say that over time his proposals have
had more success with men than with women, since today the "dark
suit and tie" formula is almost universal among businessmen and public figures around the world, although few people today would think
of this in religious terms. But Bucer, addressing King Edward VI,
had no doubts:

> Your Majesty will give to his people vestiary and sumptuary
> laws; he will control all luxury in housing, dining, dress, and
> adornment in such a way that, as he will happily arouse, pro-
> mote and strengthen a necessary modesty in Christians and
> frugality among his people, so he will also remove great public
> and private damage from his realm which results in these days
> from those extravagant luxuries in trifles that are devised both
> in foreign lands and at home.[13]

Bucer's remaining laws deal with the reform and administration of
justice. He advised the king to appoint sober and serious men to review and revise the entire legal system so as to ensure the maximum

---

[12]By *football* we mean all ball games played with the feet. The modern distinctions between
soccer, American football, and rugby were unknown in earlier times.

[13]Pauck, *Melanchthon and Bucer*, 257.

honesty and efficiency in the transaction of business, both public and private. He paid special attention to the need to appoint worthy magistrates and responsible judges because unless the laws were administered in the right way, they would be brought into disrepute and the entire reform project would collapse.

He concluded the whole work with some advice about the trial and punishment of miscreants. Bucer insisted that everyone was entitled to a fair hearing and to what we would now call due process, and he believed that punishments should fit the crimes committed. Here, however, we notice that his idea of what was a serious crime was strikingly different from anything we would be comfortable with today. Basically, he thought that anyone convicted of breaking one of the Ten Commandments should be put to death because such a person was a mortal danger to society. In his mind this meant that

> in every state sanctified to God capital punishment must be ordered for all who have dared to injure religion, either by introducing a false and impious doctrine about the worship of God or by calling people away from the true worship of God, for all who blaspheme the name of God and his solemn services.[14]

In other words, anyone who remained loyal to the pope ought to be put to death. Bucer would no doubt have included the Anabaptists in his proposed holocaust, but it is not clear whether his strictures were intended to dispose of other kinds of Protestant as well. What we can say with some certainty is that although Protestants often disagreed with one another, and sometimes came to blows, on the whole they were more tolerant of each other than they were of Catholics. That was certainly true of the English Puritans, and particularly of their leader, Oliver Cromwell (1599–1658). He was the kind of person Bucer would have wanted as a parliamentarian or magistrate in

---

[14]Pauck, *Melanchthon and Bucer*, 278.

his ideal society. He was a sincere Christian who wanted a country
that would conform to biblical principles, but he was not intolerant of
those who differed from him, as long as he thought they were filled
with the Holy Spirit. That included men like the Quaker George Fox
(1624–1691), with whom he often had theological debates but whom
he never tried to silence. But it was a different matter with Catholics.
Cromwell did not attempt to massacre them, as some hostile legends
have suggested, but he denied them civil rights and imposed harsh
penalties on them if they rebelled. Bad as that seems to us now, in his
own time he was quite restrained. Protestants who found themselves
trapped in Catholic countries quite often were put to death for reasons remarkably similar to Bucer's, and we must bear that in mind
when trying to assess Cromwell's policies and career.

Cromwell was a member of the English Parliament, but he did not
believe that it was the people who had elected him to establish the
kingdom of Christ on earth—his commission had come from God,
not from man. He thought of his armies as an instrument of divine
wrath, and he did not hesitate to exercise what he saw as godly discipline over his troops. The book of Joshua was his field manual as much
as any military handbook. Cromwell is famous, but he was by no
means unique. In the Netherlands, the struggle for independence
from Spain was led by William the Silent, prince of Orange,[15] who
had a similar understanding of his calling from God. The French
Protestants were much the same, and their great leaders were almost
all military men. So was King Gustavus Adolphus of Sweden, the
"Lion of the North" who rescued German Protestantism from near
destruction in the Thirty Years' War. These men and others like them
were fighting what to them was the Lord's battle, wanting not so much
power and glory for themselves as the freedom to develop their Protestant societies in their own way. The Reformers had not originally

---

[15]A city next to Avignon in the south of France.

envisioned this, or anything like it. Martin Luther would have preferred a Reformation based on spiritual revival in the church without any interference from lay authorities. It was only when that did not happen, and when it became apparent that without secular support he was likely to lose his life at the hands of papal heresy hunters, that he turned to the German princes for help. Those who responded to him soon discovered that they could not survive either unless they banded together and fought the emperor and his troops, which they did accordingly. They were by no means always victorious. In one notorious case, Huldrych Zwingli of Zurich was actually killed in a battle meant to protect his reformation in that city, and after Luther's death the German Protestants were so badly defeated that many of them were forced to flee the country.[16] Modern readers may deplore this recourse to arms, and the Bible could not be used to justify it, but the circumstances of the time were such that there was really no alternative. Had they not done so, they would have been crushed by their enemies, who bear at least as much responsibility for what happened.

THE STRUCTURE OF CHURCH GOVERNMENT

An important element of Reformation theology was the question of the church—what it was and how it should be governed. Virtually all the Reformers agreed that "the visible Church of Christ is a congregation of faithful men, in the which the pure Word of God is preached, and the Sacraments be duly administered according to Christ's ordinance."[17]

---

[16]Thomas Cranmer, archbishop of Canterbury, took advantage of this situation and invited several of them to England. Among those who went was Martin Bucer, who was appointed Regius Professor of Divinity in the University of Cambridge, where he died less than a year later.

[17]Article 25 of the Church of England (1563), in G. L. Bray, ed., *Documents of the English Reformation*, 2nd ed. (Cambridge: James Clarke, 2004), 298; J. Pelikan and V. Hotchkiss, eds., *Creeds and Confessions of Faith in the Christian Tradition* (New Haven, CT: Yale University Press, 2003), 2:534-35; and J. T. Dennison, *Reformed Confessions of the Sixteenth and Seventeenth Centuries in English Translation* (Grand Rapids: Reformation Heritage Books, 2008–2014), 3:762-63.

No one would take an issue with such a statement, but it was a different matter when doctrinal theory had to be translated into pastoral practice. Who was to decide what constituted the pure preaching of God's Word or the due administration of the sacraments? Before the Reformation this had not been a problem. Whatever the papacy authorized was fine, and in contrast to what would become the norm later on, the pre-Reformation church was usually quite tolerant of variety. There was no fixed form of worship, preaching was patchy and often carried out by itinerant friars rather than parish priests, and devotional practices had a way of imposing themselves over time. A good example of that was the withdrawal of the Communion cup from the laity, which occurred sometime in the fourteenth century. Nobody knows for sure how or why it happened, although in some places it may have been a measure of hygiene against the plague. The matter only came up when it was contested by the Bohemian Brethren, who insisted that it was unscriptural and should therefore be stopped. The church authorities chose to interpret this as a challenge to them, and at the Council of Constance in 1415 they decreed that it was lawful for a communicant to receive only the bread. The theological justification for this was that the bread represented the body, and since bodies all have blood in them, there is no need for a separate cup. After that was decided, Communion in one kind became the norm everywhere, although it was never made compulsory. Even the imposition of clerical celibacy was a disciplinary rule, not a doctrine, and could be dispensed with, as it was on occasion. Critics could accuse the church of inconsistency and hypocrisy in such matters, but at least everybody knew where to go for a final decision if there was a controversy.

In principle, the Reformation did nothing except change the court of appeal from the papacy to the Bible. Some of the apostles were married, so clerical celibacy could not be enforced on everyone. Communion in both kinds was practiced at the Last Supper, so it too ought to be restored. Matters of this kind were relatively easy to resolve, and almost all Protestant churches agreed on these apparently obvious points. But what if they did not? If a preacher denied the Trinity, for example, who had the right to discipline him? More importantly, who decided what qualifications a preacher ought to have and how those would be recognized? Was it enough to have a university degree, or should other things, like spiritual maturity, be taken into consideration? And who could possibly go around every church, every week, to make sure that the sermons were all faithful to Scripture? What everyone thought was desirable was in fact very difficult, if not impossible, to put into practice without clear guidelines and some means of enforcing them to prevent abuse.

When it came to setting up a viable system of church government, the Reformers were never able to agree. They all believed that what they were doing was scriptural, and in a sense it probably was. They could usually appeal to the New Testament in support of their practices, but they did so without regard to the limitations of the biblical evidence or to the context in which the first churches operated. Today most people accept that it is impossible to organize a church exclusively on the basis of what we find in the New Testament. We think that we know a lot about what went on in Corinth, for example, but in fact most of our information is circumstantial. We hear so much about it because of its dysfunction, not because Paul thought it was a model congregation. In particular, we have no idea how, when, or where its chaotic worship services took place. We know that it had elders of a kind but not how they were chosen or what they did. We have a detailed description of the Lord's Supper in 1 Corinthians 11, with one notable omission—Paul never says who ought to preside at it. We know that the celebration was often disorderly, but was keeping order the test of whether it was being duly administered? What did that actually mean?

One problem was that the Reformers never adequately addressed the fact that there were no longer any apostles to whom an appeal could be made. Paul did not hesitate to instruct churches what to do, even when he had not been there himself (as in the case of Rome, of all places), but that was what the pope did, and the Reformers rejected him. That meant that they could not re-create the New Testament church, even if they had wanted to. The only practical alternative was for each "local" church to decide for itself what to do, which opened a Pandora's box of difficulties. For a start, what did local mean? For some, each particular congregation had to formulate its own policies. That might have worked at a time when churches were widely dispersed and most people did not know what went on in neighboring congregations, but in the sixteenth century this was no longer the case. Churches were crowded together in the cities, and even in the countryside it was seldom difficult to get to the next village. If what was going on in a neighboring congregation was substantially different, who could decide whether it was acceptable? We know that the Reformers had to deal with outbreaks of pseudo-prophecy and open rebellion against the authorities, preached by self-appointed charismatic leaders whose views might include belief in the imminent return of Christ or in "free love" among consenting adults. It was all very well for others to say that these things were not the pure Word of God, but who could put a stop to them, particularly if there was a real risk that ignorant people would be caught up in a popular movement of revolt that could only end in disaster?

Faced with this kind of problem, Luther had little choice but to rely on the secular authorities for assistance. He did not care whether the church had a bishop or a council of ruling elders, as long as its affairs were conducted in a decent and seemly order. Given that Protestantism spread thanks to the support and encouragement of the German princes and city councils, it was only natural that they should be the ones to fulfill this task. As a result, the church became a department of state, governed by the same principles and the same people. This situation has been modified to some extent over time, but the traditionally Lutheran countries of northern Europe are still much more closely tied to the secular state than other Protestant churches are, even to the point where their clergy are paid as civil servants. They retain bishops, but the nature of their episcopacy is not altogether clear. The Church of Sweden, for example, claims that its bishops stand in the "apostolic succession," but the Church of Denmark rejects this, making mutual recognition of their ministries extremely difficult, even though in all other respects they are virtually the same. The problem is that one "local" church has reached a decision on this matter that is different from another, with the result that relations between them are compromised.

The Swiss Reformers found themselves in a different position, which was reflected in the way they organized their churches. The main cities of Switzerland (Zurich, Bern, Basel, and Geneva) accepted the Reformation because their councils voted for it, so they were in a strong position to determine what sort of church they wanted. This was particularly obvious in Geneva, where Guillaume Farel (1489–1565) and his younger associate, John Calvin, were both expelled from the city in 1538 because the reforms they were trying to implement were too extensive to be tolerated by the ruling class. But the Genevans soon could not maintain the Reformation they wanted without the guidance of professional pastors, and three years later Calvin was invited back and given much freer rein over church affairs. From Calvin's point of view, this freedom was never great enough, and he often sparred with the city council, but he did manage to insist that the church and the state should operate independently of one another. This was not separation in the modern sense, however, because nobody could be a councilor unless he was a member in good standing of the church, which gave the latter a degree of control over the city that Calvin thought was perfectly appropriate.

Church affairs were governed by consistories, which were established at both the parish and city levels, ensuring collective decision making both within and beyond individual congregations. Basically, the general synod of the city approved the ordination of ministers, the patterns of worship that would be used, and catechetical material for the lay people. The congregational elders would then ensure that these provisions were actually implemented, that discipline would be maintained, and that offenders would be reported to the authorities. In theory, the elders were elected by the congregations and anyone could be chosen for their office, but the social class system could not be ignored, and in practice only the more prominent citizens were elected. Even so, the duties were kept separate. A man might be a city councilor and a local church elder, but if so, he functioned in two distinct capacities that did not overlap.

This Calvinistic pattern was especially well-suited to Reformed churches that had to function in countries where Protestants were a minority, as was the case in France. We do not know whether it could have survived if the French king had become Protestant and taken his country out of the Catholic church, but it is unlikely. Collective leadership did not sit well with the monarchy, and most probably one eventually would have given way to the other. We know this because of what happened in the British Isles. When England broke with the papacy in 1534, the structures of the church were left unchanged. The king took over some of the powers previously invested in the pope, like the appointment of bishops, but for the most part, the archbishop of Canterbury was the residual legatee of Rome, and it was up to him, in concert with his fellow bishops, to determine what the doctrine and worship of the church would be. Henry VIII was never too happy with what his archbishop wanted to do, and he constrained him as much as possible, while his loyal archbishop acquiesced in that because he knew that if he did not, the Reformation itself would be endangered.

But that situation was inherently unstable and did not last. Henry VIII was succeeded by his nine-year-old son Edward VI

(r. 1547–1553), and the archbishop was appointed to the regency council, with special responsibility for church affairs. He promptly set about fashioning a genuine Reformation, which included a confession of faith (the Articles of Religion), a pattern of worship (two Books of Common Prayer, one in 1549 and another more radical one in 1552), and a book of sermons, or "homilies" that the clergy were meant to use as a means of expounding Protestant doctrine to their congregations. These reforms were cut short by the king's early death, and the country reverted to Catholicism under his successor, Mary I (r. 1553–1558). This return to Rome was initially accepted by Parliament, but it soon became apparent that it would not work. Rome wanted a degree of control over the church that even many of its supporters were reluctant to grant, and Mary started persecuting leading churchmen who had done nothing but loyally follow her father's orders. She even gave back some of the monastic property that Henry VIII had seized when he dissolved the monasteries, and that lost her the support of everyone who had gained land after the dissolution. When she died, her sister Elizabeth I (r. 1558–1603) not only restored the situation that had obtained at her brother's death five years earlier but also allowed her newly appointed bishops and senior clergy to revise the doctrinal formularies that had been adopted in his time.

To many English Protestants, the accession of Elizabeth I was an answer to their prayers. Exiles in Geneva, who had been preparing a new translation of the Bible, seized their opportunity and printed a pointed address to her in their preface to what became known as the Geneva Bible. Citing numerous examples from the Old Testament of how God had used different men to restore true worship in Israel, they told the queen,

> When we weigh . . . how much greater charge God hath laid
> upon you in making you a builder of his spiritual temple, we

cannot but partly fear, knowing the craft and force of Satan our
spiritual enemy and the weakness and inability of this our nature; and partly be fervent in our prayers toward God that he
would bring to perfection this noble work which he hath begun
in you, and therefore we endeavor ourselves by all means to aid,
and to bestow our whole force under your grace's standard,
whom God hath made as our Zerubbabel for the erecting of
this most excellent temple, and to plant and maintain his holy
Word to the advancement of his glory, for your own honor and
salvation of your soul, and for the singular comfort of that great
flock which Christ Jesus the great shepherd hath bought with
his precious blood, and committed unto your charge to be fed
both in body and soul.[18]

In particular, Elizabeth was enjoined to copy the examples of Asa,
Jehoshaphat, Josiah, and Hezekiah, kings of ancient Judah who had
banished idolatry from their realm and promoted the true knowledge and worship of God. The Reformers believed that following the
depredations of Queen Mary and her "papist" supporters, England
and Ireland were in the same dire straits as Judah had been when
those godly kings had come to the throne, and the precedent was to
serve as her example. Moreover, what Elizabeth could do in her territories would be seen and admired throughout Christendom. She
had been preserved through many dangers in her early life and was
called for this task, and she need have no doubt that God would equip
and sustain her for it:

For the eyes of all that fear God in all places behold your countries as an example to all that believe, and the prayers of all the
godly at all times are directed to God for the preservation of

---

[18]"The Preface to the Geneva Bible," para. 3, in Bray, *Documents*, 356; and Gerald Bray, ed.,
Translating the Bible from William Tyndale to King James (London: Latimer Trust, 2010),
103-4.

your Majesty. For considering God's wonderful mercies toward
you at all seasons, who hath pulled you out of the mouth of the
lions, and how that from your youth you have been brought up
in the Holy Scriptures, the hope of all men is so increased that
they cannot but look that God should bring to pass some wonderful work by your grace to the universal comfort of his
Church. Therefore even above strength you must show yourself
strong and bold in God's matters; and though Satan lay all his
power and craft together to hurt and hinder the Lord's building, yet be you assured that God will fight from heaven against
this great dragon, the ancient serpent, which is called the devil
and Satan, till he have accomplished the whole work and made
his Church glorious to himself, without spot or wrinkle.[19]

Elizabeth I no doubt knew what the Reformers expected of her,
although it is fair to say that, given their great hopes, she turned out
to be something of a disappointment. But although they would grow
impatient with the slowness of her progress in the direction they had
mapped out for her, she was closer to their way of thinking than they
may have realized. Elizabeth operated both as head of state and as
supreme governor of the church, but she kept the two roles separate.
She was not a fan of Calvin's Geneva, which was too radical for her
tastes, but she nevertheless implemented a far-reaching reformation
of the church in England. The main difference between what she instituted and what happened in Geneva was that in England lay people
had no representation in the church synods (or "convocations" as they
were called) but could express their views only through Parliament,
which Elizabeth kept firmly away from church affairs. People who
wanted a more thoroughgoing Reformation than what the queen was
prepared to allow were forced to voice their concerns in and through

---

[19]"Preface to the Geneva Bible," para. 10, in Bray, *Documents*, 359-60; and Bray, *Translating the Bible*, 108.

a largely impotent House of Commons, the lower house of Parliament, but they were relatively free to do so and gained increasing sympathy for their views as time went on.

Meanwhile, Scotland had adopted a Reformation of its own in 1560, which Elizabeth had encouraged and supported. The Scottish queen, known to us as Mary Queen of Scots, was absent in France, and although she returned after the death of her husband, King François II, her Catholicism and her female sex made her unpopular and ultimately unacceptable to the Protestant rulers of the country. They had lost no time in setting up a Geneva-style system of church government, with a General Assembly of the church paralleling Parliament and operating on Calvinist lines to a degree unknown in England. Mary was allowed to marry, but soon after she produced a son she was sent into exile and the son was proclaimed king as James VI (r. 1567–1625). James was brought up to be a model Reformed ruler, which meant that he did what the church told him. This was music to the ears of the English Protestants, who suspected that James would succeed Elizabeth when she died (because he was her closest living relative), even though Elizabeth herself refused to name a successor. Unknown to anyone, however, James grew up to resent the control exercised over him, and he longed to escape from it. His opportunity arrived when he became king of England in 1603, and a new phase in the development of the Reformed churches of Britain began.

James I (as he was called in England) wanted to unite both his crowns in a new kingdom of Great Britain, but that would also mean uniting two rather different churches. The problem was not doctrinal, but political. The English and the Scots more or less agreed on doctrine, but they differed over church government. The Scots had not abolished episcopacy, as many people now think, but they had modified it considerably. Scottish bishops had become no more than regional superintendents, charged with overseeing churches that operated on what were more or less Genevan lines. James wanted to restore these bishops to the position that their English colleagues enjoyed, which would have meant eliminating the collective leadership that prevailed lower down the scale and might even have called the existence of the General Assembly into question. Meanwhile, he also tried to improve the financial situation of the English church by restoring many of the revenues that had been confiscated or sequestered in the sixteenth century and by revitalizing a series of "high commission" courts whose task it was to implement church discipline. These courts were originally established by Elizabeth I in 1559, but they had fallen into disuse, and many English pastors were "pushing the envelope" of church discipline by abandoning the approved clerical dress, for example, or by praying in their own words instead of those of the Book of Common Prayer.

James's efforts failed, and he was wise enough not to pursue them. His one success was issuing a new translation of the Bible, although (despite what most people today think) it was never officially authorized for use. It did, however, eventually appeal to all the factions in the English church and to the Scots, so that nowadays all English-speaking Protestants think of it as the classical translation of the Bible. By then James himself had died and been succeeded by his inept and uncompromising son, Charles I (r. 1625–1649). Far from abandoning his father's policies, Charles decided to enforce them rigorously. The high commission courts became active to a degree that they had never been before, with the result that many Protestants of more "puritan" convictions were persecuted or driven to emigrate across the Atlantic. In Scotland, Charles forced an English-style episcopacy on the church and even imposed a version of the English Book of Common Prayer. The upshot was rebellion. The Scots would not accept such interference by the secular ruler in the affairs of the church, and in 1638 the General Assembly abolished episcopacy altogether.

Charles invaded the country in an attempt to restore his kind of order, but he failed. Meanwhile, the English Parliament had to be recalled (after a gap of almost eleven years) in order to vote the taxes necessary for the king to prosecute his war in Scotland. But the Parliament had other ideas. Much to the king's horror, most of its members sympathized with the Scots and refused to do as they were told. The king dissolved it and called for fresh elections, but the new Parliament was even more radical than the old. Before long the country was plunged into civil war, with Parliament fighting the king. In order to secure victory, Parliament needed the support of the Scots, which would not be forthcoming unless it adopted Scottish views on church government, which were now firmly presbyterian. In desperation, Parliament did so, but the move was never very popular in England. Presbyterianism was seen as a foreign import, much as episcopalianism was in Scotland. There were few Parliamentary defenders of the traditional episcopate, but the army preferred something else. Its generals wanted "independency," or as we would now call it, congregationalism, the right of each congregation to decide its doctrine and worship for itself. But this was anathema to the presbyterians, who argued that some form of transcongregational authority was needed in order to ensure uniformity of doctrine and prevent the spread of heresy.

In practice, state control of the church in the British Isles broke down in the 1640s. For the first time, people were allowed to think, say, and do more or less whatever they wanted, and the result was an upsurge of sects that still bewilder historians today. There were the Ranters, who shouted out whatever they felt like, claiming that they were inspired by the Holy Spirit. There were the Levellers, who practiced a primitive form of communism. The Muggletonians followed a man called Ludovic Muggleton, who thought he was one of the two witnesses promised in Revelation 11. Of all these and many more diverse movements, only two still survive, and they are very different now from what they originally were. The larger of them are the Baptists, whose early radicalism has long since been tamed.[20] The others are the Quakers, whose original claim to fame was that their leader, George Fox, would run through the streets naked whenever he felt he was full of the Spirit.[21] In this chaos, every kind of church government—and none—was permitted, the only exceptions being "popery" and traditional episcopacy, both of which were rejected as being unspiritual.

It is not hard to see why the general population got fed up with this, and when the revolutionary spirit ran out of steam, most people were relieved to welcome back the episcopal structures that had been abolished in 1646. Dissent was not completely eliminated, but it was contained, and as time went on it declined in importance. In Scotland, things took a different turn. There, the restoration of episcopacy was not welcomed, and eventually it was abolished once more. From 1690, the Church of Scotland became, as it has remained, a presbyterian church that operates along lines similar to those of the other Reformed churches in Continental Europe. The union of the crowns that James VI and I had desired in 1603 was eventually achieved in 1707, but although the parliaments of England and Scotland were merged into one, the churches were not. To this day, the monarch of the United Kingdom is an episcopalian in England but a presbyterian in Scotland, even though the churches to which she belongs are not in communion with each other. It is a unique reminder of how matters of church government could divide the Reformed world even when it was otherwise united theologically, culturally, and politically.

---

[20]For an indication of what they once were like, see J. F. McGregor, "The Baptists: Fount of All Heresy," in J. F. McGregor and B. Reay, eds., *Radical Religion in the English Revolution* (Oxford: Oxford University Press, 1984), 23-63.

[21]That he survived doing this in the English climate may be regarded by some as proof of divine protection, if not inspiration!

The Reform of Society

The necessity, and later the willingness, to defend Protestantism by force of arms shows that Protestants believed that there was something worth defending that went beyond a particular spiritual experience or hermeneutic of biblical interpretation. Protestantism was a way of life that transformed the people and the societies that adopted it, and the result was sufficiently positive that the recipients were willing to defend it with their lives, if necessary.

At the heart of the godly commonwealth, to use an expression that Protestants often adopted to describe their states, lay the pure worship of God. This consisted of regular church services on Sunday, a day of rest that was given over to religious activities. Obviously, the Reformers did not introduce Sunday worship for the first time. As far back as AD 321 the Emperor Constantine I had made it a day of rest so that Christians could meet together for worship on the day that Christ rose from the dead. But although Sunday had always been special, over the years the picture became more complex. First of all, many additional holy days were added to the calendar. Some of these commemorated events in the life of Christ, a few were set aside to honor the virgin Mary or other New Testament characters like John the Baptist and the apostles, and still others were dedicated to prominent Christians who had been canonized as saints. It is said that in some places these were so numerous that local people might have up to ninety days' holiday (a word derived from "holy day") every year, or an aggregate of three months out of twelve.

At the same time, Sunday became relatively less special as the day was set aside for playing games, socializing, and even shopping after church. In England, there was a custom for the church to sell beer after services, with the profits going to repair the building. These church ales, as they were called, were very popular with the men, and when they were sufficiently merry they would often take a ball and start playing with it—the origin of ball games as we know them today.

The Reformers were unhappy with this situation and did what they could to remedy it. They started by abolishing feast days as much as they could. The Puritans in England even got rid of Christmas, which they regarded (not unreasonably) as a survival of paganism in Christian dress. The observance of Sunday was merged with the Jewish Sabbath and made stricter than it had ever been before. It was a day of rest from normal work, but it was intended to be dedicated to the service of God. That meant several hours of church services, in which the highlight would be a sermon that might last for an hour and a half or more. This could then be followed by a form of adult Sunday school in which the Bible and Christian doctrine were systematically taught to those who attended worship. Needless to say, this conflicted with the church ales and the games that followed them. In England this was such a problem that the Puritans virtually declared war on traditional village culture, which they were determined to stamp out. King James I was so alarmed by this that in 1618 he issued the Book of Sports, which he ordered every clergyman to read from the pulpit. In it he demanded that parishioners should be free to play games on Sunday after church because that was one of the few opportunities people had for innocent recreation.

Some of the Puritans were so incensed by this that they left the country, going first to Holland (where things were not much better) and then heading for America, where they were determined to build their godly commonwealth without interference. In a sense, therefore, it is possible to say that the United States was founded by people who were trying to get away from football, which they regarded as an ungodly pursuit that detracted from Bible study. We smile at this today, but it was a serious matter at the time. In 1633 King Charles I issued the Book of Sports again, in a slightly revised version, with similar injunctions that Sunday sports must be allowed. When civil war broke out in England a decade later, the Puritans began testing local clergy to see whether they were fit to continue in office.

One of the questions they asked was whether the man in question had read the Book of Sports to his congregation. If he admitted that he had, he was sent packing, because such behavior was deemed to be inconsistent with gospel ministry.

To vigilance of this kind was added a concern to root out "heresy." This was a complex subject because few ordinary people knew enough theology to be guilty of any of the recognized Christian heresies. Occasionally somebody might be accused of one, but it was usually possible to demonstrate that the person concerned did not really know what he was talking about; in his ignorance, he could be persuaded to believe anything. This rough-and-ready approach was obviously unsatisfactory because of the injustices that it produced, but it was a different matter with popular superstition, which was rampant among the uneducated. In practice, heresy was interpreted as witchcraft, and the same penalty—death by burning at the stake— was applied to it. In England the last such burning took place in 1612, but the practice endured far longer elsewhere. The Salem witch hunts in Massachusetts took place in 1692–1693, and there was one last case in Scotland as late as 1697. By then there was a general revulsion at the thought of putting people to death for religious reasons, especially since many of them were innocent victims denounced by jealous neighbors and the like. But there can be no doubt that, sad as this history is, it was the product of a genuine desire to root evil out of society so that the godly commonwealth could flourish as the Reformers had wanted it to.

Social discipline of this kind was seen to be necessary for the gospel to thrive unhindered, but it should be said that it was not decided arbitrarily by the local clergyman. On the contrary, justice was normally in the hands of laymen, and in many places it was the responsibility of a consistory of elders who met together for the purpose. These men could be stricter than the theologians, as the case of Calvin's Geneva reminds us. Contrary to popular belief, Calvin was quite tolerant of those who disagreed with him, and he did not believe in persecution. But the city council in Geneva was not so generous. The majority of its members were determined to enforce social and theological conformity, and when someone came along who upset that, there was trouble. That is what happened in the case of the unfortunate Miguel Servetus, a Spaniard who had denied the Trinity and fled to Geneva, wrongly believing that the city would offer him sanctuary. Calvin naturally condemned his heresy, though he pleaded for Servetus to be beheaded instead of burned at the stake. It would have been a more humane punishment, but the city council refused his request.

Poor Calvin took the blame for that, an injustice that has been perpetuated ever since, but the incident proves at least one thing: the Reformation was not a clerical conspiracy to take control of the church. On the contrary, it was very much a lay movement in which church members with no special theological training were fully prepared to judge doctrinal questions and impose what to them was the appropriate penalty. The Servetus case demonstrates that the Reformation was a genuine social movement in which all members of the church were involved, not just the specially trained clerical caste or people who were cut off from wider society.

This participation was made possible by the Reformers' belief in the priesthood of all believers. Everybody had a part to play in the godly commonwealth, and those in positions of power were expected to use it for the glory of God. This is how a ship's captain or an army commander could become a pastor to his men, as many of them were. But the practical effects of this were sometimes rather curious. For example, the authority granted to prominent lay people often meant that the official church was bypassed if those lay people did not like it for some reason. In England local town councils would appoint lecturers to their parish churches who would be paid out of public (or other) funds to preach and teach the gospel when the local minister was thought to be inadequate. These lecturers were all Puritans, of course, and they encouraged a spirit of independence with respect to the official church that made the English Civil War possible. It also meant that practical moral issues were often more important than strictly theological disputes. Unitarians were officially censured but often tolerated at the local level because few people understood what they were saying. But drunkenness and disorderly behavior were clearly diabolical and had to be suppressed, as they often were. The records of the time are full of cases in which ordinary people were censured for things like swearing, and women were often accused of wearing indecent clothing—skirts that revealed their ankles, for example. On October 16, 1634, a certain John Elkins of Isham (Northamptonshire) was fined a hundred pounds for wearing his hat during church services, for using the Communion table as a counter for business transactions and—perhaps worst of all—for telling people that a ploughman was as good as a priest.[22] Mr. Elkins's behavior was boorish, to be sure, but what motivated him? Was he a Puritan, trying to desacralize the church and eradicate the last vestiges of popery? Or was he just a common troublemaker? We have no idea, but the court records are full of similar cases, and it is unlikely that a single cause lay behind them all. Religious radicalism and antisocial conduct shaded into one another, and distinguishing them is often far from easy—or even possible.

The village school was another way in which Reformation values were inculcated in the minds of the population. The sixteenth century was a golden age for the production of primers and catechisms designed to teach reading and writing with the aid of the Bible and theology. The ability to read the Scriptures was fundamental in a church that relied on them for its doctrine and practice, and children were regularly tested on their knowledge of the sacred texts. A book like Proverbs, which few people read today, was popular because of

---

[22]See J. P. Kenyon, *The Stuart Constitution: 1603–1688*, 2nd ed. (Cambridge: Cambridge University Press, 1986), 65.

the practical wisdom it inculcated. Most pupils learned their morality from it and from selected portions of the New Testament, like the Beatitudes in the Sermon on the Mount (Mt 5).

The effectiveness of these methods was striking. There was a genuine correlation in people's minds between Protestantism, education, and intelligence that was virtually impossible to escape. A few rich people were able to retain pre-Reformation habits and practices because they could afford private tutors, and there were remote places where the state did not reach, but these were exceptional. In the British Isles the old ways lingered longest in those regions where most people did not speak English—Wales, the highlands of Scotland, and most of Ireland. This presented the Reformers with a dilemma. Should they translate the Bible and other writings into the local languages, a task that was often costly and laborious, or should they try to persuade people to learn English instead? Here, the reaction was mixed. In several European countries, the Reformation provided the stimulus for translating works into languages that had not previously been written down or disseminated to any great extent. As a result, some of the earliest extant texts in Finnish, Slovenian, Estonian, Latvian, Lithuanian, and even Romanian are portions of Scripture or catechetical materials that were produced at the time of the Reformation for evangelistic purposes.

In the British Isles, translation was encouraged in Wales, but books in Welsh were expensive and the country was poor, so the effect was less than it might otherwise have been. In Scotland, missionaries were sent out to the Gaelic areas, with some success. In Ireland it proved to be much harder to reach the native population, which was still largely tribal in social organization, even though an Irish-language Bible was eventually prepared. The Puritans despaired of these remote places, which seemed to them to be culpably resistant to the truth, and they never made much headway there, despite frequent pleas to Parliament to provide preachers to bring light to "the dark corners of the land." In the eighteenth century, Wales and Scotland were touched by Protestant revival movements that completed the job the Reformers had been unable to finish, but that did not happen in Ireland. The sad result was that Protestants there often regarded the local Catholic population as a lesser breed of humanity and treated it accordingly, which did nothing to improve the situation. They justified this by a rather strange application of the doctrine of election—Protestants were God's chosen people and Catholics were reprobates, made all the more so by the fact that they had rejected the offer of the gospel that had been made to them, even though it had been made in an unknown tongue by people whom they regarded as foreigners.

The real contribution of Protestantism to the development of learning can be measured by the way in which nontheological disciplines progressed after the Reformation. In the early days, Catholics as well as Protestants had been interested in the natural sciences and taken part in the discoveries of the sixteenth century. But as time went on, Catholics were increasingly encouraged to turn their minds elsewhere. Their clergy and monks continued to produce vast tomes of theology and law, and they were superb editors of ancient texts and the like. But when it came to subjects like biology and chemistry, the Protestant world was much more curious and willing to experiment. Sometimes historians account for this by saying that Catholic countries censored new ideas, but that is an oversimplification. In reality, it was the priesthood of all believers, the belief that all vocations were sacred even if they appeared to be secular and that the people of God should be allowed to pursue knowledge wherever it could be found, that tipped the scales in favor of the Protestants. In the sixteenth century the Italian cities and Spain were the centers of European culture, but by 1700 they were in decline and the light of learning had moved north—to the Netherlands in particular, and by extension to Germany and Britain. The modern world would be a Protestant creation, and eventually even the Catholic countries would succumb to it.

The godly commonwealth was a Protestant ideal that came to fruition in northern Europe and Switzerland, but it was not the only kind of Reformation that could be found. Alongside it there was a more radical streak that had appeared at the very beginning and continues to manifest itself as a minority movement (or series of movements). The first wave of these appeared in Switzerland and in the Rhineland within a few years of the outbreak of the Reformation. Today we group them together as Anabaptists because they rebaptized their members as believing adults and rejected the practice of infant baptism, but this is misleading. Rather like modern charismatics, Anabaptists were relatively easy for others to recognize but hard to define precisely. Many of them were primitive communists, holding all their goods in common and therefore necessarily living apart from wider society. Others were social revolutionaries who were determined to overthrow the established order and set up what they claimed was absolute freedom but was in fact a vicious tyranny. Some of their leaders were educated and competent theologians, but others were rabble-rousers who had been thrust into prominence because of their big mouths and compelling personalities. They shared a basic set of beliefs but found it hard to agree on a common platform for social action, so they fell out with each other even more than other Protestants did. They were never able to secure a dominant position in any secular state and were usually persecuted, although in a few places like the Netherlands they were grudgingly tolerated, at least as long as the authorities had other, more serious enemies to fight.

Leaving aside their more extreme traits and representatives, the Anabaptists said that Christianity proclaims a new life that is not of this world. In that respect they were the heirs of the monastic tradition, but they applied it in a new way. Instead of encouraging individual spirituality, they advocated community life. They were profoundly anticlerical and stressed the priesthood of all believers, even to the point of weakening their own internal organization. They rejected all recourse to violence and kept their distance from the secular state. Their insistence on believers' baptism produced a high level of commitment in their members, and those who did not share that were excluded from their fellowship. All Christian churches believed in excommunicating those who did not conform to their beliefs, but the Anabaptists followed through on this to a degree that set them apart. The fact that they were mostly fairly small and gathered congregations, not national churches, made it easier to administer discipline, and they did so with a vigor that resembled the inquisitorial practices of Rome. Article 36 of the Waterland Confession of 1580 states,

> Those excluded from the church are by no means admitted (as long as they persevere in sins) to the communion of the Holy Supper or other ecclesiastical actions, but we deprive them of these and all other privileges by which any communion, fraternity or spiritual participation in sacred things is signified.[23]

A generation later we find the same principle stated even more forcefully in Article 17 of the Mennonite Dordrecht Confession of 1632:

> As regards the withdrawing from, or the shunning of, those who are expelled, we believe and confess, that if anyone, whether it be through a wicked life or perverse doctrine, is so far fallen as to be separated from God, and consequently rebuked by, and expelled from, the church, he must also, according to the doctrine of Christ and his apostles, be shunned and avoided by all the members of the church.[24]

Shunning could cause hardship at times, especially when a community exercised discipline against one of its members but not against

---

[23]W. L. Lumpkin and B. J. Leonard, eds., *Baptist Confessions of Faith*, 2nd ed. (Valley Forge, PA: Judson Press, 2011), 59.

[24]Lumpkin and Leonard, *Baptist Confessions*, 72-73.

his (or her) spouse and children, thereby splitting up families that should have stayed together. But these were exceptions, and although they are regrettable, they do not look so bad when set against the kinds of persecution that those who fell out with the mainline (or "magisterial") Reformers were sometimes subjected to. In the modern world, where church and state have grown apart and where individual profession of faith counts for more than inherited tradition, many aspects of the Anabaptist heritage have come to be appreciated as a witness and a blessing to the whole church. They are certainly more highly regarded today than they ever were in the past, even if some of their ideas have failed to catch on more widely. Their pacifism, for example, is often admired and regarded as an ideal that it would be nice to attain if it were possible, but most people recognize that in a fallen world it is necessary to arm oneself against the threat of evil, however painful and anti-Christian that might appear to be.

Modern Christians mostly live in a secular, pluralist society where church and state are functionally separate and religious beliefs play little part in politics. In some ways this is a good thing, as religious conflict does nothing to further the cause of the gospel and may even be counterproductive, but the absence of spiritual values in the public square has created an atmosphere that is openly hostile to all forms of Christianity, and individual believers face discrimination if they express their convictions publicly. The states we live in usually claim to be liberal, in the sense that they do not impose a particular set of religious beliefs on their populations, but in practice they are often more totalitarian than their sixteenth-century predecessors were. It may be impossible to go back in time and resurrect the conditions that prevailed in those days, but modern Christians, in particular those who believe in the ever-present need for reformation, must surely agree that we must be allowed to find a voice in our pluralist age and use the opportunities we have to proclaim the gospel and persuade others to accept it as the only sure basis for a truly free society.

Six

The Emergence
of Confessional Theology

From Confessing to Confessions

The era of the Protestant Reformation stands out as one of confessional theology. Between 1530 and 1700 at least a hundred formal confessions of faith saw the light of day, and virtually every Protestant group, large or small, produced one or more as statements of its particular beliefs.[1] Many of these confessions have since fallen by the wayside and are little known today, even among historians of the period,

---

[1]The most important of these can be found in J. Pelikan and V. Hotchkiss, eds., *Creeds and Confessions of Faith in the Christian Tradition* (New Haven, CT: Yale University Press, 2003). The second of its three volumes is devoted to the Reformation era, but the Eastern Orthodox confessions that were written in response to Protestantism are in the first volume. The Lutheran confessions are grouped together in Robert Kolb and Timothy J. Wengert, ed., *The Book of Concord: The Confessions of the Evangelical Lutheran Church* (Minneapolis, MN: Fortress Press, 2000). See also Charles P. Arand, Robert Kolb, and James A. Nestingen, *The Lutheran Confessions: History and Theology of The Book of Concord* (Minneapolis, MN: Fortress Press, 2012); and F. Bente, *Historical Introductions to The Book of Concord* (St. Louis, MO: Concordia Press, 1965). The most comprehensive collection of non-Lutheran Reformed confessions is J. T. Dennison, *Reformed Confessions of the Sixteenth and Seventeenth Centuries in English Translation* (Grand Rapids: Reformation Heritage Books, 2008–2014). See also the original texts in H. Faulenbach and E. Busch, eds., *Reformierte Bekenntnisschriften*, 8 vols. (Neukirchen-Vluyn: Neukirchener Verlag, 2002–2016). For a comparative presentation of the Belgic Confession (1561), the Heidelberg Catechism (1563), the Second Helvetic Confession (1566), and the Westminster Standards (1646–1648), see Joel R. Beeke and Sinclair B. Ferguson, eds., *Reformed Confessions Harmonized* (Grand Rapids: Baker, 1999). For Anabaptist and Baptist confessions of the Reformation era, see W. L. Lumpkin and B. J. Leonard, eds., *Baptist Confessions of Faith*, 2nd ed. (Valley Forge, PA: Judson Press, 2011).

but others attained iconic status and are still in use. Among these are the Lutheran Augsburg Confession (1530), the French Reformed Confession of La Rochelle (1559), the Anglican Thirty-Nine Articles (1571),[2] and the basically Presbyterian Westminster Confession of Faith (1646), which spawned a number of other confessions that are more or less revisions of it, like the Baptist Second London Confession of 1689.[3] There were even confessions of faith produced by the Eastern Orthodox churches, which felt that they had to respond to the upheaval in the West. One of these, the Confession of Cyril Lucaris, patriarch of Constantinople (1629), was strongly influenced by Calvinism.[4] Two others, that of Peter Moghila (1642) and that of Dositheus, patriarch of Jerusalem (1672) were essentially reactions to Lucaris and closer in tone to the teaching of the Roman Catholic Church.[5] Rome, interestingly enough, did not produce a confession of its own, but the canons of the Council of Trent (1545–1563) had much the same effect.[6] They were conceived as anti-Lutheran but were broad enough in scope to cover all other forms of Protestantism, and so the church never felt a need to supplement them in order to take account of later developments in Reformed theology.

In a sense, the composition of systematic confessions of faith went back to the early church. The ancient creeds can be viewed in that

---

[2]An earlier version was drafted in 1563, which in turn was a revision of the original Forty-Two Articles of 1553. For the text of all three compared, see G. L. Bray, ed., *Documents of the English Reformation*, 2nd ed. (Cambridge: James Clarke, 2004), 284-311. The final (current) version is printed at the end of the Book of Common Prayer (Cambridge: Cambridge University Press, 2004).

[3]Bray, *Documents*, 486-520; Pelikan and Hotchkiss, *Creeds and Confessions*, 2:601-49; Dennison, *Reformed Confessions*, 4:230-72.

[4]Dennison, *Reformed Confessions*, 4:154-63; Pelikan and Hotchkiss, *Creeds and Confessions*, 1:549-58. On Lucaris, see George A. Hadjiantoniou, *Protestant Patriarch* (Richmond, VA: John Knox Press, 1961); and Steven Runciman, *The Great Church in Captivity* (Cambridge: Cambridge University Press, 1968), 259-88. Lucaris wrote his confession in 1629.

[5]For Moghila's confession, see Pelikan and Hotchkiss, *Creeds and Confessions*, 1:559-612. For that of Dositheus, see Pelikan and Hotchkiss, *Creeds and Confessions*, 1:613-35.

[6]See N. P. Tanner, ed., *Decrees of the Ecumenical Councils* (Washington, DC: Georgetown University Press; London: Sheed and Ward, 1990), 2:660-99.

light, and for many centuries they served as the basis of Christian teaching. The creeds had the great advantage of being short and could be easily memorized by people who were either illiterate or had limited access to written material. From the time of Charlemagne (around AD 800) they were included in the church's liturgies—the Apostles' Creed in the daily offices and the so-called Nicene Creed in the Lord's Supper—so they became familiar to most people. The Reformers adopted them as their own and interpreted them in much the same way as their medieval forebears had done, a fact they used in order to underline their essential orthodoxy in matters of faith. Protestantism might have been a new kind of Christianity, but it was not heretical, at least not by the standards of the early church.

Whether Martin Luther would ever have written a confession of faith on his own initiative is impossible to say. His Ninety-Five Theses were propositions for theological debate, not a confession in the true sense of the word, and composing a statement of his basic beliefs was not one of his priorities. He was much more concerned with expounding the Bible and explaining the importance of the key doctrine of justification by faith alone, as well as with refuting the charges laid against him by his opponents, both Catholic and Reformed. The secular state, in the person of the Emperor Charles V, forced his hand and must be credited with originating the Protestant tradition of confessionalism.

Charles had to know what Luther and his followers believed. They could be neither tolerated nor legally persecuted unless it was clear who they were, and that could be known only by their doctrines. He therefore required Luther to draw up a statement of his theological principles, which he would present to the German diet (parliament) that met at Augsburg in 1530. What we call a confession took the form of a protestation, or an affirmation of what the Reformation stood for. Those who subscribed to it were therefore dubbed Protestants, and the name stuck. Nowadays the label is applied much more widely than it was at the time, since for much of the sixteenth century it referred only to those who accepted the Augsburg Confession as their basis of faith. In 1555 the Holy Roman Empire granted toleration to these Lutherans in German states but not to others. Other kinds of Reformed theology were not taken into account, nor were the divisions among the Lutherans themselves, and opponents of Rome who thought differently from Luther either hid behind the Augsburg Confession or continued to suffer persecution.

By the time of the Augsburg Confession, Luther's reformation was already more than a decade old, and it was no longer unique. The Swiss city of Zurich had initiated a reformation of its own, more or less at the same time as Luther's original protest in Wittenberg, and in the following years there had been a number of outbreaks in different parts of Germany. Some of these, like the rebellion of Thomas Müntzer (1489–1525), who originally followed Luther but broke with him because he thought that Luther was too conservative, were highly contentious and instrumental in provoking a peasants' revolt that threatened to undo the entire social order. Luther could not support that, partly because his notion of the kingdom of God was spiritual rather than political but also because he relied too much on the support of the German princes whose authority Müntzer was undermining. In these circumstances, Luther found himself increasingly under pressure to dissociate himself from such extremism, and a clear statement of his own beliefs helped to do that.

Meanwhile, the Zurich reformers, led by Huldrych Zwingli, were developing their own agenda. Luther had been motivated primarily by abuses arising from the sale of indulgences, which led him to examine the theological structure on which they were built. Before long, he condemned the system of works righteousness, of which indulgences were a part, and proclaimed that justification before God was by faith alone. Zwingli, however, had a different background. He was more concerned with the relationship between spirit and matter, the infinite and the finite. In what way could physical elements like the water of baptism or the bread and wine of the Lord's Supper convey the grace of God? He concluded that they cannot, and although he too arrived at a doctrine of justification by faith alone, he did so by another route. Could these two different approaches be harmonized?

At first there was considerable expectation on both sides that a meeting of minds was possible and should be pursued. Under the auspices of one of Luther's secular supporters, Philip of Hesse (1504–1567), Luther and Zwingli met at Marburg in October 1529, where they managed to agree on fourteen out of fifteen items on the agenda.[7] The first eight were relatively uncontroversial. They covered such things as the Trinity, the incarnation of Christ, the life and work of Christ, original sin, and justification by faith alone. They also agreed, in opposition to radicals like Müntzer, that faith is given by the Holy Spirit in and through the preaching of the Word, not by charismatic (and uncontrolled) interventions.

Somewhat more remarkably, they managed to reach common ground regarding the nature and administration of baptism, saying that "it is not merely an empty symbol or sign among Christians, but a sign and act of God by which our faith is fostered. Through it we are born again to life."[8] This was in answer to the radicals of Zurich, who had repudiated infant baptism on the ground that it was meaningless without faith and had rebaptized themselves as adult believers. They had already produced their own Schleitheim Confession (1527) that outlined their position, so it was necessary for both Luther and Zwingli to state their opposition to it.[9]

---

[7]For the text, see Pelikan and Hotchkiss, *Creeds and Confessions*, 2:791-95; and T. F. Lull, ed., *Martin Luther's Basic Theological Writings*, 2nd ed. (Minneapolis, MN: Fortress Press, 2005), 277-79.

[8]"The Marburg Colloquy," 8, in Lull, *Luther's Basic Theological Writings*, 278; and Pelikan and Hotchkiss, *Creeds and Confessions*, 2:94.

[9]For the text of the Schleitheim Confession, see Pelikan and Hotchkiss, *Creeds and Confessions*, 2:694-703; and Lumpkin and Leonard, *Baptist Confessions*, 22-31.

The two Reformers also concurred on the place of good works in the Christian life, on the voluntary (but also potentially beneficial) nature of private confession, and on the validity of secular government, which some of the more extreme Anabaptists, as well as certain supporters of the papacy, were inclined to reject.[10] Finally, they both agreed that traditions with no basis in Scripture were optional, apart from clerical celibacy, which was condemned as satanic.[11] It is important to recall this broad area of agreement because it throws into relief the one issue in which they could not reach a consensus: the nature of the Lord's Supper. They did agree that it should be administered in both kinds, as Christ had instituted it, and that it was not a work by which one person could obtain grace on behalf of someone else, whether that person was alive or dead. More remarkably still, they both affirmed that

> the sacrament of the altar is a sacrament of the true body and blood of Jesus Christ, and the spiritual reception of this body and blood is particularly necessary for every Christian. Similarly, the use of the sacrament, like the Word, is given and ordained by God Almighty so that weak consciences might be moved to faith through the Holy Spirit.[12]

To the modern mind, such a high degree of convergence would seem to be good enough, but not for those who met at Marburg. They pointed out that "we have not at this time agreed whether the true body and blood of Christ are bodily in the bread and wine," a question to them that was fundamental. Nevertheless, they did not give up hope of eventually finding a formula on which they could make

---

[10]Needless to say, the Anabaptists and the "papists" came at this question from opposite angles. The former were essentially anarchists, whereas the latter wanted a papal monarchy that was superior to earthly states.

[11]"Marburg Colloquy," article 13, in Lull, *Luther's Basic Theological Writings*, 279; and Pelikan and Hotchkiss, *Creeds and Confessions*, 2:95.

[12]"Marburg Colloquy," article 15, in Lull, *Luther's Basic Theological Writings*, 279; and Pelikan and Hotchkiss, *Creeds and Confessions*, 2:95.

common cause. As they put it, "Each side is able to display Christian love to the other (as far as conscience allows). Both sides are praying diligently to Almighty God, that he would confirm us in the right understanding through his Spirit."[13] Tragically, their prayers were not to be answered, and the Marburg Colloquy, instead of being the harbinger of a unity to come, became the moment that later generations would regard as a parting of ways which would eventually produce separate and apparently irreconcilable traditions.

The experience of the Marburg Colloquy taught Luther and his colleagues that further definition of their position was necessary, and they did not hesitate to respond to the emperor's request when it came. They had remarkably little to say regarding the disagreement that had prevented the formation of a common front at Marburg, although the anti-Zwinglian bias was clear: "Of the Supper of the Lord they [the Lutherans] teach that the body and blood of Christ are truly present, and are communicated to those that eat in the Lord's Supper. And they disapprove of those that teach otherwise."[14]

The Augsburg Confession elaborated on what had been agreed at Marburg, along with some other things that Luther and his colleagues evidently thought had to be emphasized in their disagreement with Rome. It is divided into two main sections: the first consisting of twenty-two articles, being a more or less systematic outline of basic doctrines, and the second containing seven much longer headings covering "abuses that have been corrected."[15]

The doctrinal section can be broken down fairly easily according to the subject matter being treated. It starts with four articles dealing

---

[13]"Marburg Colloquy," 15, in Lull, *Luther's Basic Theological Writings*, 279; and Pelikan and Hotchkiss, *Creeds and Confessions*, 2:95.

[14]Augsburg Confession 10, in Bray, *Documents*, 610; Kolb and Wengert, *Book of Concord*, 44-45; and Pelikan and Hotchkiss, *Creeds and Confessions*, 2:64. The Latin original of the last sentence reads, "et improbant secus docentes."

[15]See J. M. Reu, *The Augsburg Confession* (St. Louis, MO: Concordia Publishing House, 2005).

with God, original sin, the incarnation of the Son, and justification by faith. Next come four more articles covering the church, although the order seems somewhat odd to a modern reader. It starts with the ministry of the church, moves to the "new obedience" of the Christian, and only then defines what the church is, in two separate articles. After that, six articles deal with the sacraments, followed by seven more that appear to be in no particular order. These deal with church ceremonies, civil affairs, the return of Christ, free will, the origin of sin, good works, and the "worship" of saints.[16] Finally, there is a concluding summary, which also serves as an introduction to the second section.

The Lutherans were concerned to point out that they did not advocate the abolition of all ceremonies, only a reformation of the way they were performed that would remove superstitious and other inappropriate elements that had crept into them. The items covered are Communion in both kinds, the marriage of priests, the Mass,[17] confession, tradition(s), monastic vows, and the nature and extent of church authority.[18] All of these things were hotly contested by the Reformers, but they were not strictly doctrinal matters and could (at least in theory) be modified or abandoned by the papacy if it chose to do so. As we know, however, it did not, so these essentially secondary items became boundary markers between Protestants and Catholics that have mostly endured to this day.

Luther and his associates insisted on subscription to the Augsburg Confession as proof of genuine Reformed convictions, and it became the touchstone for accepting other Reformed bodies, both in Germany and elsewhere. This caused problems for the Zwinglians

---

[16]The Latin term used for "worship" is *cultus*, which is ambiguous because it can mean either "adoration" (normally used only of God) or "veneration" (a broader concept). Protestants have often interpreted it to be the former, whereas Catholics have always insisted that it is the latter.

[17]The confession retained this word (*missa* in Latin) for the Lord's Supper.

[18]The word used for "authority" is *potestas* (power).

and the other Swiss Reformers who followed his lead, but Luther was not ready to give up on them just yet. Zwingli's unfortunate death in 1531 delayed attempts to follow up the intention of the Marburg Colloquy to find a solution to the question of the presence of Christ in the Lord's Supper, but the discussion was resumed, largely thanks to the intervention of Martin Bucer, who was determined to find a form of words that all could accept. The result was the so-called Wittenberg Concord, thrashed out in May 1536, which stated,

> This institution of the sacrament is efficacious in the church, and depends upon the worth neither of minister nor communicant. Wherefore, as Paul says that the unworthy also eat, so they hold that the body and blood of the Lord are truly extended also to the unworthy, and that the unworthy receive, where the words and institution of Christ are retained. But these partake for judgment, as Paul says, because they abuse the sacrament when they use it without repentance and faith.[19]

Philipp Melanchthon continued to work on the vexed question of the real presence of Christ in the Lord's Supper, and in 1540 he issued a revised version of article 10 in the Augsburg Confession. It now read, "On the Lord's Supper they teach that with the bread and wine the body and blood of Christ are truly exhibited to those who eat in the Lord's Supper."[20]

Luther was still alive at the time, and as far as we can tell, neither he nor anyone else expressed any reservation about Melanchthon's version. They believed it was the same as what was found in the Wittenberg Concord,[21] but in the Smalcald Articles of 1538, Luther had written, "We maintain that the bread and the wine in the Supper are

---

[19]Pelikan and Hotchkiss, *Creeds and Confessions*, 2:799. The Pauline allusion is to 1 Cor 11:27.
[20]Cited from Arand, Kolb, and Nestingen, *Lutheran Confessions*, 75.
[21]See Kolb and Wengert, *Book of Concord*, 320n37.

the true body and blood of Christ and that they are not only offered to and received by upright Christians but also by evil ones."[22]

The assertion that the body and blood of Christ were received by the ungodly, a belief known in Latin as the *manducatio impiorum*, was the tipping point. Those who had been influenced by Zwingli could agree that the sacramental elements revealed the body and blood of Christ to believers who received them by faith, but to say that unbelievers also received the body and blood meant that there must have been some change in the elements themselves, irrespective of the faith of those who received them. This the Zwinglians could not accept. In 1561 Frederick III, elector of the Palatinate in the Rhineland, introduced a Calvinist (in effect Zwinglian) view of the sacrament into his dominions, claiming that Melanchthon's revised text of the tenth article of the Augsburg Confession was broad enough to include it. By then, both Luther and Melanchthon were dead, so no direct appeal could be made to either of them. But to many outside the Palatinate it was clear that Frederick III's understanding of the revised Augsburg text was out of line with what Luther had written in the Smalcald Confession, and they insisted that the original Augsburg text must be restored. That was done in the Formula of Concord (1577) by theologians who deliberately wanted to exclude any possible Calvinistic interpretation. Those who held to the latter opinion were anathematized in article 7, and the door to reconciliation was firmly closed.[23]

The Lutheran attachment to the Augsburg Confession could also create political difficulties. The best example occurred in England after Henry VIII broke with Rome in 1534. Henry was not a Protestant in any doctrinal sense, but he needed allies in his struggle against the pope, and the German Protestants were the only reliable ones available.

---

[22]Smalcald Articles 3.6, in Kolb and Wengert, *Book of Concord*, 320; and Pelikan and Hotchkiss, *Creeds and Confessions*, 2:119-49.

[23]Formula of Concord 7.114; Kolb and Wengert, *Book of Concord*, 13.

They were happy to help but required conformity in matters of doctrine for a genuine alliance to be possible. Henry accordingly sent a small group of theologians to Germany, where they debated with the Lutherans and tried to work out a common basis of faith to which the Church of England would be prepared to subscribe.

In English eyes, the Augsburg Confession was unacceptable for two reasons. First, they saw it as a political document that had been conceived within the framework of the Holy Roman Empire and ratified by its governing authorities. Henry VIII had not broken away from Rome to submit to the Germans (and still less to his nephew Charles V), so signing it was a nonstarter. Henry also did not subscribe to its teachings, or at least not to all of them. A new confession was therefore required that was compatible with Augsburg but tailored to the English scene. The result was the Wittenberg Articles. They were probably composed by Philipp Melanchthon and received Luther's approval, although they were never adopted by any German church. Nor did they get very far in England. In the end, the English theologians who had gone to Wittenberg adapted the articles to their own requirements. The result was the so-called Ten Articles of 1536, which became the first confessional document of the independent Church of England.[24] These articles were a very watered-down version of the Augsburg Confession, but they managed to slip by the eagle eye of Henry VIII. They were subdivided into two different kinds of article. The first five were devoted to doctrinal questions—inherited belief in the Bible, creeds, and early councils of the church; the three sacraments of baptism, penance, and the "Altar" (Lord's Supper); and justification by faith. The second section covered devotional practices—the use of images, the way of honoring the saints, the appropriateness of praying to them, the validity of particular rites and ceremonies, and, finally, purgatory.

---

[24]For the full text, see Bray, *Documents*, 162-74; Pelikan and Hotchkiss, *Creeds and Confessions*, 2:296-310.

The Protestantism of the Ten Articles is most obvious in what they say about justification by faith and about purgatory, the existence of which was called into question, if not actually denied. Yet the article expounding the Lord's Supper is treated in such a way as to make transubstantiation the natural reading:

> Under the form and figure of bread and wine, which we there presently do see and perceive by outward senses, is verily, substantially and really contained and comprehended the very selfsame body and blood of our Savior Jesus Christ . . . and that under the same form and figure of bread and wine the very selfsame body and blood of Christ is corporally, really and in the very substance exhibited, distributed and received unto and of all of them which receive the said sacrament.[25]

Archbishop Thomas Cranmer and his reform-minded colleagues tried to put a Protestant gloss on the Ten Articles in a book called *The Institution of a Christian Man*, published in 1537 and popularly known as the *Bishops' Book*, but much of what it said was controversial and unacceptable to the king, who remained theologically conservative. The result was a revised version that appeared in 1543 and is popularly known as the *King's Book*, which removed most of the earlier volume's Protestant features while continuing to condemn the more obvious abuses of the late medieval church.[26]

Cranmer himself continued to work privately to adapt the Augsburg Confession for English use, and its influence can be seen in the various sets of articles that he drew up over the years. An extensive draft adapting the Augsburg Confession to the English situation has survived among his papers, but it was never published, and England's

---

[25]"Ten Articles," 4, in Bray, *Documents*, 169-70; and Pelikan and Hotchkiss, *Creeds and Confessions*, 2:305.

[26]For the text of both books and a clear examination of the revision process, see G. L. Bray, ed., *The Institution of a Christian Man* (Cambridge: James Clarke, 2018).

"Lutheran moment" passed.[27] When the Church of England was finally free to adopt a clearly Protestant confession of faith, Luther was dead, his followers were dividing, and the theological world had moved on.

By then the Council of Trent had begun its sessions and was producing confessional statements that the Protestants had to answer—Augsburg was no longer sufficient. There was still some hope that the Swiss Reformers, who had never been in full agreement with Luther, might be accommodated in a broader Protestant alliance, and as we have already noted, both Martin Bucer and Philipp Melanchthon were working to that end. The French Reformers based in Geneva and the Swiss Germans in Zurich managed to conclude an agreement in 1549, known as the Consensus Tigurinus.[28] This addressed the question of the real presence of Christ in the Lord's Supper in a way that clearly challenged the stand taken in the Augsburg Confession and subsequently reiterated, albeit in a more moderate way, the Wittenberg Concord of 1536:

> Besides the fact that nothing is received in the sacraments except by faith, it is also necessary to hold that the grace of God is certainly not so tied to them that whoever has the sign receives the thing itself. For the signs are administered to the reprobate as well as to the elect, but the reality only reaches the latter.[29]

---

[27]Bray, *Documents*, 184-221. See H. E. Jacobs, *The Lutheran Movement in England During the Reigns of Henry VIII and Edward VI, and Its Literary Monuments* (Philadelphia, PA: G. W. Frederick, 1890). The question of Lutheran-Anglican relations (and compatibility) was raised again in 1714 when the Lutheran George I inherited the British crown. An argument against their basic harmony was put forward by Thomas Brett, *A Review of the Lutheran Principles* (London: Henry Clements, 1714) and countered by John Lewis, *A Second Review of the Lutheran Principles* (London: J. Baker, 1714). George I became king but had to conform to the Church of England in accordance with the Act of Succession (1701).

[28]For the full text, see Pelikan and Hotchkiss, *Creeds and Confessions*, 2:802-15; and Dennison, *Reformed Confessions*, 1:537-45.

[29]Consensus Tigurinus 17. See Pelikan and Hotchkiss, *Creeds and Confessions*, 2:810; and Dennison, *Reformed Confessions*, 1:43.

In an apparent recognition of the Lutheran point that the same sacrament is administered to all, whether they are worthy to receive it or not, the Consensus Tigurinus goes on to say,

> It is quite certain that Christ, with his gifts, is offered communely to all, and that the truth of God is not overthrown by the unfaithfulness of men, the sacraments always retain their power, but all are not capable of Christ and his gifts and so, on God's part, nothing is changed; but as for men, each receives according to the measure of his faith.[30]

This article respects the objectivity of the sacrament itself, which is duly administered according to a set procedure that is applicable to everyone without discrimination but limits its effect to those who receive it in faith. As the Consensus concludes, "The use of the sacrament is no more profitable to the unfaithful than if they abstained."[31]

For good measure, the Consensus Tigurinus went on to discount any notion of the ubiquity of Christ's ascended body:

> It is particularly necessary to reject every idea of a local presence. For as the signs are present in this world and are perceived with the eyes and touched with the hands, so Christ, as man, is nowhere but in heaven and is to be sought in no other way than by the mind and the understanding of faith.[32]

As the authors of the Consensus Tigurinus understood it, the difference came down to the nature of the connection between the signs (bread and wine) and the things signified (body and blood of Christ). To them, the signs pointed to the realities they signified but were not

---

[30]Consensus Tigurinus 18. See Pelikan and Hotchkiss, *Creeds and Confessions*, 2:810; and Dennison, *Reformed Confessions*, 1:43.

[31]Consensus Tigurinus 19. See Pelikan and Hotchkiss, *Creeds and Confessions*, 2:810; and Dennison, *Reformed Confessions*, 1:43.

[32]Consensus Tigurinus 21. See Pelikan and Hotchkiss, *Creeds and Confessions*, 2:811; and Dennison, *Reformed Confessions*, 1:44.

inseparably bound to them. This only served to exacerbate divisions within the Lutheran camp, where a movement of so-called authentic or Gnesio-Lutherans repudiated the attempts that had been made to reconcile Wittenberg and the Swiss. They succeeded in this, but at the cost of alienating Melanchthon and his followers, the so-called Philippists. A new pattern of alliances was forming, in which the Gnesio-Lutherans claimed the mantle of Luther for themselves and the Philippists united with the Swiss and the French to create what we now call the Reformed branch of the Protestant movement. Unfortunately, instead of looking for a middle way that would unite them, dogmatists on both sides preferred to develop theological systems that would accentuate their differences, leading to a split in the Reformed world that, in one form or another, persists to this day.

Needless to say, all this activity called forth new confessions of faith in which the differences of opinion were spelled out, and those who dissented from whatever line was being promoted were duly anathematized. As Reformed churches sprang up in different places, each of them composed its own confession, so that we now have confessional documents stemming from "Belgium" (the Protestant Netherlands), Scotland, and other places. These confessions were very similar to one another, and there was no sense that they represented rival theologies, but they were geared to the needs of local churches and were not considered to be universal in the way that the Augsburg Confession had been.

The articles adopted by the Church of England have a special interest, not only because in their final form they have remained foundational for the worldwide Anglican Communion but also because they went through a process of revision that is easy to follow and that allows us to measure the changing pulse of Reformed theology in the middle years of the sixteenth century, when Protestant confessionalism was taking root. When the articles were first published in 1553 there were forty-two of them, but ten years later the number had been reduced to thirty-nine, and that remained the same in the final revision of 1571.[33] This was not done simply by dropping three of the original articles but rather by a more thorough revision that took account of theological developments that had occurred in the interim.

The first section of the Thirty-Nine Articles (1-8) expounds "catholic" doctrines that all Christians had traditionally accepted. These included the Trinity, the incarnation of Christ, his descent into hell, his resurrection, the canon of Scripture, the place of the Old Testament in the Christian Bible, and the authority of the three ancient creeds. The 1563 revision added an article on the Holy Spirit that had somehow been overlooked ten years earlier but was in no sense a new doctrine. The most interesting thing about this section is the way that certain traditional beliefs were re-expressed in 1563. For example, the article on Christ's descent into hell, which in 1553 had quoted 1 Peter 3:18 in support of the doctrine, omitted it ten years later, probably because John Calvin had pointed out that it was a misinterpretation of the biblical text. Similarly, in the article on Holy Scripture, the original tolerance for some traditional but unbiblical beliefs "as godly and profitable" was left out because the emphasis was to be placed on Scripture alone (*sola Scriptura*) without any such distraction.

The middle section of the articles (9-34) is by far the most extensive and deals with the controversies prompted by the Reformation. It can be subdivided into those articles that deal with salvation (9-18) and those that touch on the church (19-22), including its ministry (23-26), the sacraments (27-33), and other aspects of worship (34).

---

[33]Bray, *Documents*, 284-311. It should be noted that the Thirty-Nine Articles are officially dated to 1562 because they were approved by the convocation of Canterbury on February 19, 1563 (1562 in the old calendar, where the New Year began on 25 March). The revisions of 1571 were considered to be too unimportant to warrant calling them a new edition, but it is in that form that they have come down to us today. Note, however, that the Protestant Episcopal Church of the United States enacted a further revision in 1801, in which it deleted the reference to the Athanasian Creed in article 8 and all mention of the traditional church-state connection.

Here it is noticeable that the article on grace that had been accepted in 1553 was omitted in the revision, as was one on blasphemy against the Holy Spirit and another on the need to keep the moral law. The first of these dealt with the thorny question of free will, which the revisers evidently thought was too controversial for one formulation of it to be imposed on the church as a whole. Similarly, doubts about what constituted blasphemy against the Holy Spirit seem to have influenced the revisers into dropping any reference to it. The article on the moral law is fully in line with what the Reformers generally taught about it, but again, the question of the ongoing use of the law by Christians seems to have been too controversial for it to be included, and so it too was left out in the revision.

The third section of the articles (35-37) concerns matters directly related to the English Church. Here the most surprising thing is the omission of any reference to the Book of Common Prayer in the 1563 revision, which is particularly interesting in light of subsequent claims by many modern Anglicans that their prayer book is more authoritative than the articles in matters of faith and doctrine. That is obviously not what the revisers thought at the time. Finally, four of the six miscellaneous articles that were appended in 1553 were dropped altogether. These concerned the resurrection of the dead, the question of "soul sleep" after death until the final judgment, millenarianism, and universalism. It is not clear why they disappeared, but they were probably felt to be too controversial and ultimately unnecessary. The last two of the present articles (38-39) deal respectively with the right to hold private property and the legitimacy of oath-taking, two matters that some of the more radical Anabaptist sects had called into question.[34] On the whole, the final version of the articles was a streamlining of the original text that continued to

---

[34]It may be noted in passing that the English Baptists were (and still are) quite happy to accept these articles and have always rejected the more extreme views of some who claim the Anabaptist heritage.

highlight and define the key doctrines of justification by faith and its consequences for the life of the believer and the church, while paring away statements that may have been true in themselves but that ran the risk of distracting the church from its main purpose and creating controversy where none need exist.

When we look at these confessions today we find that they share a broadly similar structure. They begin with general theological principles that for the most part were agreed by all sides in the debates— the doctrines of God, the Trinity, the Scriptures, Christology, the Holy Spirit, and so on. They then move on to the specific issues at stake in the Reformation—the doctrine of salvation, justification by faith, election and predestination, the church, the ministry, and the sacraments. Here we find real differences between Protestants and Roman Catholics as well as disputes among Protestants. Broadly speaking, Protestants tended to agree with each other on the doctrines of salvation but differed when it came to questions relating to the church, the ministry, and the sacraments. Finally, many of the confessions conclude with articles relating to the local situation in which they were composed, or what we would now call denominational distinctives. These might cover church-state relations, the nature of church discipline, and such questions as the lawfulness of taking oaths and the proper observance of the Sabbath.

THE SECOND GENERATION OF PROTESTANT THEOLOGY

In some ways, Luther's death in 1546 marked a turning point in the history of the Reformation. Without his guiding hand, the Protestant movement was set adrift and soon suffered some serious political reverses. The Schmalkaldic (Smalcaldic) League, which had been formed by Protestant princes as a defense mechanism against the emperor Charles V, was smashed in 1547 and forced to disband. In an effort to conciliate the Protestants, Charles V persuaded the German diet, which was meeting once more at Augsburg, to issue a temporary directive that would govern the beliefs and practices of the German churches until the conclusion of the Council of Trent. This temporary solution, or interim, as it was called, was basically Erasmian in tone. It accepted the need for widespread church reform but insisted on recognition of the papacy and of transubstantiation in the Lord's Supper. It also rejected Luther's teaching of justification by faith alone. Several Protestant princes, traumatized by their defeat, accepted the Augsburg Interim and imposed it on their lands, but Melanchthon rejected it, and his example was followed across most of northern Germany. As an alternative, Melanchthon drew up his own interim under the auspices of the elector of Saxony, whose capital was Leipzig, after which his interim came to be named.[35]

The Leipzig Interim relied heavily on the concept of *adiaphora* (things indifferent). Clerical vestments, the use of Latin in worship, and a range of traditional pious practices were not essential to the gospel, so they could be tolerated for the sake of the peace of the church. Justification by faith was compromised by omitting the key word *alone*, and good works, by which Melanchthon meant the practice of the cardinal virtues of faith, hope, and love, were decreed to be necessary for salvation. Many of his erstwhile supporters were shocked by what seemed to them to be apostasy from the teachings of Luther. Melanchthon was trying to make the best of a bad job and was playing for time because he knew that the emperor would not reign for much longer, but others did not see things the same way.[36] Matthias Flacius Illyricus (1520–1575) was so incensed that he resigned his teaching post at Wittenberg and went to join his friend Nicolaus Gallus (ca. 1516–1570), who had taken up a pastoral charge in Magdeburg. The two men made common cause with Nicolaus von

---

[35]See Arand, Kolb, and Nestingen, *Lutheran Confessions*, 175-89, on which what follows is based.

[36]Charles V abdicated on August 27, 1556, and died in Spain two years later (on September 21, 1558).

Amsdorf (1483–1565), who had once been close to Melanchthon but later diverged from him on a number of points, including the "compromise" revision of the Augsburg Confession. Working together, these men criticized the whole concept of *adiaphora*. Perhaps in the refined atmosphere of a university common room it was possible to make light of things like clerical vestments, but in the real world of ordinary people, they mattered. The Gnesio-Lutherans insisted on a radical interpretation of Luther's teaching, with no compromises and no *adiaphora*. If they were persecuted for their dogmatism, then so be it; it was better to suffer for their faith than to compromise merely in order to be tolerated by those who did not share it. As a result of their intransigence, the Lutheran movement was split into warring factions, which was made more complicated by the fact that some people moved back and forth from one to another and Gnesio-Lutherans not infrequently quarreled with the Philippists.

This quarrel had international repercussions when in 1563 Queen Elizabeth I suppressed article 29 of the newly minted Thirty-Nine Articles of the Church of England because she was afraid that it might alienate the Gnesio-Lutherans. This was because the article claims that although unbelievers may receive the sacrament of the Lord's Supper, "in no wise are they partakers of Christ."[37] The Gnesio-Lutherans thought otherwise, and the queen did not want to risk alienating them.[38]

Things got so bad that there was even a resurgence, among some of the Philippists, of the belief that good works were necessary for salvation. The whole question of the relationship between faith and works was reopened, with every conceivable view of the subject being advocated by someone as the correct teaching of the Bible.

---

[37]Bray, *Documents*, 302; Pelikan and Hotchkiss, *Creeds and Confessions*, 2:536; Dennison, *Reformed Confessions*, 3:64.

[38]Eight years later (in 1571) that fear had been overcome and article 29 was restored, placing the Church of England firmly on the side of the Philippists.

Even Flacius came to believe that the grace of God, necessary as it was, nevertheless built on human efforts. The Gnesio-Lutherans tore themselves apart over this. In the process, the notion of the third use of the law, which Melanchthon shared with Calvin, was discounted because it seemed to open the door to belief in the validity of human works in the process of salvation. They believed that those who were born again of the Spirit would live a good life freely and spontaneously, with no need for any sort of law or coercion. That, of course, provoked a counterblast from the Philippists, who claimed that the freedom and spontaneity of which the Gnesio-Lutherans spoke could be produced only by submission to the law.

In this instance the Formula of Concord came down on the side of the Philippists, which was also the view of many Gnesio-Lutherans, but it was sensitive to the charges laid against this position by those who rejected law in any form and did its best to accommodate their view. After stating their own opinion, the authors of the formula went on to state,

> However, in order to avoid all misunderstanding as much as possible and to teach and maintain the real difference between the works of the law and the works of the Spirit, it must be most diligently noted that, when we speak of good works that are in accord with the law of God (for otherwise they are not good works), the word "law" has one single meaning, namely, the unchanging will of God, according to which human beings are to conduct themselves in this life.[39]

On this basis, the Lutherans were united at last, though at the cost of permanently alienating many of the more determined Philippists, who were henceforth identified more closely with what we now call the Reformed churches. This is somewhat ironic, in that the order of

---

[39]Formula of Concord 6.15; Kolb and Wengert, *Book of Concord*, 89.

the twelve articles of the Formula of Concord follows Melanchthon's *Loci Communes* more closely than it does the Augsburg Confession, which up until then had been the chief Lutheran confessional document. Each article, except the last, is presented according to a common formula. First of all, the nature and current status of the controversy is set out briefly. Then the authors explain their own teaching in two series of theses, the first one being a list of the things they want to affirm and the second one detailing opinions that they reject.

The first article covers original sin and is followed by one on free will, then another on the righteousness of faith. The fourth article is devoted to the ever-controversial theme of good works, the fifth to the contrast between the law and the gospel, and the sixth (very short one) to the third use of the law. Next comes an article dealing with the Lord's Supper, followed by one on the person of Christ and another short one on his descent into hell. Finally, the tenth article is devoted to the so-called *adiaphora* of church practices, the eleventh to predestination and election, and the twelfth to the denunciation of various sectarian groups, particularly the Anabaptists and the anti-trinitarians, who are described as "a completely new sect, never before heard of in Christendom."[40] It seems most likely that they were referring to the Socinians, who were just beginning to make their mark at this time, but they may well have been thinking also of men like Miguel Servetus.

The Formula of Concord is followed by a lengthy appendix in which its authors asserted the primacy of the original text of the Augsburg Confession over the modifications that Melanchthon had subsequently made to it. They then went on to provide a detailed commentary of each of the twelve articles in turn, giving the Scriptural basis for them and showing how they tied in with the teaching of Luther himself. Here the authors expounded the history of the controversies that had arisen among Protestants from the early days

---

[40]Formula of Concord 12.29-30; Kolb and Wengert, *Book of Concord*, 522-23.

of the Reformation onward, and they made their strongest claim that
their opinions were the same as those held by Martin Luther. To
them that was the criterion of orthodoxy, and they had no desire to
develop their theology any further. The controversies that had arisen
since Luther's death had forced them to clarify his thinking, but it
was his thinking (and not theirs) that they were claiming to expound.
Today, of course, we have a greater sense of historical context and are
less willing to accept such claims at face value, but it is important to
understand the mentality behind them. Lutheran theology in effect
became the interpretation of Luther's teaching, and to this day
Lutherans are more inclined than other Protestants are to give the
opinions of their founding father a preeminent and decisive role in
determining what their orthodox doctrine should be.

Among the non-Lutheran Reformed, a rather different development took place. In 1566 the Swiss churches produced the Second
Helvetic Confession, which is notable for being the first confession to
put the doctrine of Scripture at the beginning instead of the doctrine
of God.[41] This alteration, which was more important for its form
than for its substance, was copied by other Reformed churches, and
by the seventeenth century it had become standard among them.
Thus the Irish Articles of 1615, which were intended to be an adaptation of the Thirty-Nine Articles for the use of the Church of Ireland,
followed the Helvetic model, as did the later Westminster Confession.[42] The great exception to this rule was the Anabaptist tradition,
which both in its Continental European and in its English forms remained faithful to the earlier order of presentation.[43]

---

[41]See Dennison, *Reformed Confessions*, 3:810-11.

[42]For the Irish Articles, see Bray, *Documents*, 437-52; Pelikan and Hotchkiss, *Creeds and
Confessions*, 2:551-68; and Dennison, *Reformed Confessions*, 4:88-107. Bray, *Documents*,
661-64 contains tables comparing the Augsburg Confession to the Thirty-Nine Articles,
and the articles to the Westminster Confession.

[43]For the evidence, see Lumpkin and Leonard, *Baptist Confessions*. The last Baptist confession to follow the ancient pattern was the Somerset Confession of 1656 (Lumpkin and

By 1650 the confessional movement had reached maturity and was running out of steam. The Thirty-Nine Articles were frozen in 1628 when King Charles I forbade any further alteration of them, and seven years later they were imposed on the Church of Ireland as well. The Westminster Confession started life as an attempt to revise and update the Thirty-Nine Articles, but the assembly divines soon realized that a fresh start was required. It was their aim to produce a systematic confessional theology that would stand the test of time and make further confessional statements more or less unnecessary.

The Westminster Confession begins with three foundational chapters devoted to Scripture, the Trinity, and the divine decree (of predestination). To those trained in the classical theological tradition, this order may seem odd, but it reflects the priorities of mature Reformed theology. The Bible comes first because it is the source of all other doctrines. God comes second because he is the chief subject of the written revelation, and everything else depends on him. Finally, the divine decree comes third because the plan of God is the foundation for everything that exists and also for everything that happens in the world. Nothing escapes the divine mind.

The second section covers the work of creation, including the providential ordering of the universe and the fall of humanity into sin. This provides the backdrop for the third section, in which the pattern of salvation is outlined according to the principle of covenant. The Westminster Confession is rightly regarded as the supreme monument of covenant theology, and it is in chapters 7 through 18 that the effects of this are most clearly seen. After expounding the basic covenant principle, the confession goes on to present Christ as the Mediator, an ingenious way of combining both Christology (the one person and two natures of the Son of God) and soteriology (the saving work of the incarnate Son). After that, the confession rehearses

---

Leonard, *Baptist Confessions*, 184-98). After that, the Baptists fell into line with the pattern of the Westminster Confession of Faith.

the history of salvation, starting with the loss of Adamic free will and divine election.

The confession avoids the classic debate over whether election occurred before or after the fall of man by espousing both ideas, each in its proper place. In the chapter on the divine decree it is clearly stated that "God from all eternity did, by the most wise and holy counsel of his own will, freely and unchangeably ordain whatsoever comes to pass," and that he predestined certain angels and men to salvation "before the foundation of the world was laid, according to his eternal and immutable purpose."[44] This is the doctrine that theologians call supralapsarianism—that is to say, the belief that election to salvation occurred even before the fall of Adam. But at the same time, the confession also affirms that the "effectual calling" of the predestined takes place only after the fall, the doctrine that is classically known as infralapsarianism.[45] The two points of view are reconciled by saying that they represent a single saving work of God, seen from different perspectives. Supralapsarianism bears witness to his inner, secret will whereas infralapsarianism explains how that will is manifested in our experience. Understood in this way, there is no contradiction between the different points of view, each of which expresses an important aspect of God's saving plan.

Following this, the confession deals with each stage of the saving work of God in turn. First comes justification (11), then adoption (12), sanctification (13), the gift of saving faith (14), repentance (15), good works (16), the perseverance of the saints (17), and the assurance of salvation (18). The order is broadly sequential, but it is probably a mistake to press this order too far—it seems strange to put repentance, for example, after sanctification. But great caution is

---

[44]Westminster Confession of Faith 3.1, 5; Bray, *Documents*, 490; Pelikan and Hotchkiss, *Creeds and Confessions*, 2:610; Dennison, *Reformed Confessions*, 4:38.

[45]Westminster Confession of Faith 10; Bray, *Documents*, 495-96; Pelikan and Hotchkiss, *Creeds and Confessions*, 2:619-20; Dennison, *Reformed Confessions*, 4:246-47.

required here because it can always be argued that the work of God (justification, adoption, sanctification) necessarily precedes and produces the response of the creature (repentance, good works) and that it is the gift of saving faith that makes the former bear fruit in the latter. The apparent oddity of the order may reflect our modern prejudices rather than the theological outlook that guided the Westminster divines and their contemporaries, to which we have become relatively insensitive.

The next set of chapters (19-24) covers the Christian life, a most important aspect of later Reformed thinking. It begins with the law of God, the famous "third use" of which is the foundation of Christian conduct. From there it proceeds naturally to the subject of liberty of conscience, because the law is written on our hearts and is no longer an external constraint forcing us to act against our will. That in turn leads to worship and the observance of the Sabbath, which assumed great importance in covenant theology, not least because it was intimately connected with creation and the eternal rest of God. Next comes social behavior—the taking of lawful oaths (22), the duties of the civil magistrate (23), and the nature of marriage (24). The last of these also deals with the sensitive subject of divorce, allowing not only adultery as a just cause for dissolving a marriage but also "such wilful desertion as can no way be remedied by the Church or civil magistrate."[46] That sounds reasonable enough today, but it was a remarkably liberal position to adopt in the seventeenth century and a reminder to us that the Puritans were not nearly as "puritanical" as later generations have made them appear. Of course, defining what constitutes irremediable "wilful desertion" is not easy, and experience has shown that the vagueness of the definition leaves the door open to a wide variety of interpretations that go far beyond what the original framers of the confession had in mind.

---

[46]Westminster Confession of Faith 24.6, in Bray, *Documents*, 506; Pelikan and Hotchkiss, *Creeds and Confessions*, 2:638; and Dennison, *Reformed Confessions*, 4:263-64.

The next section (25-31) deals with the church, including the communion of saints (26), the sacraments (27-29), church discipline (30), and the role of synods in decision making (31). It is all fairly straightforward, although the omission of any regulations governing the ordained ministry is striking. It is clear from the way in which the administration of the sacraments is described that the Westminster divines accepted the need for lawfully ordained ministers, but who they should be is left undetermined. Particularly intriguing is the provision made for "church officers, distinct from the civil magistrate" to whom "the keys of the kingdom of heaven are committed, by virtue whereof they have power respectively to retain and remit sins."[47] Powers that the original Reformers wrested from the hands of the pope are here accorded to "church officers," but we are not told who they are or how they should be chosen. This probably reflects divisions within the Westminster Assembly itself, wherein the majority favored what became presbyterianism but a considerable number preferred congregationalism, and there was even one advocate of episcopacy.

The last two chapters (32-33) deal with the state of the dead and the last judgment, both matters that had been briefly touched on in Cranmer's Forty-Two Articles (1553) but then dropped from the revision ten years later, presumably because they were either too controversial to handle or of secondary importance. The most important point to notice here is that the notion of "soul sleep" after death, which had been entertained by some of the early Reformers, is specifically excluded.[48]

A curiosity of the confession is the large number of Scripture prooftexts—nearly one thousand in all—that support the assertions made in the main body of the confession itself. These texts were not

---

[47]Westminster Confession of Faith 30.1-2, in Bray, *Documents*, 510; Pelikan and Hotchkiss, *Creeds and Confessions*, 2:644; and Dennison, *Reformed Confessions*, 4:6.

[48]Calvin wrote a treatise against soul sleep called *Psychopannychia*.

part of the original document but were added at the request of the English Parliament, whose members (not unreasonably) thought that a document that claimed to be based on Scripture alone ought to demonstrate its biblical credentials in this way. Unfortunately, modern exegetes are by no means always persuaded that the texts cited in support of particular assertions in the confession really support the arguments being advanced, with the result that what was originally conceived as a strength has sometimes (although by no means always) turned out to be more of a weakness instead. But modern readers who notice this should not jump to overhasty conclusions. The misapplication of some Bible verses does not invalidate the method in general, and rather than criticize the confession on this score, it would be wiser and more fruitful to look for alternative texts that do support the doctrines being asserted. Only if they cannot be found are we justified in rejecting what the Westminster Confession has to offer in this respect.

In its own time, the Westminster Confession was so successful that, although the Puritan movement that spawned it was checked by the restoration of the British monarchy in 1660, it survived to become the official doctrinal standard of the Church of Scotland in 1690. In 1689 the English Baptists adopted a revised version of the Westminster Confession, followed later on by their American counterparts, who produced a similar version at Philadelphia (1742).

Tinkering of a minor kind continued into the early nineteenth century, when American Episcopalians modified the Thirty-Nine Articles to suit conditions in the newly independent United States, and Presbyterians did the same with the Westminster Confession, but neither group thought it necessary to write a new statement of faith. By then, the confessional era of mainline Protestantism was well and truly over.

Much the same can be said for the situation in the more radical forms of Protestantism. The early Anabaptists produced a number of confessions of varying length and quality, but by the middle of the seventeenth century even they had lost their earlier vigor. Meanwhile the Eastern Orthodox churches adopted the Confession of Dositheus as normative, although it never received official sanction and gradually faded into the background. Rome continued to rely on the canons of Trent and made no further dogmatic pronouncements until the mid-nineteenth century. Theological arguments continued, of course, and in the Protestant world numerous attempts were made to defend the historic confessions of the Reformation era, but creative theological thought had moved elsewhere and the conservatives were increasingly faced with attempts from within their own communions to downgrade or even to abolish the statements of faith that had originally defined them.

Looking back after three centuries, we can see that very often different denominations felt obliged to spell out secondary matters because those things set them apart from other Protestants, and this ultimately discredited the confessional movement in the eyes of many. Contrary to the original intentions of those who composed the confessions, these secondary matters came to be regarded as more important than the weightier items of doctrine on which everyone was agreed. It was a lopsided approach in which denominational distinctives often took center stage and produced controversies over things that should never have divided the church. The eighteenth-century evangelical movement began at least in part as a reaction to this kind of theological nitpicking and quickly developed an interdenominational character that it still retains. Presbyterians and Baptists might argue about all manner of things, but they are usually prepared to cooperate in evangelism, Bible translation, and the like, and nowadays few people would allow their historic differences to interfere with their fellowship at such practical levels.

Conclusion

The Core Doctrines of Protestantism

The confessions of the Reformation era are an important reference point for establishing the key doctrines of the Reformation, and in this respect, their essential unity of approach is more significant than the differences that particular statements of faith contain. It is immediately apparent that the distinctiveness of the Reformation can be seen most clearly in what the confessions have to say about the way of salvation. This can be summarized as follows.

The radical character of the fall. The present condition of the human race is one of separation from God, caused not by him but by the disobedience of the first human beings. Nobody in the sixteenth century questioned the historical veracity of the biblical account; both Protestants and Catholics believed that there had been a real Adam and Eve who had lived in a Garden of Eden that was located somewhere in what is now Iraq. Sin had entered the world because this couple had jointly succumbed to the temptation of Satan, who promised them that if they ate the forbidden fruit of the tree of the knowledge of good and evil they would become like God. They listened to his temptation, and as a result God expelled them from the garden, although not without giving them some hope that eventually they would be redeemed.

The question then became, How complete was the separation between God and his human creatures? Adam and Eve had been created in the image and likeness of God, and they retained a special status in creation even after they fell. Before the Reformation, most theologians gravitated toward the belief that the first human beings had lost the likeness of God but preserved his image, making it possible to envisage the restoration of the likeness at some future point. That belief was based on the assumption that the words *image* and *likeness* referred to two different things, but the recovery of a knowledge of Hebrew made such a distinction untenable. The Hebrew language works by using synonyms in parallel, so *image* and *likeness* are in effect two words meaning the same thing. The image/likeness was either corrupted or destroyed by the fall, but it could not be divided into two constituent parts.

The most common belief among Catholics was that the image/likeness of God had been marred but not destroyed. The fundamental structure was still there and the damage could be repaired by the operation of divine grace, which is what the church existed for. The minority view was that the image/likeness had been ruined beyond repair. No amount of grace could restore it to what it had been before the fall, and that was not what the gospel message promised. Instead, a new birth was required, a fresh beginning that would put the "old man" (the ruined image/likeness) to death and replace it with the indwelling Holy Spirit. This is essentially what the apostle Paul had said when he wrote to the Galatians (2:20): "I have been crucified with Christ. It is no longer I who live, but Christ who lives in me." The "old man" did not disappear, of course. It continued to exist and to cause problems for the Christian, who had to fight against it in a pattern of spiritual warfare that is fully described in the New Testament, especially in Paul's epistles. Only physical death and spiritual resurrection will put an end to that struggle, but the presence of Christ in a person's life will enable him or her to live according to God's will here and now—the firstfruits of eternal life are present and active in this one.

If this radical view of sinfulness is accepted, then it is obvious that there can be no place for human cooperation or improvement in the spiritual life. Any achievement of that kind would be building on an insecure foundation, and like the house built on sand, it would eventually collapse, however solid and beautiful it might appear to be. The Reformation argument, following the apostle Paul, was that we are a "new creation" in Christ—the old has passed away and all things have been made new in him.

The radical character of salvation. Because it is not possible to grow into a new life in incremental stages, that new life must be complete in itself from the very beginning. To be a Christian is therefore to be born again. New birth does not rule out the need for growth, but it is growth of what is already there in principle, not the addition of new elements that effect a gradual transformation from one kind of life to another. This new life is not autonomous. We are not re-created as little Adams and Eves but rather integrated into the life of the new Adam, who is Christ. It is in him, and in him alone, that we are saved, because thanks to his righteousness, revealed above all in the perfect sacrifice that he made for our sins, we can stand in the presence of God the Father and be accepted by him as his children. What had previously been conceived as the end result of a long process that would most probably have to continue after our physical death by a further period of cleansing in purgatory was now seen as a gift, bestowed on us not as a reward for anything we have done to deserve it but in the light of our faith in Christ. It is because we have recognized our need and accepted that it has been met in Christ that we have received the gift of salvation. This is what the Reformers meant by justification—acceptance in the presence of God, not as people who have overcome sin in their lives but as sinners who have been clothed in the righteousness of Christ.

The radical character of the church. The church is not a spiritual empire presided over by an infallible leader who represents Christ on

earth, but an invisible company of faithful believers who are united
by the Holy Spirit. This fellowship incarnates itself in visible forms,
but none of them can claim exclusive authority or spiritual perfection, and they are all essentially provisional. The ordained ministry
in this invisible church is primarily that of preaching the Word of
God, which simultaneously evangelizes the unconverted and ministers to believers. The sacraments of baptism and the Lord's Supper
are extensions of the ministry of the Word and cannot be separated
from it. In no sense are they magical carriers of divine grace that can
be granted or withheld by a hierarchy determined to assert its own
control. In the church every member is equal, although some have
particular gifts and responsibilities that are meant to accompany
them. Church order is flexible and can be adapted to meet different
circumstances. Protestants disagree about how much compromise is
possible or desirable in practice, but they have sometimes been able
to work out a pattern of church government that is acceptable to a
broad majority. Many important activities, like Bible translation and
evangelism, are carried out by interdenominational or parachurch
organizations that can dispense with some of the requirements of
particular church bodies, and they usually unite on a common basis
of faith that all can adhere to with a good conscience. Nowadays, lay
people can usually move from one denomination to another with
little difficulty, and mutual recognition of ordained ministries is
growing, although it is still far from universal. In a secular world,
especially in places where the church is persecuted by hostile regimes,
Protestants have proved to be highly adaptable and have often thrived
in the face of opposition, a curious development that in some respects
has brought them closer to the reality of the early church than the
Reformers ever envisaged.

   The radical character of spiritual authority. Finally, and perhaps
most importantly, all Protestants believe that spiritual authority rests
with God alone and is revealed to us in his Word, the Bible. Today,

everyone accepts that the Bible must be interpreted in its original languages, with due regard for the context in which the revelation was given. There is vast scope here for detailed analysis, and it is hardly surprising that many different theories have been proposed regarding the composition and interpretation of the sacred texts. This has led to an exaggerated emphasis on details that are open to question and may contradict the overall witness of the Reformation, even on central matters like the doctrine of justification by faith alone. A distinction has to be made here between the theses of individual scholars and teachers, which must remain open to debate, and the consensus of the Protestant theological tradition, which, while not infallible, remains the benchmark for measuring new ideas. There is always a danger that individuals will take things to an extreme, and aberrant spiritual movements are not uncommon in the Protestant world, but most people believe that the truth will emerge when their teachings and practices are subjected to the test of conformity to the Bible, and for the most part offbeat or heretical views tend to fade away once that test is applied. There is therefore no need for an infallible magisterium to exercise church discipline, which will usually emerge of its own accord and be accepted by consensus. Remnants of such oddities may survive on the margins of Protestantism, but they are seldom strong enough to produce long-lasting movements of their own.

The work of the Protestant reformers of the sixteenth and seventeenth centuries was not perfect, as they themselves would have been the first to admit. Their watchword was that the church was always in need of reform (*ecclesia semper reformanda est*), and it probably would have puzzled them if they had known that their particular formulations of Christian truth would acquire a canonical status, even a de facto infallibility, in later times. But on their core principles, they believed that they had discovered the truth that God had revealed, and that truth would remain essentially the same through time and space. If they could return to earth today, they would doubtless be surprised by the outward forms of the churches that claim their inheritance, but on the gospel of salvation by grace through faith alone they would be at one with those who have succeeded them, and in many cases they would probably be urging them to be even more faithful to their message than they claim to be, not in order to glorify their Reformation ancestors but so that the name of Jesus Christ might truly be proclaimed and exalted on earth until he comes again.

WORKS CITED

PRIMARY SOURCES

Beeke, J. R., and S. B. Ferguson, eds. *Reformed Confessions Harmonized*. Grand Rapids: Baker, 1999.

Bray, G. L., ed. *The Book of Homilies: A Critical Edition*. Cambridge: James Clarke, 2015.

———. *Documents of the English Reformation*. 2nd ed. Cambridge: James Clarke, 2004.

———. *Translating the Bible from William Tyndale to King James*. London: Latimer Trust, 2010.

Calvin, John. *Institutes of the Christian Religion*. 2 vols. Edited by J. T. McNeill. Translated by F. L. Battles. Philadelphia, PA: Westminster Press, 1960.

Dennison, J. T., ed. *Reformed Confessions of the Sixteenth and Seventeenth Centuries in English Translation*. Grand Rapids: Reformation Heritage Books, 2008–2014.

Faulenbach, H., and E. Busch, eds. *Reformierte Bekenntnisschriften*. 8 vols. Neukirchen-Vluyn: Neukirchener Verlag, 2002–2016.

Friedberg, Emil, ed. *Corpus iuris canonici*. 2 vols. Graz: Akademische Druck- und Verlagsanstalt, 1955.

Kenyon, J. P., ed. *The Stuart Constitution: 1603–1688*. 2nd ed. Cambridge: Cambridge University Press, 1986.

Kolb, R., and T. J. Wengert, eds. *The Book of Concord: The Confessions of the Evangelical Lutheran Church*. Minneapolis, MN: Fortress Press, 2000.

Lombard, Peter. *Sententiae in IV libris distinctae*. 2 vols. Grottaferrata: Editiones Colegii S. Bonaventurae ad Claras Aquas, 1971–1981.

Lull, T. F., ed. *Martin Luther's Basic Theological Writings*. 2nd ed. Minneapolis, MN: Fortress Press, 2005.

Lumpkin, W. L., and B. J. Leonard, eds. *Baptist Confessions of Faith*. 2nd ed. Valley Forge, PA: Judson Press, 2011.

Luther, Martin. *Luther's Works: American Edition*. 55 vols. Edited by J. Pelikan et al. Philadelphia, PA: Fortress Press, 1957–1975.

Mears, N., A. Raffe, S. Taylor, P. Williamson, and L. Bates, eds. *National Prayers: Special Worship Since the Reformation*. 2 vols. Woodbridge, UK: Boydell and Brewer, 2013–2017.

Milton, John. *Judgment of Martin Bucer Concerning Divorce*. London: Matthew Simmons, 1644.

Ozilou, Marc, trans. *Pierre Lombard: Les quatre livres des Sentences*. Paris: Cerf, 2012–2015.

Pauck, W., ed. *Melanchthon and Bucer*. Philadelphia, PA: Westminster Press, 1969.

Pelikan, J., and V. Hotchkiss, eds. *Creeds and Confessions of Faith in the Christian Tradition*. 3 vols. New Haven, CT: Yale University Press, 2003.

Silano, Giulio, trans. *Peter Lombard: The Sentences*. 4 vols. Toronto, ON: Pontifical Institute of Mediaeval Studies, 2007–2010.

Tanner, N. P. *Decrees of the Ecumenical Councils*. 2 vols. Washington, DC: Georgetown University Press; London: Sheed and Ward, 1990.

Wendel, F., ed. *Martini Buceri Opera Latina XV: De Regno Christi*. Paris: Presses Universitaires de France; Gütersloh, Ger.: C. Bertelsmann Verlag, 1955.

William of Ockham. *Predestination, God's Foreknowledge, and Future Contingents*. 2nd ed. Translated by M. M. Adams and N. Kretzmann. Indianapolis, IN: Hackett, 1983.

Wyclif, John. *De eucharistia*. Edited by J. Loserth for the Wyclif Society. London: Trübner, 1892.

———. *On the Truth of Holy Scripture*. Translated by I. C. Levy. Kalamazoo, MI: Medieval Institute Press, 2001.

Secondary Literature

Allen, David L. *The Extent of the Atonement: A Historical and Critical Review.* Nashville, TN: Broadman and Holman Academic, 2018.

Aquinas, Thomas. *Summa theologiae* 3.75.4. Available online at www .newadvent.org/summa.

Arand, C. P., R. Kolb, and J. A. Nestingen. *The Lutheran Confessions: History and Theology of The Book of Concord.* Minneapolis, MN: Fortress Press, 2012.

Augustine, *Tractates on the Gospel of John*, 80.3.

Bente, F. *Historical Introductions to The Book of Concord.* St. Louis, MO: Concordia Publishing House, 1965.

Book of Common Prayer. Cambridge: Cambridge University Press, 2004.

Bray, G. L., ed., *The Institution of a Christian Man.* Cambridge: James Clarke, 2018.

Brett, T. *A Review of the Lutheran Principles.* London: Henry Clements, 1714.

Brewer, B. C. *Martin Luther and the Seven Sacraments: A Contemporary Protestant Reappraisal.* Grand Rapids: Baker Academic, 2017.

Calvin, John. *Institutes of the Christian Religion*, 2 vols., Edited by J. T. McNeill. Translated by F. L. Battles. Philadelphia, PA: Westminster Press, 1960.

Cheney, C. R., ed. *Councils and Synods: With Other Documents Relating to the English Church.* Oxford: Clarendon Press, 1964.

Evans, G. R. *Mediaeval Commentaries on the* Sentences *of Peter Lombard.* 2 vols. Leiden: Brill, 2002.

Goudriaan, Aza, and Fred Lieburg, eds. *Revisiting the Synod of Dordt (1618–1619).* Leiden: Brill, 2010.

Gregory of Nazianzus, *Epistula* 101.

Hadjiantoniou, G. A. *Protestant Patriarch.* Richmond, VA: John Knox Press, 1961.

Hooykaas, Reijer. *Religion and the Rise of Modern Science.* Vancouver, BC: Regent College Publications, 2000. First published 1972 by Scottish Academic Press (Edinburgh).

Jacobs, H. E. *The Lutheran Movement in England During the Reigns of Henry VIII and Edward VI, and Its Literary Monuments.* Philadelphia, PA: G. W. Frederick, 1890.

Kolb, R., I. Dingel, and L. Batka. *The Oxford Handbook of Martin Luther's Theology*. Oxford: Oxford University Press, 2014.

Kolb, R., and C. R. Trueman. *Between Wittenberg and Geneva: Lutheran and Reformed Theology in Conversation*. Grand Rapids: Baker, 2017.

Le Goff, Jacques. *The Birth of Purgatory*. Chicago: University of Chicago Press, 1984.

Levy, Ian C. *John Wyclif: Scriptural Logic, Real Presence and the Parameters of Orthodoxy*. Milwaukee, WI: Marquette University Press, 2003.

Lewis, John. *A Second Review of the Lutheran Principles*. London: J. Baker, 1714.

Macy, G. *A Companion to the Eucharist in the Reformation*. Leiden: Brill, 2014.

McCracken, G. E. *Early Medieval Theology*. Library of Christian Classics, 9. Philadelphia, PA: Westminster Press, 1957.

McGregor, J. F., and B. Reay, eds. *Radical Religion in the English Revolution*. Oxford: Oxford University Press, 1984.

Muller, Richard A. *Post-Reformation Reformed Dogmatics*. 4 vols. Grand Rapids: Baker, 2003.

Reu, J. M. *The Augsburg Confession*. St. Louis, MO: Concordia Publishing House, 2005.

Runciman, S. *The Great Church in Captivity*. Cambridge: Cambridge University Press, 1968.

Selderhuis, H. J. *Marriage and Divorce in the Thought of Martin Bucer*. Kirksville, MO: Thomas Jefferson University Press, 1999.

Vignaux, Paul. *Luther, commentateur des Sentences*. Paris: Vrin, 1935.

Wengert, T. J. *Dictionary of Luther and the Lutheran Traditions*. Grand Rapids: Baker, 2017.

General Index

Scripture Index

Reformation Commentary on Scripture

Timothy George (General Editor)

and Scott Manetsch (Associate General Editor)

Retrieved for the Sake of Renewal

"Although it will be of use to students of the Reformation, this series is far from being an esoteric study of largely forgotten voices; this collection of reforming comments, comprehending every verse and provided with topical headings, will serve contemporary pastors and preachers very well."

Elsie Anne McKee, Princeton Theological Seminary

"This commentary series is a godsend!"

Richard J. Mouw, president, Fuller Theological Seminary

"Why was this not done before? The publication of the Reformation Commentary on Scripture should be greeted with enthusiasm by every believing Christian—but especially by those who will preach and teach the Word of God."

R. Albert Mohler Jr., president, The Southern Baptist Theological Seminary

"This series will strengthen our understanding of the period of the Reformation and enable us to apply its insights to our own day and its challenges to the church."

Robert Kolb, Concordia Theological Seminary

For more series information go to: www.ivpress.com/rcs

InterVarsity Press

Downers Grove, Illinois 60515